The Belgian RAF Pilot
Who Defied the Gestapo

The Belgian RAF Pilot Who Defied the Gestapo

The Fearless Baron de Selys Longchamps

Marc Audrit

First published in Belgium in 2023 by Weyrich Édition as *Sur les Traces de Jean de Selys Longchamps: Une Vie au Galop*
This edition published in Great Britain in 2025 by
Air World
An imprint of Pen & Sword Books Limited
Yorkshire – Philadelphia

Copyright © Marc Audrit, 2025

ISBN 9781036119775

The right of Marc Audrit to be identified as
Author of this Work has been asserted by him in accordance
with the Copyright, Designs and Patents Act 1988.

A CIP catalogue record for this book is
available from the British Library.

All rights reserved. No part of this book may be reproduced or
transmitted in any form or by any means, electronic or mechanical
including photocopying, recording or by any information storage and
retrieval system, without permission from the Publisher in writing.

Typeset by Mac Style
Printed in the UK by CPI Group (UK) Ltd, Croydon, CR0 4YY.

Pen & Sword Books Limited incorporates the imprints of After the Battle, Atlas, Archaeology, Aviation, Discovery, Family History, Fiction, History, Maritime, Military, Military Classics, Politics, Select, Transport, True Crime, Air World, Frontline Publishing, Leo Cooper, Remember When, Seaforth Publishing, The Praetorian Press, Wharncliffe Local History, Wharncliffe Transport, Wharncliffe True Crime and White Owl.

For a complete list of Pen & Sword titles please contact

PEN & SWORD BOOKS LIMITED
47 Church Street, Barnsley, South Yorkshire, S70 2AS, England
E-mail: enquiries@pen-and-sword.co.uk
Website: www.pen-and-sword.co.uk
or
PEN AND SWORD BOOKS
1950 Lawrence Road, Havertown, PA 19083, USA
E-mail: uspen-and-sword@casematepublishers.com
Website: www.penandswordbooks.com

*To my brother Michel, an extraordinary source of inspiration.
To my two sons, Tanguy and Antoine, endless sources of pride.
To the memory of Michel 'Mickey' de Selys.*

Contents

Foreword		ix
Introduction		x
Chapter 1	Blood Will Tell (*1622–1912*)	1
Chapter 2	My Father, My Hero (*1880–1939*)	11
Chapter 3	The 400 Blows (*1918–1939*)	23
Chapter 4	18 Days and Then It's Gone (*10–28 May 1940*)	31
Chapter 5	Into the Wild (*29–31 May 1940*)	43
Chapter 6	Catch-22 (*1 June–14 December 1940*)	52
Chapter 7	The Sky is the Limit (*16 December 1940–7 March 1941*)	71
Chapter 8	'Maggie' (*8 March–13 May 1941*)	81
Chapter 9	Wings of Desire (*14 May–28 September 1941*)	91
Chapter 10	'Tally Ho!' (*28 September 1941–26 April 1942*)	107
Chapter 11	'Tiffy', the Plane of a Lifetime (*27 April 1942–19 January 1943*)	135
Chapter 12	Befehlshaber der Sipo-SD, 453 Avenue Louise, Brussels, Belgium (*1940–1943*)	160
Chapter 13	Don't Stop Me Now (*20 January 1943*)	178
Chapter 14	'The Special One' (*21 January–15 August 1943*)	204
Chapter 15	Bad Moon Rising (*16 August 1943*)	226
Chapter 16	The Remains of the Day (*From 1946 to Today*)	244
Chapter 17	The Incredibles (*1939–1948*)	257
Acknowledgements		276
Notes		277
Selected Bibliography		283
Index		286

Jean de Selys Longchamps.

Foreword

First and foremost, I would like to sincerely thank and congratulate Marc Audrit for this impressive contribution to the history of Belgian aviation. Gathering all the information about the life of Jean de Selys Longchamps was no easy task. The result, being unique and simply remarkable, is even more commendable.

This biography reveals the story of his exceptional career as an officer and fighter pilot during the Second World War. The author also gives us a very comprehensive account of the environment in which his notable personality developed: his family, education, studies, passion for horse riding, and professional experiences.

The war would reveal exceptional qualities in this great patriot. After the capitulation on 28 May 1940, he was determined to continue the fight against the occupier at all costs, and with motivated and unconventional means, this cavalry officer became an excellent fighter pilot in the Royal Air Force. The spectacular solo raid on 20 January 1943, against the Sipo-SD building at 453 Avenue Louise in Brussels, took place in this context.

More than eighty years later, Marc Audrit provides us with a very precise insight into these events, which still have a profound resonance today. His thorough research also finally dispels the false rumours and inaccuracies regularly spread about this extraordinary exploit.

I especially hope that this biography of one of the leading figures among Belgian Royal Air Force aviators will inspire the younger generation, often overwhelmed by ephemeral and superficial information. These aviators shaped our present society through their brilliant commitment throughout the Second World War. The heavy price they had to pay deserves our profound and lasting gratitude.

Gerard Van Caelenberge
Belgian Air Force general (ret.)
Honorary Vice-President 609 Squadron Association

Introduction

This biography of Jean de Selys Longchamps was written to address a twofold anomaly. The first is indeed surprising: eighty years after his death, no biography had yet been dedicated to the man who signed off on what many consider one of the boldest feats ever achieved by a Belgian officer during the Second World War. The second anomaly is no less disconcerting due to an overwhelming truth: Jean de Selys' life is often condensed to the mere handful of seconds during which he strafed the headquarters of the Sipo-SD on 20 January 1943. When he conducted his raid, Jean de Selys was already 30 years old, yet one rarely, if ever, hears about the person he was or the life journey that led him to exhibit heroism and courage that nobody, not even his close acquaintances, suspected he had in him.

One cannot grasp why de Selys would override orders (his raid was not sanctioned) and risk everything to 'boost the morale of the Belgians' without delving into his family history and the life filled with precipices that he traversed, sword drawn, from May 1940. At the time of mobilisation, Jean de Selys was an unfinished man. War, the ultimate trial to reveal one's character, would birth him anew, plunging him back into the impatience and innocence of beginnings.

In her brilliant essay 'The Beginnings: Where to Start Again', Claire Marin skillfully encapsulates what characterises these unexpected dice throws that break or divert the course of life: 'The beginning is when reality scratches us, provokes us, jostles us; it's the moment when an idea is born by infringement, from the fortuity of the world.' Armed with this renewed fervour, Jean de Selys would approach his second life, which would alas, last only 1,193 days, from 10 May 1940 to 16 August 1943.

It is also crucial to clarify that this biography is anything but hagiographic. Aviators, real or fictional, are often portrayed as knights of the sky. Comic book writer Yann has a charming expression that perfectly summarises the dominating archetype: 'Buck Danny [a fictional American navy pilot featured in a long-running comic series] is a scout with wings.' None of this applies to Jean de Selys: he is an avowed individualist, mostly concerned with fulfilling his path and furious at being forced into inactivity. His profile—noble, royalist, Catholic, from Brussels, francophone—is polarising and earns him a few enmities. He could not care less. However, as we prepare to track de Selys' steps in the pages that follow, we also uncover an unexpected facet of his personality when he reveals, especially in his writings, a skin-deep sensitivity.

The work of a biographer is often said to be inherently hybrid, carved into three professions: detective, historian, and writer. The 'investigation' part was thrilling because, beyond 20 January 1943, little information was available. Fortunately, the de Selys family granted me access to significant collections, rich in precious documents (flight log, personal journal, photo albums…) and multiple dives into Belgian, British, and German archives have unearthed gems of information, some quite novel. This essential detective work has also allowed us to deliver a hefty slap to the snout of our certainties, nourished by an impressive array of rumours, fake news, approximations, and little dealings with reality that contaminate most narratives related to Jean de Selys Longchamps. If this biography succeeds in clearing a portion of this miasmic halo, my efforts will have been rewarded.

Becoming the father of two children, I have come to understand the importance of the duty of transmission. I am convinced that we are the insolvent heirs to yesterday's heroes, to those who sacrificed themselves to defend our freedom. It is therefore vital to take the time to keep their memory alive and ensure they are not forgotten. This book is thus a modest act of resistance against the tyranny of immediacy that dominates our society and tends to confine us to an increasingly epileptic world, and, sadly, a despairingly amnesic one.

Marc Audrit

Chapter 1

Blood Will Tell

(1622–1912)

It was in Brussels that the story of an extraordinary man began, a man who would forge a path through the thorns of life and transform, against all odds, a languid youth into an epic odyssey. On Friday, 31 May 1912 Jean Michel Paul Ghislain de Selys Longchamps was born in the heart of the Belgian capital. In a mischievous nod to the one who would later excel at the controls of a combat aircraft, the day's newspapers echoed the death of a most illustrious pioneer of aviation, the American Wilbur Wright. The Wright brothers – Wilbur and Orville – were indeed the first to have achieved a flight in a closed circuit, performing a controlled turn and covering 4,080 feet in 1 minute and 36 seconds on 20 September 1904. Those were figures that could have coaxed a first smile from the newborn had he known that one day he would himself master a fighter capable of flying at over 410mph and covering more than 497 miles.

But on that last day of May 1912, what mostly stirred the Belgian daily press were the legislative elections scheduled for Sunday, 2 June. The preceding campaign was often described as one of the most virulent in history, peppered with numerous incidents and during which passionate crowds flocked en masse to pre-election meetings. Against all odds, it was the Catholic Party that triumphed two days later and won a strong majority in both the House of Representatives and the Senate. The announcement of the results did not occur without turmoil, sparking a violent strike in the major industrial centres of Wallonia. Buffeted by the demonstrations, the police did not hesitate to open fire. The strike eventually ended on 9 June, marked by several deaths and many injuries.

In the wake of all this tumult, on 15 August 1912, MP Jules Destrée published a letter to the King on the separation of Flanders and Wallonia, revealing the communal tensions that we still know a century later. This open letter made a lot of noise in the country and reflected a deep unease, originating from an indisputable demographic fact: the Flemish, predominantly Catholic, outnumbered the French speakers, and the weight of their claims increasingly exasperated the mostly socialist and liberal

One of the earliest known photographs of Jean de Selys Longchamps (he was 2 years old at the time).

Walloon population. Those fierce tensions would only temporarily subside due to the strong patriotic surge that would accompany the outbreak of the First World War two years later.

One could have dreamed of a slightly more peaceful world to welcome little Jean de Selys Longchamps. But contrary to what the events surrounding his first weeks of life suggest, he was fortunate to be born in a country in full bloom. Even though it was one of the smallest nations in terms of area (11,373 square miles, placing it eighteenth among European countries, just ahead of Montenegro), Belgium boasted the world's highest population density (603 people per square mile) and was a model envied by many countries for its infrastructure, railways, and roads.

The secondary sector had clearly overtaken the primary sector. Trade was flourishing. And colonial expansion harboured the greatest hopes since the Congo became Belgian in 1908. Lastly, at the head of the country, a young King, Albert I, had reigned since 23 December 1909 over a kingdom of 7 million people and would soon reveal his extraordinary panache by leading of Belgium and its army.

Upon his birth, Jean joined a family already composed of a sister six years his senior and a brother born two years earlier: Monique Eusébie Ghislaine Charlotte Marie had come into the world on 9 February 1906, and Michel François Raphaël Marie Ghislain, on 2 April 1910.

Their parents, Raymond de Selys Longchamps and Émilie de Theux de Meylandt et Montjardin, were married on Tuesday, 23 May 1905, a year that also marked the grand seventy-fifth anniversary of Belgium's independence. The de Selys family was among the most representative old nobility of the ancient Principality of Liège.[1] Its origins were in Maastricht, and its known lineage traced back to a certain Michel de Selys, who died around 1622. From his union with Claire Boex, a son was born: the very first Jean de Selys. The descendants of the latter obtained from Emperor Ferdinand III of Habsburg letters patent of nobility of the Holy Roman Empire and confirmation of the ancient coat of arms on 29 May 1656. A little more than forty years later, Walter, Lord of Frère, d'Heure, and Wihogne, who would ensure the lineage of the de Selys, was ennobled as a baron of the Holy Roman Empire on 26 July 1699, by letter of Emperor Leopold I, Archduke of Austria. It was thanks to this distant ancestor that the de Selys family obtained the baronial title, which descendants would proudly carry over the following centuries. It is worth noting that Longchamps was added later to the family name when a nobility title related to this village in the Liège region was acquired.

The family's coat of arms is described as follows: azure, a cross argent charged with five escallops sable; its motto, '*Virtus in cruce*' [virtue grows under the cross], azure on a scroll argent.

Raymond de Selys Longchamps and Émilie de Theux de Meylandt et Montjardin, Jean's parents.

It would be tedious and irrelevant to list here the impressive procession of mayors, aldermen, canons, senators etc. that the de Selys Longchamps family can boast of, but it is, however, appropriate to pause at two of them, as they will help better frame the familial context in which Raymond de Selys Longchamps, the happy father of little Jean, would grow up, with the infant's cooing now resonantly echoing in the family home during the summer of 1912.

The first individual it is useful to become more acquainted is Baron Edmond de Selys Longchamps, Jean's great-grandfather, born in 1813 in Paris. His extraordinary multi-faceted personality grants him a special place in the family saga. He distinguished himself in politics, becoming successively deputy, senator, vice-president, and then President of the Belgian Senate from 1880 to 1884. But his remarkable intelligence and thirst for discovery also established him as one of the most eminent specialists in odonatology (the study of dragonflies and damselflies), mammals, and birds. He published his first scientific article on the birds and insects of Belgium in 1831 at the age of 18. His work earned him international recognition, notably from Charles Darwin, with whom he regularly corresponded. An inveterate traveller, Edmond de Selys is associated with the identification of more than 700 species of dragonflies in Europe. The passion of this great-grandfather for these elegant insects that have successfully conquered the air may have subliminally given the desire to fly to the future Royal Air Force pilot that is little Jean, who knows? What is certain is that Edmond de Selys was a character of great charisma and presence, as attested by the testimony of a 15-year-old boy – Auguste Lameere, future eminent professor of Zoology – who met him for the first time in 1880 (Edmond was then 66 years old):

Coat of arms of the de Selys Longchamps family.

> Big and sturdy, he was at once old and amusingly young. His long hair hung over his ears and his collar and gave him the appearance of someone from another century. He looked as if he had stepped out of an old Flemish painting. When he spoke to give an opinion, his words immediately made me understand that it was him.[2]

Edmond de Selys, after having left his mark on almost the entire nineteenth century, died on 11 December 1900, at the age of 87. It was predictable that a character of such stature would educate his children – he had four – by passing on a love of nature and the virus of insatiable curiosity. This would indeed be the case with his son Raphaël, the father of Raymond and the grandfather of Jean, who was born in 1841. Raphaël de Selys Longchamps was raised in a liberal and republican spirit, marked by the philosophy of the Enlightenment and Jean-Jacques Rousseau. In many respects, his life would embody the tensions related to the numerous changes that occurred during the last quarter of the nineteenth century. For most people, the thirst for progress is opposed to the contradictory desire to keep the world as it is. Many, in his comfortable

Portrait of Edmond de Selys Longchamps, Jean de Selys' great-grandfather.

situation – Raphaël is indeed a wealthy landowner – would be content with the status quo. But of course, that is without counting on the values his father Edmond passed on to him, and Raphaël would make a point of satisfying a true appetite for discovery.

His adult life began in 1862 with his entrance to the Royal Military School of Brussels. There he became a lieutenant of cavalry, inaugurating a long family tradition. Like his future descendants, Raphaël would even have the opportunity to brush with conflict – albeit from a distance – as he took part in the Franco-Prussian War of 1870. The Belgians did not actively participate in this conflict, but the fear of invasion by the two belligerents prompted them to actively protect their borders with Prussia and France. Although significant battles took place in the immediate vicinity of Belgian territory, such as the Battle of Sedan where 320,000 men would clash just 8 miles from the border, Belgium maintained its neutrality and was never drawn into the conflict.

In 1872 Raphaël married Eusébie de Brigode-Kemlandt, a young woman of French nobility born in 1850. The bride's father – Pierre de Brigode-Kemlandt – was a hero of the war of 1870, during which his service at the head of 9th Battalion of the Northern National Mobile Guard earned him the Legion of Honour. The de Brigode-Kemlandt family, one of the richest in the Lille region, owned the Château de Luchin, which thus became one of the de Selys Longchamps family's holiday retreats.

The de Selys Longchamps family in front of the Château de Luchin.

Self-portrait of Raphaël de Selys Longchamps, Jean's grandfather.

However, this traditional course of life took on a new dimension when Raphaël discovered his great passion: photography. He began in 1876, and for twenty-five years he took shots that today's experts consider to be the work of a pioneer in amateur photographic practice.³ Being a photographer at that time was anything but a sinecure.

When taking outdoor shots, one had to carry a portable laboratory, while a scientific background in both chemistry and optics was essential to succeed. Raphaël de Selys Longchamps' group photographs attest to an astonishing mastery of spatial composition. His works also include numerous snapshots and shots that show he did not hesitate to venture into experimental techniques, photomontages, or superimpositions. More than 2,000 of his shots are now preserved at the Charleroi Photography Museum. This abundant body of work undoubtedly inspired Jean de Selys, who partly inherited this photographic instinct that would lead him to slip a miniature camera into his flight suit many years later.

One of photographer Raphaël de Selys Longchamps' favourite subjects was undoubtedly his family. He did not hesitate to enlist in his compositions and enjoyed dressing up his offspring to stage them. He and Eusébie had six children, three girls and three boys. Among these was Raymond de Selys Longchamps, born in 1880, the fourth child of the couple. The time has now come to become better acquainted with the man who would become, thirty-two years later, the father of Jean de Selys Longchamps.

Raymond, Jeanne, and Hélène de Selys dressed up at the Château de Borgharen.

Chapter 2

My Father, My Hero

(1880–1939)

Raymond de Selys' childhood remains something of an enigma, yet the veil is partially lifted by a series of photographs taken by his father. Beyond the charming vignettes in which he is seen donning a variety of costumes – here a Pierrot, there sporting an elegant eighteenth-century wig– we glimpse pieces of a comfortable life unfolding within the family's castles, chiefly Longchamps (Waremme), Borgharen (Maastricht), and Luchin (Lille). Numerous snaps also capture moments in Liège, where the family maintained a grand winter residence in the heart of the city.

Undoubtedly, hunting and horse riding – cherished pastimes of the de Selys Longchamps – were the bedrock of Raymond's upbringing.

In 1898, aged 18, he followed in his father's footsteps, enrolling in the Royal Military Academy.[1] By 20 December 1899, he had committed to an eight-year stint in the army. A year on, Raymond earned his stripes as a second lieutenant of infantry and was posted to 3rd Line Regiment where his tenure was brief; soon he was detached to the riding school, where his equestrian prowess and officer's mettle were put to the test – and he excelled with flying colours. (He was noted for being 'a vigorous rider', 'performs all his duties exceedingly well. Despite his stature, he has achieved excellent results in horsemanship. Of very good character.') By late 1904, his dream was realised: he transferred to the cavalry, joining the 2nd Lancers.

Spring 1905 saw the union of Raymond and Émilie de Theux de Meylandt et Montjardin, both 25 years of age. Émilie bore the name of an ancient Belgian family, ennobled in perpetuity by Emperor Leopold I in 1703. With fourteen siblings, her lineage was as distinguished as it was extensive. For their honeymoon, Raymond sought military leave, planning an extensive tour across France, Switzerland, Italy, Germany, Austria-Hungary, Luxembourg, and the Netherlands. The nuptial blessing was bestowed on 23 May at 11:30am, in the parish church of Saint-Boniface in Ixelles.

1905 was indeed a banner year, as on 27 December, Raymond was assigned to the prestigious 1st Guides Cavalry Regiment.

Raymond de Selys began his military career in 1898.

Émilie de Theux de Meylandt et Montjardin, Jean's mother.

Monique, François, and Jean at Harlue (1914).

The couple welcomed their first child, Monique, in 1906, their happiness seemingly untouchable, their life's trajectory idyllic among the well-born.

But 1909 was to be a mixed bag. The good? Raymond was promoted to lieutenant, and Émilie's second pregnancy promised a son, François (born April 1910). The bad,

Raymond de Selys in Belgian cavalry uniform.

however, cast a pall: Raymond's health raised grave concerns, and by the summer, he was placed on inactive duty due to a non-service-related heart condition. A bureaucratic way of saying his military career was effectively over. One can only imagine his dismay; nothing had prepared him for such a setback. His stellar performance in physical training and fencing in 1905 – 'a skilled instructor with a talent for physical exercise' – stood in stark contrast to this downturn.

Raymond retreated to his family, watching his children Monique and François grow up. By the time their third child, Jean, arrived in late May 1912, Raymond's joy was marred by the army's decision on 26 September 1912, to medically retire him for his heart condition – a bitter blow for a 32-year-old man, seeing his cavalry dreams utterly dashed. Remember the photograph by his father Raphaël, capturing him in uniform, up on his horse, pride incarnate? To forge a path, distinct from the towering legacies of his grandfather Edmond and father Raphaël, was no easy feat, and the army had offered him that chance.

By the end of 1912, the Belgian army was under the microscope. King Albert I was set on revolutionising its resources and structure. A bill tabled on 5 December sought to muster 33,000 men annually, augmented by 2,000 volunteers, aiming for a 340,000-strong field army in short order. The bill's passage in 1913 triggered tax hikes, including on alcohol, a government ploy to tackle what many saw as a national scourge. By early 1914, the War Ministry's budget reached nearly 14% of the state's total, almost 30% of extraordinary expenses. But was it too little, too late?

The two years leading up to the First World War were deceptively tranquil, nothing like the fevered build-up to the conflict in 1939. The year 1914 actually began under what Churchill would describe as 'an exceptional tranquility'. On 28 June, the assassination of Archduke Franz Ferdinand in Sarajevo, a protest against Austrian presence in Bosnia-Herzegovina, barely rippled through the summer calm. Belgians were unfazed; it was another gunshot that caught the public's imagination, a scandalous crime involving blood and sex splashed across the newspapers: Henriette Caillaux, wife of the French Finance Minister, had murdered the director of *Le Figaro* newspaper in March, and her trial was set to open on 20 July 1914 – a riveting prospect.

Yet, the machinery of war was fast assembling: on 23 July, Austria-Hungary's untenable ultimatum to Serbia; Russia's indignation the next day, soon echoed by France; Austria-Hungary's general mobilisation was met by Russia's, prompting Germany's ultimatum and subsequent declaration of war on 1 August. France declared mobilisation on the same day. By 3 August, after a mere ten-day sequence, Germany declared war on France, and the conflict ignited with lightning speed.

Belgium's neutrality was supposed to be a shield against the looming war. Yet, cautiously, on 27 July, the government halted all military leave, and two days later, the army was put on heightened peacetime alert – a sadly prescient move.

On the morning of 3 August 1914, at 6am, the German Minister Claus von Below-Saleske delivered to Foreign Minister Julien Davignon a terse letter declaring war on Belgium following its refusal to allow German passage through its territory, a demand made the previous evening. Within 3 hours, General Otto von Emmich's forces crossed the Belgian border at Gemmenich, and by 1pm, German troops were already at Visé. England, guarantor of Belgium's neutrality, found itself de facto at war.

Few observers in Europe's fevered capitals believed Belgium could truly withstand the German juggernaut. Yet under King Albert I, Belgium displayed remarkable tenacity, earning the respect of all its allies.

The Belgian army, amid its reformation, counted only 190,000 men and 19,000 volunteers against Germany's 3.84 million soldiers. It was a disparate, poorly equipped, and undisciplined force, sorely lacking in officers. This disconcerting weakness in the Belgian order of battle precipitated the unlikely return of Raymond de Selys Longchamps to combat duty.

The tumultuous prelude to conflict stirred his patriotic spirit, and Raymond fought to be reinstated. Pensioned off with a heart condition? No matter – more was needed to stop a de Selys Longchamps.

His efforts bore fruit; by 2 August 1914, he was recalled as a reserve lieutenant for the duration of the war. Assigned to fortress cavalry, he was stationed at the PFA (Fortified Position of Antwerp), a strategic bulwark housing the army's food and ammunition reserves. This National Redoubt, Europe's mightiest fortress, bristled with defences: twenty outer and eight inner forts, armed with 1,000 guns, divided into five defensive sectors. Raymond joined the squadron in the second sector, east of Antwerp, near the outer forts of Olegem, Broechem, and Kessel.

The National Redoubt soon became a battlefield focal point: the last fort at Liège fell on 16 August, and the Germans entered Brussels four days later. Political institutions and the field army retreated to Antwerp, hoping for swift relief from France and Britain.

Yet the Belgians did not remain idle behind their defences, making two daring sorties on 25–26 August and 8–15 September, boldly striking German forces and disrupting their lines. Likely on a reconnaissance mission for these assaults, Raymond, lacking recent military training, suffered an inguinal hernia after a gruelling 110-km patrol. The medical officer in Schilde wanted him evacuated for surgery, but Lieutenant de Selys Longchamps refused, determined to remain with his unit without exception. Nothing seemed to stop a man reinvigorated by the uniform he donned once more.

A letter in his military file noted his distinction in numerous reconnaissance missions and patrols, highlighting that he 'volunteered for the most dangerous spots'. Strikingly, similar words would describe the zeal of his son Jean in the RAF three decades later – indeed, the apple did not fall far from the tree.

Raymond's file also records missions undertaken with 'great judgment and bravery' in Retie, Kasterlee, and Mol. His superior, Major Emmanuel de Blommaert – a baron, noted horseman (bronze medalist in equestrian jumping at the 1912 Stockholm Olympics), and a military man highly regarded by his peers (later a major general) – clearly held Raymond in high esteem. He must have been gratified to command such driven officers, as German pressure on Antwerp's stronghold intensified.

General Hans von Beseler was tasked with capturing the port city. A veteran of the 1870 war and victor at Liège, von Beseler did not immediately throw his five infantry divisions into battle but used heavy artillery to bombard the forts around Antwerp. One by one, the fortifications were devastated by a deluge of German shells.

On 1 October at 4pm, the artillery fire ceased abruptly, and von Beseler ordered his infantry to storm the Belgian lines. The final offensive phase had begun.

On 2 October 1st and 2nd Belgian divisions counterattacked to reclaim lost positions along the fort line. That day, a patrol led by Raymond de Selys Longchamps was ambushed by about forty German cyclists hidden in the underbrush near the Flemish town of Lille (north of Herentals). Raymond, leading the patrol, was taken by surprise; his horse was killed, and he was wounded in the hand. Struggling to free himself from beneath his dead horse, his hernia painfully reasserted itself amid the intense effort. Capture loomed, but Raymond did not entertain the thought for a second, taking advantage of the confusion to escape on foot with the Germans in hot pursuit. For over a mile, he dodged through the pines, badly out of breath, saved only by his men and a 2nd Mounted Chasseurs patrol, who fought on foot to scatter the pursuers. Two of his brigadiers (corporals), distinguished in combat, were promoted on Raymond's recommendation. Back with his squadron, his wounds were treated but once more he refused evacuation.

On 3 October, Winston Churchill, Britain's First Lord of the Admiralty, arrived in Antwerp to assess the increasingly dire situation. The next day, the fearsome German siege artillery, Big Bertha, pounded the fort at Kessel within Raymond's defence zone, the direct hits shattering the fortress.

On 5 October, Raymond de Selys Longchamps' squadron was ordered to the left bank of the Scheldt, but his health prevented him from riding again. Major Blommaert

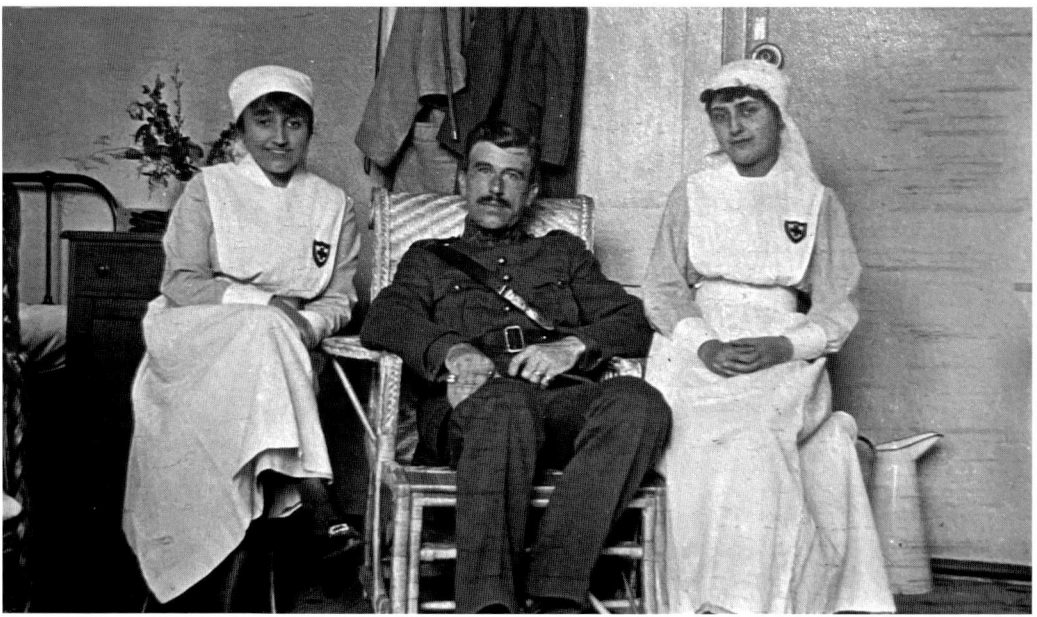

Raymond de Selys during his convalescence in England.

Monique, Edé, Jean and François in Harrington (1915).

now formally ordered him hospitalised, commanding him to make for England via Ostend on 7 October. He arrived on the 13th and was treated at the Royal Naval Hospital in Gosport (Portsmouth) for four weeks.

Meanwhile, the fortress of Antwerp fell on 10 October 1914. The field army and King Albert I retreated to the Yser Plain to continue the conflict for three gruelling years.

During his recovery, Raymond was reunited with his family, whom he had prudently secured in England just before the outbreak of the war. Émilie, Monique, François and little Jean were overjoyed to share with him the delight of welcoming a new boy to the family: Edmond Georges Marie Michel Ghislain, affectionately known as Edé, born on 9 December 1914, in Newmarket, Suffolk.

Many thought Raymond's military career was conclusively over, but they underestimated his renowned tenacity.

By early April 1916, he resumed service as a staff officer for the London garrison. Appointed assistant treasurer of the 'Relief for Belgian Prisoners in Germany', he struggled to find fulfillment in an administrative role while the war raged on. He tirelessly petitioned for active duty and was finally sent to the Remount Service in Calais in December 1916. This service was responsible for cataloguing, supplying,

Raymond de Selys back in service (1916).

and preparing horses needed by the army units. Raymond was closer to the front, yet he remained discontented.

His persistence paid off when he was appointed liaison officer to the British GHQ on 14 March 1917. On 26 September 1918, he was commissioned as a reserve second captain of cavalry for the rest of the war. His service record was once again lauded by his superiors:

> This officer, in his dealings with the British, has shown skill and sound judgment; he has maintained the advantage of his excellent relationships despite often bitter conflicts. From the Belgian perspective, Captain de Selys served with great zeal and dedication. He spared no personal risk, especially during the crossing of the Lys, to provide timely aid to civilians. The right bank of the river was subjected to interdiction fire, and it took real contempt for danger to search the localities for civilian authorities sheltered in cellars.[2]

Raymond de Selys Longchamps earned multiple decorations, and his citation for the French Croix de Guerre, dated 25 January 1920, is particularly telling:

> A Belgian cavalry officer who fulfilled the duties of liaison officer with 14th French Army Corps in Flanders in April, May, and June 1918, with much diligence, zeal and tact. He rendered notable services to the staff of this corps through his perfect knowledge of Dickebusch. Called upon by his duties to undertake missions in areas under heavy bombardment or gas attack, he always stood out under fire for his absolute disregard for danger and his composure.

Raymond de Selys Longchamps continued his career in the Belgian cavalry until 1930 and was named an honorary major a year after finally retiring. Had he been younger, he might well have been mobilised in 1939, but he left the reserve corps on 1 April 1939. No doubt he would have relished being part of it once more, but this time, it would be his four children's turn to distinguish themselves.

Monique, François, Jean, and Edé (1918).

Chapter 3

The 400 Blows

(1918–1939)

Edmond, Raphaël, Raymond… The de Selys Longchamps family was rife with illustrious figures to inspire the four children who, emerging from the war in 1918 at the ages of 12 (Monique), 8 (François), 6 (Jean), and 4 (Edé), finally returned to Belgium.

Back in their homeland, they lived for a short while in the Château de Longchamps in Waremme. They then moved to Spa, where their father was stationed. A tutor was entrusted with their education, polishing their French after four years in England. The three boys all boarded at the Benedictine College of Maredsous. François began in 1920, followed by Jean and then Edé. For the de Selys who attended Maredsous, it was 'a somewhat mythical place: a closed world that one seldom leaves, where singular rules of honour and trust prevail, with a unique vocabulary.'

Yet Maredsous' milieu was not for every temperament, and while François and Edé completed their schooling there, Jean proved markedly resistant to the institution's strictures, revealing a pupil less enthralled by academics than his brothers and even a bit hard headed. One day, Jean absconded from the college (family legend has it his brother Edé covertly brought him supplies), leading to escapades that landed him in other schools, such as Saint-Michel College in Etterbeek, where he consistently displayed the same lackadaisical approach. Yet he was beloved by his classmates and was a storyteller par excellence. Indeed, his best grades came in reading and recitation. As a post-war journalist wrote, 'Jean de Selys was neither a brilliant student nor a model of compliance. But he had enough pride and willpower to clear the hurdles of exams, confounding his kin, who were deprived of the chance to chide him.'[1] Jean completed his scientific studies and spent two years at the University of Louvain studying commercial and financial sciences.

Jean was acutely aware of the anxiety his erratic youth and extreme indecision caused his parents. On Good Friday 1941, while still a trainee pilot in the RAF, he confessed: '… I write this page tonight so that papa and mama know I've been graced to end this life, whose youth had given them some worry, in a way I'm sure they'd approve of…'

Jean de Selys as a model student (1926).

Jean de Selys during a training session on a Belgian racecourse.

There were, however, signs of hope in his demeanour, hinting at his mettle and iron will. A natural horseman, Jean embraced horse racing with a passion. By 16 he was competing admirably against the realm's best jockeys, accruing impressive Gentleman-Rider results until the outbreak of the war (winning fifteen races in 1939). Observers praised his innate grace, in flat races and jumping alike. His remarkable tenacity shone through during a race in Ostend, which he won despite suffering from acute appendicitis. Tall at 6 feet, with chestnut hair, lively brown eyes, a radiant gaze brimming with desire, a slim and elegant figure, beneath his affable dilettante airs Jean de Selys Longchamps hid a steely resolve. Yet his heroic spirit would manifest during the eighteen-day campaign and later still at the helm of a fighter plane.

But let us not leap ahead. His equestrian prowess made him a natural fit for 1st Regiment of Guides, the prestigious cavalry unit his father and brothers also served in. The 1st Guides are an institution in the Belgian army, famed for deeds like the charge at Burkel (19 October 1918), the last planned cavalry charge by such a force in the First World War. With sabres drawn, shouting 'Forward, my children. For the King!', the Belgians routed the Germans near Bruges. Officers at their Etterbeek barracks cherished a relic from that charge: the bullet-riddled saddle Captain-Commander

Count Francis de Meeus used in the assault that was to prove fatal for him.

In 1933, when Jean joined the training squadron of 1st Guides as a voluntary enlistee for three years,[2] the regiment was a bastion of the Belgian aristocracy's offspring, all keenly attuned to splendour and tradition. Stationed at the imposing Witte de Haelen barracks on Géneral Jacques Boulevard in Brussels, opposite a vast parade ground now occupied by VUB university, Jean de Selys made his initial foray into the military cavalry during a period that marked the difficult end of an era; there was a heated debate between advocates of horse cavalry and proponents of complete motorisation.[3] Predictably, the latter would prevail, but the cavalry corps' reorganisation commenced only sluggishly from 1935. Unlike the French and British, who favoured tanks, the Belgians chose a far more modest plan involving motorcycles, with or without sidecars, to mechanise their cavalry. The Belgian motorcycle industry was renowned, with Liège-based brands such as FN, Gillet, and Saroléa starting to militarise civilian motorcycles. The phase-out of horses was completed in March 1938, and the six active cavalry regiments were then designated as motorcycle regiments. Armoured capabilities were introduced gradually, but far too late to significantly influence the conflict that began in 1940. Thus, Jean de Selys Longchamps was among the last generation to join a cavalry regiment still true to its historical roots, which undoubtedly pleased him. He even took this opportunity to hone his riding skills and push the envelope even further, as evidenced by a letter to his sister Monique in September 1934, detailing a jumping accident that knocked him out, with half his face battered, a broken nose, a hip injury, and an inability to walk. The competitor in him did not complain, but merely lamented his absence from a contest the following week. Through letters to his sister from his hospital bed, written between 28 August and 8 September following his accident, Jean revealed two sides of his character. There was a bright, humorous side – 'I believe I can say goodbye to waltzing for a while' – and a darker, more troubled side, found in some of his future writings – 'the trouble, you see, is that we always imagine ourselves different from other men.' It is noteworthy that Jean maintained a close relationship

Jean de Selys in the uniform of 1st Guides Regiment.

Jean de Selys and his brother, Edé.

with his sister Monique, to whom he had written since his earliest years and confided in without hesitation.

Jean's equestrian adventures brought him close to a legendary figure in the racing world: Sam Heapy. This English jockey, with a breathtaking track record (achieving a record-breaking 3,000 victories in 1937), had lived in Belgium since the turn of the century and raced under the colours of Baron Brugmann. It was in the latter's stables, where Jean sometimes trained, that the two men forged their friendship. Sam's impressive career made him a natural mentor for Jean de Selys, who saw horse racing as the great affair of his life.

But Jean remained Jean, and after fourteen months with 1st Guides, marred by a few punishments (for example, eight days confinement in May 1934 for 'having skulked from horse duty by deceiving his platoon leader's good faith'), he requested and was granted an indefinite leave without pay. He returned to the regiment in June

Jean de Selys in action at an equestrian competition, wearing his 1st Guides uniform.

1935 for one month before taking another nine-month leave until March 1936. And so it continued. Jean seemed more preoccupied with his exploits on the racecourses, his role as an escort at high-society parties, and family hunting gatherings than with the rigours of a military career to which he paid little mind. He had a touch of Peter Pan about him. His mischief and rogue charm were much appreciated in the circles he frequented. To fully grasp his character, consider this anecdote: one evening, Jean went to a party with Louisette Thys (the future Mrs de Roubaix), his lady companion. Deeming her hat not to his taste, Jean stopped the car, grabbed the hat, opened the bonnet, and wiped the oil dipstick with the infamous hat. He then threw it in the boot and resumed driving, satisfied: 'Here we go, that's much better!' His companion was stunned. His delightful impudence was quite the hit.

In 1936, he was also found among the staff of Crédit Anversois, a banking establishment located on the Avenue des Arts in Brussels, not far from his parents' home at 118 rue de Trèves. In 1937, despite his intermittent military career, a royal decree of 26 June heralded his promotion to the rank of reserve second lieutenant.

Jean fulfilled all his military recalls between 1935 and 1939. A special ten-day recall in June and July 1939 offered him a glimpse into the beginnings of cavalry motorisation, as evidenced by a photograph where he is seen donning a motorcycle helmet and leather jacket amidst a group of similarly dressed 'cavalrymen'. It was clearly the end of an era, with sabre charges now nothing but a distant memory. Only a few Polish brigades would experience the chilling thrill of a cavalry charge during the German invasion of their country in September 1939.

Baron Jean de Selys Longchamps, with service number 38160, was mobilised on 3 October 1939, and assigned by 1st Guides to the Cyclist Group of 17th Infantry

Jean de Selys, a dandy whose charm left no one indifferent.

Jean de Selys (third from left) in a motorcycle uniform during manoeuvres in 1939.

Division (17th DI),[4] a second reserve infantry division, upon the activation of Phase D of the mobilisation plan. Reserve cavalrymen from the classes of 1931 to 1934 were indeed used to form reconnaissance units for the infantry divisions. While the active infantry divisions and the first reserve infantry divisions had only one cyclist squadron each, the less well-equipped second reserve divisions were bolstered by a cyclist group composed of three squadrons. Thus, 17th DI comprised two fusilier squadrons and one machine-gunner squadron, all mobilised by bicycle. However, Jean avoided the somewhat ignominious fate that turned cavaliers into cyclists in the spring of 1940, as his rank of second lieutenant earned him the role of quartermaster officer within the headquarters staff of the Cyclist Group 17th DI. This spared him the jibes that invariably accompanied the Guides when they pedaled their steeds and the laughingly offered encouragements – 'Give it the spurs, my lad!' – that never failed to wound the pride of the dignified cavaliers.

Chapter 4

18 Days and Then It's Gone

(10–28 May 1940)

The sequence leading up to the beginning of the Second World War clearly differed from what was observed in 1914. What strikes most is its length and the resulting astonishing immobility.

On 1 September 1939, Germany invaded Poland without a declaration of war and remained deaf to the ultimatum of the British and French governments, who demanded the withdrawal of its troops from Polish territory. Their ultimatum ended on 2 September. The next day, Great Britain and France declared war on Nazi Germany. This at least clarified a situation that had been deteriorating month after month since the mid-thirties, with Germany increasingly – and blatantly – violating all the treaties and agreements previously concluded under the anesthetised gaze of statesmen who greatly overestimated their diplomatic capabilities and continued to consider Adolf Hitler as a little brute who needed to be tamed. This marked the peak of sterile appeasement policies that only those naive enough to believe them were deceived by. What everyone was unaware of on 3 September, however, was that at that very moment, an endless length of time began where the future belligerents would observe each other for eight long months: it was the beginning of the 'Phoney War', which would only end on 10 May 1940.

As Great Britain and France declared war on Germany, Belgium was pressed to take a stance: either it allied with one of the belligerents, implying an immediate entry into war, or it opted for neutrality. The latter option was chosen, carried by the slim hope of escaping the threatening conflict. As a neutral country, Belgium could safely carry out the mobilisation of its troops at a relatively slow pace, staggering its war footing until May 1940.

In 1939, the Belgian army had already put in place various improvement programmes (motorisation of cavalry divisions, the adoption of new motorised 120mm artillery pieces, the purchase of excellent 47mm anti-tank guns, modernisation of the fortifications network…) begun in the previous years. When King Leopold III officially took command on 3 September, the field army was already 550,000-men strong. But the decision to have a mass army should not deceive us: there were indeed many shadows surrounding the picture, starting with the lack of competent officers, which the hurried swelling of the ranks would significantly highlight, and an air force whose equipment had only been modernised in homeopathic doses and in no way met the standards now imposed by the formidable Luftwaffe. Let us also add that the second reserve units, like the one Jean de Selys would join upon his mobilisation, suffered from the poor quality of most of their equipment. It can thus be assumed that almost all means of transport of 17th DI Cyclist Group were requisitioned vehicles. Within the squadrons, there was a heterogeneous set of cars, trucks and bicycles, which would sometimes not even be painted in khaki before 10 May to avoid damaging them. Barely mobilised, the first task assigned to Reserve Lieutenant Georges Remi (better known as Hergé, the father of Tintin) would be to requisition bicycles.

The Cyclist Group of the 15th DI, giving a good idea of the general appearance of a unit similar to Jean de Selys' in May 1940.

The standard weapon of an officer like Jean de Selys was the pistol, the most modern being the FN GP 1934 9mm, but it was not uncommon to find FN Browning 1910s, Colt 1903s, and FN Browning 1900s used during the First World War. For reserve officers concerned about having quality armament, it was common to buy their pistol from a civilian gunsmith. The lack of military weapons even required mass requisitioning of pistols and revolvers from civilians for reserve units. Many of these requisitions were still carried out by the gendarmerie or the police during the first days of the invasion.

Although Jean de Selys Longchamps had to contend with makeshift equipment, he benefited from the guidance of an experienced officer, Major Henry Van Derton.[1] At the dawn of the conflict, the 38-year-old Van Derton was also a decorated cavalryman from the First World War, where he had fought mainly in the 2nd Regiment of Horse Hunters. He joined the 1st Guides in September 1938, and it was this last posting that led him to cross paths with Jean during the 1939 mobilisation. His military file notes that Van Derton was 'kind but firm' with his subordinates. His work at the head of 17th DI Cyclist Group was also very favourably appreciated: 'He has managed to make his unit, composed only of recalled soldiers, a homogeneous whole over which he exerts a real ascendancy.' An experienced officer with proven leadership was a precious resource because from September 1939 until the start of hostilities in May 1940, a growing laxity was observed within most of the mobilised units, and discipline inevitably dulled to worrying proportions. A spirit of tolerance and goodwill prevailed, and permissions were increasingly considered rights rather than rewards. The small size of the country made it easier to abuse these privileges, as mobilised men could quickly return home. Moreover, soldiers became demotivated over the months due to the monotony of the tasks assigned to them (watches, chores, constructing earthworks…) as well as the subversive propaganda of the VNV* that contaminated some Flemish regiments.

Yet, the reasons to believe in the imminence of a German attack were evident. Right after the end of the Polish campaign (on 6 October 1939), a progressive reinforcement of German forces was observed: initially, thirty divisions were deployed facing the Grand Duchy of Luxembourg and the Maginot Line, but these quickly increased to eighty, then 120 by February 1940, deployed along the borders adjoining the Netherlands, Belgium, and France. On 10 May, no less than 140 divisions would participate in the assault. Merely five days after its creation in Laarne (east of Ghent), 17th DI Cyclist Group was already leaving the 17th DI and heading towards the Turnhout region.[2] Major Van Derton positioned his unit in Retie (near the Dutch border) and placed his men at the disposal of 9th DI. On 12 January 1940, the group was moved to Kasterlee. After another operational deployment in Campine, the unit headed to

---

* The Vlaamsch Nationaal Verbond (VNV) or Flemish National Union was a significant nationalist political party in Belgium.

Officers of Cyclist Group 17th DI (April 1940). Jean de Selys is standing (second from right) and Georges Van Derton is sitting (third from left).

Kortrijk on 5 March with the mission of guarding a section of the Belgian-French border between the Scheldt and Lys rivers.

On 28 April 17th DI Cyclist Group was relieved by 13th DI Cyclist Group and resumed the positions defended by the latter in Lanaken, near the Dutch border (3 miles from Maastricht). Once in position, the unit was placed under the command of 1st Army Corps.

The defence of the Vucht/Briegden sub-sector was entrusted to 17th DI Cyclist Group. Its mission consisted of monitoring the east bank of the Meuse over about 9 miles, alerting the advanced intelligence centre in Hasselt in case of a German invasion, and proceeding with the destruction of a series of strategic bridges to hinder the enemy offensive. The command post of 17th DI Cyclist Group, where Jean de Selys was based, was in Neerharen at the centre of the defence apparatus, for which the cyclist group was responsible.

On 9 May, the 1st Squadron of fusilier cyclists of the Van Derton group took up position in the northern zone (extending from Vucht to Oud-Rekem), while 2nd Squadron oversaw the southern zone (from Oud-Rekem to Briegden). The machine gunners of 3rd Squadron were distributed between the two squadrons of fusiliers.

S/Lt de Selys, Major Van Derton, Lt Colman (Van Derton's deputy), and Lt de Halleux (commander of 2nd squadron) (March/April 1940).

It is worth noting that on the eve of the conflict, the Belgian army counted twenty-three divisions, or 650,000 soldiers under arms. The mobilisation effort was impressive: Belgium had never had so many soldiers to defend its territory. However, this impressive total needed to be nuanced: barely half the forces could be considered as real combat units. Thus, in the eyes of the general staff, second reserve units such as Jean's were not intended to be on the front line. The storm unleashed by the Nazi forces' assault would, of course, swiftly sweep away this eminently theoretical view of the order of battle.

Lt Colman, S/Lt de Crayencourt (2nd Squadron), Lt de Crawhez, and Major Van Derton (March/April 1940).

On the early morning of Friday, 10 May 1940, without any ultimatum or formal declaration of war, German forces invaded Belgium. The Luftwaffe not only attacked the Albert Canal defences and major airfields, but also sowed chaos in the central part of the country by destroying railway stations, bridges, and communication networks. The attack on Belgium and the Netherlands was a large-scale diversion manoeuvre to draw French and British allies to the north. No one within the general staffs understood that it was in the south, in the Ardennes, that the bulk of the Nazi push would exert itself.

Everything happened very quickly, and the Belgian forces were stunned by what turned out to be a demonstration of the best principles of blitzkrieg. Alongside speed of execution and abundance of resources, the Germans also exhibited audacity. In an unprecedented move, gliders landed on the fort of Ében-Émael to allow parachutist commandos to neutralise the fortification with shaped charges in just a few minutes.

In the area of 17th DI Cyclist Group, Van Derton's command post in Neerharen received a general alarm at 12:17am, and orders were given to take up combat positions along the Zuid-Willemsvaart and the Briegden-Neerharen canal. At 4:30am, the cyclists' barracks at Lanaken were heavily bombed, and its telephone exchange was destroyed: direct communication with HQ was severed, and the local connection between 17th DI Cyclist Group's command post and its detachments tasked with bridge destruction was also lost. Great confusion now reigned over what needed to be done and within what timeframe. Major Van Derton took the initiative to blow up the bridge over the Zuid-Willemsvaart at Smeermaas around 6:30am. The unit in charge of destroying the bridge, located 650 feet from the Belgian-Dutch border, was then captured by German forces.

Orders for the destruction of the other bridges finally arrived at Van Derton's HQ at 7:30. The bridges of Vucht, Maasmechelen, Boorsem, Oud-Rekem, Neerharen, Tournebride, and Lanaken were swiftly destroyed to attempt to slow down the German offensive. The Oud-Rekem bridge was the last to explode, at 8am. Around 9am, the enemy reached the Zuid-Willemsvaart in the northern part of the sector defended by the fusiliers of 17th DI Cyclist Group, near Vucht. Enemy detachments crossed the Meuse with rubber boats and gained ground. While the enemy rapidly advanced north of the defensive line, it also succeeded in making a major breach in the southern zone, near the Veldwezelt bridge. By 3pm, the enemy was already at the gates of Rekkem. The situation for Van Derton's men became increasingly dire as the group was now on the verge of being surrounded. Around 5:30pm, the order to retreat was finally given by the corps. The losses suffered during the day were serious, ammunition reserves were already depleted, and 17th DI Cyclist Group was positioned at the eastern edge of Tongres on the night of 10–11 May.

The unit paid a heavy price for its deployment as a covering force between the Belgian-Dutch border and the Albert Canal. The group counted ten killed and many others wounded or taken prisoner. This first day had already seen Jean de Selys distinguish himself.[3] When, around noon, he ensured communication between the headquarters of his unit and that of 1st Army Corps in Tongres, driving, despite the danger, through machine gun fire barrages and bomb carpets that the Luftwaffe multiplied on the increasingly congested Belgian roads. During his journey, Jean observed that the Briegden bridge had not been blown up – the lieutenant in charge of the mission confessed to him not knowing how to do it – and he informed Van Derton. His superior's dismay struck him: chaos seemed total. Around 2:30am, Jean was exhausted when he finally came to a stop near Hasselt, where his unit had established its quarters. As he dozed off for a handful of hours at the end of this first day of war, Jean was no longer quite the same man: he had experienced combat. Like his father twenty-six years earlier, Jean had seen men die around him. The men were sometimes friends, such as Baron Raymond de Crawhez, a lieutenant leading 4th Platoon who lost his life alongside him in the Neerharen sector. During the following morning, the unit was violently bombed by Stukas. Retreat orders multiplied, and the cyclist group began a long journey of over 60 miles that passed through Waremme, Leefdaal, and Tervuren, before finally arriving in the village of Relegem, located between Wemmel and Zellik, northwest of Brussels, on Monday, 13 May.

That same day, 13 May, was also marked by a speech King Leopold III addressed to his troops through the following proclamation:

Soldiers,
Suddenly assailed by an unprecedented surprise attack, grappling with forces overwhelmingly equipped and benefiting from formidable aviation, the Belgian army has been executing a difficult manoeuvre for three days, the success of which is of the utmost importance for the overall conduct of operations and for the fate of the war. This manoeuvre requires exceptional efforts from all, officers and soldiers, sustained day and night, amid a moral tension pushed to the extreme by the sight of the ravages caused by a ruthless invader. However harsh the ordeal,

King Leopold III reviews a cyclist group before the start of hostilities.

you will overcome it with courage. Our position improves by the hour, our ranks are closing. On decisive days, you will stiffen all energies, consent to all sacrifices to halt the invasion. As on the Yser in 1914, French and British troops cooperate there: the salvation and honour of the country command it.

LEOPOLD.

It is uncertain whether this proclamation sparked much enthusiasm within 17th DI Cyclist Group, whose soldiers were already in a dismal condition, and which now had to be completely reorganised due to the heavy losses suffered. Henceforth, the unit consisted of only two squadrons, with the men and equipment of 3rd Squadron being redistributed between 1st and 2nd. Jean de Selys' role evolved within the group and he became the leader of a platoon attached to the protection of the headquarters and responsible for ammunition resupply of what remained of 17th DI Cyclist Group.

During the night of 16–17 May, a week after the start of the conflict, the Cyclist Group retreated once more and joined the rest of the army on the new defensive line from Terneuzen to Audenarde, passing through Ghent. On Saturday, 19 May, Van Derton established his HQ in the village of Afsnee, west of Ghent. Still attached to 1st Corps, the group was tasked in the following days with guarding all bridges between Nevele and Vinderhoute. This mission lasted until 23 May, when Major Van Derton received the order to withdraw starting at 9:30pm to the left bank of the Lys. The bridges of Drongen, Mariakerke, Vinderhoute, and Landegem were destroyed in the evening, and the cyclists withdrew. After a journey passing through Nevele, Poeke, and Wingene, Ruddervoorde was reached on the morning of 24 May. The men were dirty, tired, and their uniforms were no longer fresh in that sunny spring of 1940.

The following day, Saturday, 25 May, Van Derton and his unit moved again and ended the day by taking up positions at the northern limit of Wervik, less than 12 miles from Ypres and a stone's throw from the French border. There, the cyclists faced the enemy again. Around 11pm, gunfire erupted in the area where 1st Squadron was located. During the evening, the last British troops withdrew south of Wervik to move towards the border without informing the Belgians. The southern flank of the Belgian army was now constantly exposed. As they fell asleep, one could hear soldiers softly sobbing, exhausted and anxious about what the future held. The psychological shock was severe: everything that had been meticulously built up had collapsed in an instant. Even the French army, touted as the strongest on the continent, experienced a dizzying collapse, while the British seemed to have completely disappeared…

At dawn on Sunday, 26 May, the Germans infiltrated between the first and second Belgian lines, and around 5:30am, the enemy attacked the cyclists near kilometre post 1 on the Geluwe–Wervik road.

Captain Le Court, commanding officer of 1st Squadron, 17th DI Cyclist Group, was overwhelmed and decided to raise the white flag on his forward position, even though his resistance capabilities were not fully exhausted. This attitude infuriated Van Derton, and Le Court was relieved of his command that same evening. Nothing seemed to be able to stop the Germans, who managed to cross the road and continue their breakthrough. At 7:30am, 1st Corps ordered a general retreat to the Roeselare-Ypres railway line, where an immense improvised anti-tank barrier had been hastily constructed using 2,000 freight wagons placed buffer to buffer. Fifteen minutes later, Van Derton's 1st Squadron was heavily attacked. Jean de Selys Longchamps distinguished himself once again, which, after the war (on 16 February 1946) would earn him a citation in the Army Order of the Day and the award of an additional Palm on the 1940 War Cross: 'Through his personal and audacious action, armed with a submachine gun, he enabled certain elements of his group to disengage on the verge of being encircled on 26 May 1940, during the battle of Geluwe.'

The group still tried to establish contact with the British, but Van Derton realised with horror that they had left the area without informing him. His men could only escape the enemy fire at the cost of heavy losses (three-quarters of his troops were killed, wounded, or missing, about 300 men in total) and they managed to flee to Zonnebeke. Around 9:30am, the cyclists reached Westrozebeke, from where the unit was sent to new quarters at Vijfwegen, near Roulers.

The next day, the group licked its wounds after the tough battle it had just fought. Due to the large number of stragglers and wounded, the unit was now reduced to a single squadron of 180 men, equipped with only one machine gun and seventeen or eighteen submachine guns. They soon needed to set out again, as a new mission awaited Van Derton's men: the group was once again called upon to participate in yet another defence setup orchestrated by Colonel Charles d'Orjo de Marchovelette (commander of 2nd Lancers) between Zonnebeke and Langemark-Poelkapelle. The 17th DI Cyclist Group therefore headed towards Langemark and reinforced the lines starting at 2:30pm. The men took up positions on the right flank, along the Steenbeek. Seventeen days after the start of hostilities, Jean de Selys Longchamps and what remained of the unit to which he belonged, found themselves more than 140 miles away from their initial position. They were far from imagining that their very last combat position would be near a place that Adolf Hitler himself would visit five days later, on 1 June, when he made a brief tour of his troops in Belgium and stopped at a German military cemetery where 44,300 soldiers who fell during the First World War were buried, in Langemark.[4] The Führer had not forgotten that it was in that region where he experienced baptism by fire on 28 October 1914.

In the previous days, the Belgian army had been engaged in a defensive battle of attrition. All its units still fit for combat were on the front lines, plugging enemy penetrations as best they could. The defensive setups attempted to form a cohesive whole with the heterogeneous units that were still available, but the front line had been irreparably breached. Also, logistical problems with supplies and the evacuation of the wounded posed nearly insoluble challenges at the rear. The railways were inaccessible, and the roads were extraordinarily congested. More than 3 million individuals (soldiers, refugees, civilians) were concentrated in a resistance pocket of 650 square miles, less than a twentieth of Belgium's total territory.

On Tuesday, 28 May, the day dawned under a low and rainy sky looking like an old rag. The news of unconditional surrender spread among the troops, leaving a taste of ash in the mouths of all those soldiers with wan faces. The Belgian army still deployed sixteen divisions against the thirteen German divisions, but their position had become untenable.

German propaganda did wonders to present a modern, ultra-motorised army. The reality was more nuanced, and horse-drawn units were just as numerous during the invasion.

The day before, King Leopold III had sent a delegate to the German High Command to inquire about the conditions for ceasing hostilities. At 11pm, the sovereign accepted the conditions imposed by the enemy and proposed the ceasefire be set for the following day at 4am. It was at this moment the combat units ceased fire along the entire Belgian front, except for a few areas notified later, which would continue fighting until 2:30pm.

The eighteen-day campaign was indeed over, leaving hundreds of thousands of dazed and incredulous soldiers to their sad fate. Within all the units, there was now a strange mixture of relief and stupefaction. At the end of the eighteen days, the army counts 6,624 dead and around 20,000 wounded. Some 225,000 prisoners would soon be in German hands.

Jean de Selys Longchamps was in Sint-Juliaan, north of Ypres, when the surrender was announced to his unit around 6:30am. A chasm could have opened under his feet, but it did not. Those few days of war had given him in life experiences that were unknown to him until then, he who had lived a sheltered life in a cozy bubble that had enveloped his existence since birth. There was fear, of course, a lot of fear even, but also exhilarating surges of adrenaline as only true adventure can provide. He took risks and he loved it. War seemed to exert a kind of fascination on him. For de Selys, there is no doubt that the fight had to continue in one way or another. As a fervent Catholic, he could not ignore the fact the Nazis represented a real threat to Christian civilization, and that was viscerally unbearable to him. The prospect of seeing his country dissolve into the German Reich was equally unbearable. Jean had always been somewhat resistant to orders, so this incongruous call to lay down arms would not change his mind, even if it came from an authority his family had taught him to respect to the highest degree: that of the King.

Not everyone in the group was as resolute as him, and Major Van Derton was captured by the Germans on 28 May near Snellegem (near Bruges). For him, the war was already over, and he would not return from captivity until five years later, in June 1945.

At this time, Jean was 25 miles from the Belgian coast. He did not yet know that the British forces had launched a vast operation to evacuate troops to England. Operation Dynamo - also known as the more epic 'Miracle of Dunkirk' - was indeed initiated by Churchill on 26 May, just before 7pm, without the French and Belgian general staffs being informed. The Belgians, whose crumbling defensive lines deeply concern their allies, were simply kept in the dark deliberately. The French were informed at the political level - Winston Churchill mentioned it to Paul Reynaud on 26 May - but Reynaud, Prime Minister and Minister of Foreign Affairs, did not pass on the information to the military, who would only truly understand the extent of the plan the British were executing on 29 May.

Chapter 5

Into the Wild

(29–31 May 1940)

I t was to De Panne, the last town on the Belgian coast before France, located 12 miles from Dunkirk, where de Selys Longchamps decided to head, lacking any real alternative options. Unknowingly, Jean had made the right choice and was about to join the place where the British forces had recently moved their HQ. Indeed, the Belgian locality was preferred to Dunkirk because an underwater cable connected the continent to Great Britain, allowing for good-quality telephone communications with

The heart of the seaside town of De Panne is unrecognisable.

Dover and London. The bigwigs of the British staff thus set up shop in De Panne on the seafront. Among them was the man who would distinguish himself many times during the conflict and who would lead the liberation of Belgium four years later, Field Marshal Bernard Montgomery, who now commanded the entire eastern sector from De Panne.

When de Selys finally reached the coast, he discovered a topsy-turvy town that had lost all the charm of the peaceful seaside resort it had been just a few days earlier under the name of De Panne les Bains. The indescribable chaos that accompanied his journey from Sint-Juliaan to De Panne was indeed a harbinger of the worst, yet Jean was nonetheless struck by the sight of streets brimming with abandoned military equipment, through which one sometimes struggled to navigate due to their sheer abundance. Even the boardwalk was clogged with a massive number of trucks and other vehicles left by desperate troops, whose only obsession now was to escape. The beach was likewise littered with all sorts of materials, ammunition boxes and machine guns pitifully lined up on the sand, as if it was a huge open-air flea market. It all seemed unreal. The town was overflowing with weary soldiers and panicked civilians. The explosions, screams, smells, smoke, and even fire in some places oozed a sinister foretaste of the apocalypse and thickened the atmosphere. The waterfront, which just hours earlier represented an escape route to England, now seemed like a gateway to hell. Famed writer and journalist Joseph Kessel, who was in the Dunkirk area at the same time trying to embark, reported that it was 'the biggest fright of my life, the one that knots the guts and paralyzes.' Whilst the Belgian army had laid down its arms a few hours earlier, De Panne was still at the heart of the fierce battle unfolding in the tiny Dunkirk resistance pocket. The French and British threw their last forces into covering the evacuation with all the energy of despair. Anti-aircraft batteries were scattered throughout the city and on the beaches.

In the sky, the Royal Air Force, which had been rather discreet during the eighteen-day campaign, threw itself wholeheartedly into protecting the rescue zones of the British Expeditionary Force (BEF). The Luftwaffe was in difficulty, for the first time they did not have complete control of the sky. British planes, taking off from their advanced bases in southeast England, could fly up to three operations a day. Meanwhile, the Germans, who had not yet set up air bases in Belgium, had to operate from western Germany and could only carry out one mission daily. Therefore, aerial combats ensued above the troops massed on the beaches, and perhaps Jean was inspired by the sight of the Hurricanes and Spitfires valiantly engaging the swastika-crossed fighters and bombers? This is plausible, as it is probably the very first time Jean witnessed the frenzied dogfights that surely tickled the soul of the fighter that had revealed itself in him over the previous few days. It is very likely that he was flown over by planes from 609 Squadron, in which he would distinguish himself thirteen months later.

In addition to Dunkirk, which concentrated the bulk of the operations, the British had established evacuation zones from three beaches: Malo-les-Bains, Bray-Dunes Plage, and De Panne, at the eastern end of the area.

For Jean de Selys Longchamps, salvation came from meeting other Belgian officers who, like him, had decided not to lay down their arms and to cross the lines to reach the beaches. In the midst of the debacle that seemed to sweep everything around them, fate had them cross paths with Colonel Jules Bastin, a cavalry officer as well and a true legend of the First World War (imprisoned by the Germans in 1914, he made ten escape attempts, the last of which succeeded). Among the Belgian officers gathered at De Panne alongside Jean de Selys, Lieutenant Doctor Albert Guérisse[1] was well acquainted with Bastin, who had commanded his regiment (1st Lancers) a few months earlier, and he solicited Bastin to agree with the British that the fifteen or so Belgian officers stranded at De Panne alongside him could embark for England. It did not promise to be easy, as priority was clearly given to the British. Even the French had been ordered to evacuate the entire Bray-Dunes – De Panne sector to leave it exclusively for the British.

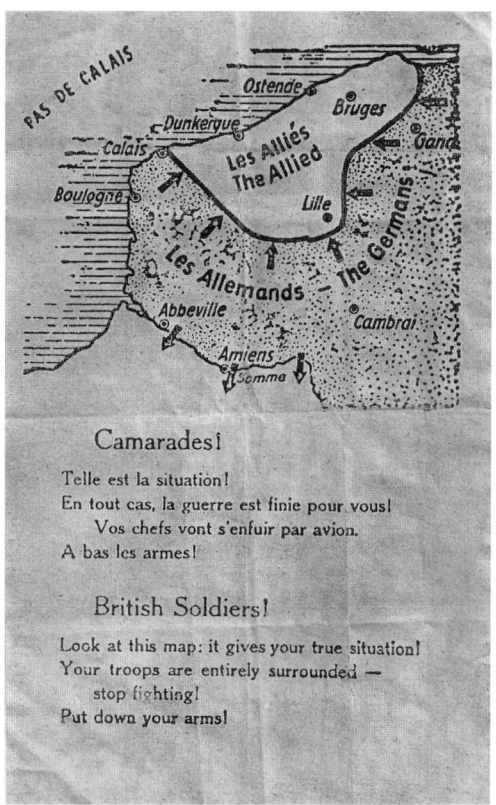

Psychological warfare raged, and the Germans dropped leaflets to demoralise their enemies.

Posted in a bomb crater on the beach, de Selys Longchamps, surrounded by other Belgian officers, remained hopeful and impatiently awaited the long-expected moment of embarkation, which still seemed just as uncertain. They were about 100 feet from a Bofors 40mm anti-aircraft defence battery that tirelessly scanned the sky for Luftwaffe predators. To pass the time, they observed the incredible logistical ballet unfolding before their eyes. As De Panne is not equipped with a jetty, the British had to build three makeshift piers consisting of a long column of trucks stuck together at low tide. Their tyres were burst to prevent them from floating, and they were heavily weighted with sandbags to ensure their stability. These improvised piers stretched far enough into the sea – sometimes up to twenty-five trucks – so that troops could embark on

Hidden in a bomb crater on the beach, Jean de Selys (far left) waits with his companions in misfortune. Albert Guérisse is third from the right.

Facing the group of Belgian officers, the English are busy on the beach. An anti-aircraft gun is visible on the left.

One of the long columns of trucks lined up to serve as an improvised pier.

small boats which took them to ships moored a little further offshore. To reach these boats, soldiers walked on ordinary planks hastily fitted to the roofs of the trucks. It was unorthodox, but effective.

In the morning of 29 May, the backwash made it difficult to embark on the beaches of De Panne, Bray-Dunes, and Malo-les-Bains. In the late afternoon, the Luftwaffe repeatedly bombed and strafed the beach and the which had come to the aid of the soldiers trapped in the pocket. The town itself was not spared, and firefighters fought for more than ten hours on twelve large fires that day. It was not until 3 June that all the fires would be completely under control in the severely wounded seaside town.

But let us return to the day of 30 May, which was again punctuated by new air raids and bombings. Louis Gregorius, a refugee who arrived in De Panne from Brussels on the 27th, testifies:

> At noon, we go to dine with villagers. For dessert, the Germans serve us an airplane attack. Whistling sounds reveal that bombs are being dropped. Terrible explosions shake the ground. We race to our boarding house. Long black columns of smoke rise into the sky. Houses burn. Cries are heard, calls from panicked people. They run and gesticulate like madmen. Then, a plane emerges. Its engine sputters. The craft descends and opens fire with all its machine guns. It sweeps the streets. We lose sight of it. Suddenly, it reappears. It's been hit by anti-aircraft fire. It loses altitude, skims our roof, hits the ground, crashes, and bursts into flames. Its remnants burn. Its ammunition explodes. A fireworks display couldn't do better.[2]

The beach of De Panne littered with debris. In the background can be seen one of the improvised piers built by the English to reach boats offshore.

The nerves of all were constantly tested, as explosions went off on all sides. This time, it was the bomb disposal experts who detonated a marine mine stranded on the beach. Gregorius describes the scene: 'A tremendous explosion shakes the ground and sends a huge flame toward the sky. Then a cloud of smoke and dust and it's over.'[3]

By now, the entirety of the British Expeditionary Force was within the perimeter set around Dunkirk, whose defence now falls solely to French units. Colonel Bastin's efforts to get the Belgian officers and non-commissioned officers embarked were thwarted by the impossibility of getting a Belgian ship from Dover to De Panne. After new and difficult negotiations with the British, Bastin finally obtained permission to have forty Belgians embark on a British ship in the western zone of the beach. However, their boarding could only happen once all the British military were aboard. The Belgians, therefore, joined a line on the beach, which moved desperately slowly.

The next day, Friday, 31 May, before sunrise, de Selys Longchamps and his companions in misfortune observed Dunkirk burning in the distance: the fire was impressive. In a twilight atmosphere, the Belgians gradually made their way towards the makeshift piers. It is not clearly established whether Jean de Selys Longchamps managed to embark with Albert Guérisse on the British ship HMS *Westward Ho*,[4] but it seems very likely since their destinies would continue to cross during the following weeks. It is enlightening to linger for a moment on HMS *Westward Ho*, as an example of the extraordinary heterogeneity of the fleet that would repatriate the troops to England.

The *Westward Ho* on which Belgian officers left De Panne just in time to join England.

HMS *Westward Ho* was a paddle-wheel ship, built in 1894, which had been used as a minehunter since the First World War and experienced its last great feat of arms with Operation Dynamo. Nearly 900 vessels of all sizes took part in Operation Dynamo, with only a quarter belonging to the Royal Navy: from cruisers to dinghies, and even yachts, over twenty different types of ships were involved.

A remarkable photograph taken by war correspondent Otto Kropf showing a Wehrmacht soldier posing on the remains of a pier in De Panne.

At about 4am, embarking was still far from easy. Non-British military personnel sometimes suffered from hostile and even brutal incidents at the hands of certain British officers, who treated other nationalities with little respect and were often uncompromising in enforcing the 'British only' rule that prevailed in the zone. A British officer, pistol in hand, even threatened de Selys and attempted to prevent him from boarding.[5] The details of how Jean managed to persuade him to allow him on board are unfortunately unknown, but one can imagine his legendary eloquence, coupled with audacity and resolve, made the difference.

Once aboard HMS *Westward Ho*, Jean was among the 150 soldiers embarked in De Panne, before the ship headed for Dunkirk, where it came under attack from German aircraft. Nonetheless, it succeeded in taking on 602 additional soldiers.[6]

De Selys was thus one of the 338,226 soldiers (including 139,911 non-British) evacuated as part of Operation Dynamo. Two-thirds of the evacuees left from Dunkirk, and a third from the three beaches, including De Panne. The British losses were significant: some 68,111 men of the BEF were killed or captured, while 243 ships and

The victors discovered the unimaginable chaos left on the beaches by their defeated opponents.

106 aircraft were lost. Also abandoned were 2,472 cannons, 63,879 vehicles, 76,000 tons of ammunition, and 500,000 tons of fuel and provisions. On the French side, 40,000 soldiers ultimately surrendered to the Germans in the Dunkirk pocket. Since the start of the German invasion on 10 May, the Allies had lost the equivalent of 71 divisions: 30 French, 22 Belgian, the equivalent of 10 Dutch, and 9 British.[7]

Operation Dynamo, nonetheless, deserves to be described as a miraculous success; one that far surpassed the expectations of the British Chief of the Imperial General Staff, General Edmund Ironside. On 26 May, he had set a goal to evacuate 30,000 soldiers. In the end, ten times that number were rescued. The baffling halt of the German armoured advance – having taken only fourteen days to cover the 240 miles from Bastogne to Gravelines, and then requiring twelve days to progress from Gravelines to Dunkirk, a mere 12.5 miles away – along with the surprising confusion that appeared to afflict the German High Command as of 21 May, certainly contributed to this outcome.

Other factors also account for this unlikely accomplishment: the unexpected Belgian resistance that held firm until 27 May, the adverse weather conditions over the English Channel, and the ferocity of a Royal Air Force that disrupted Luftwaffe operations, as well as the remarkable British logistics and the bravery and sacrifice of the French troops, especially those of 16th Corps, covering the evacuation. However, Winston Churchill remained pragmatic, tempering any celebratory sentiments when he declared in the House of Commons on 4 June: 'Wars are not won by evacuations.'

Chapter 6

Catch-22

(1 June – 14 December 1940)

On 31 May, Jean de Selys Longchamps made his entrance onto British soil via the pier at Margate, a quaint port town in the Thanet district of Kent. Just days prior, on 27 May, this location was thrust into the evacuation endeavour famously dubbed Operation Dynamo. In a striking tally, between the end of May and the start of June 1940, some 46,722 survivors funnelled through here. Fate held an unnoticed twist for Jean: Margate lies just 3.5 miles from the Manston base, from where he would take off on 20 January 1943, to strike at the Gestapo headquarters in Brussels.

Postcard depicting the Margate pier where the survivors of De Panne took their first steps on English soil.

Upon landing in Margate, the Dunkirk pocket survivors were shepherded towards the town's railway station, where volunteers welcomed them with tea and snacks in a makeshift yet effective arrangement.

Jean's stint in Margate was fleeting; he promptly headed to Ramsgate, and from there, made his way to London in the afternoon, only to be quickly redirected to Tenby, 170 miles further west, at the southwestern extremity of Wales. The Belgian Military Camp for Regrouping (CMBR) had been established there since 28 May,[1] spurred by the initiative of the Belgian ambassador, Émile de Cartier de Marchienne. Lieutenant General Van Strydonck de Burkel, a charismatic figure from Antwerp aged 63 in May 1940, famous for participating in the last cavalry charge at Burkel in 1918, led the camp. In June 1940, Tenby housed only 462 Belgians, but numbers soon swelled to 700 by August and 900 by November. There, the Belgian army was reborn like the phoenix, and the roots of what would become the legendary Piron Brigade began to take hold. Indeed, Tenby was set to become a pivotal location in military history, though such a future was hard for Jean to envision at the time as he passed through.

The legendary Lieutenant General Van Strydonck de Burkel.

As June 1940 dawned, Tenby embodied the very essence of being 'in the middle of nowhere': a bleak town of 4,000 souls, its only treasure was a modest fishing harbour. The locals spoke a dialect baffling to foreigners, and the rain seemed unending. It was hardly the sort of place to boost morale, especially as the British, who were still fighting, offered the Belgians scant respect. Their army having surrendered, the Belgians were often viewed by the locals as nothing more than refugees.

At the time of Jean's arrival, Tenby was barely more than a landing spot for a diverse collection of soldiers suffering from low spirits, from the hardcore patriot itching for more action to the bewildered conscript who found himself there more out of happenstance than conviction. The air was thick with toxicity: contradictory reports spread across Tenby and the most despondent voices easily tainted those struggling to figure out who was leading their country, which now seems to lack both government and an army.

Yet Belgium had not uttered its final words. Resistance formed on all fronts, and as early as 31 May, 190 Belgian parliamentarians convened in Limoges (France) to pass a motion condemning 'the capitulation initiated by Leopold III'. It was a modest start, but it signified that the Belgians, albeit reeling, were beginning to raise their heads.

In Tenby, rumour even had it that the Belgian army was planning to reconstitute combat units in France.[2] Considerable forces retreated to France at the time of capitulation, including many militiamen from the class of 1940 who are already at work reconstituting the 7th Infantry Division, battered during the battles along the Albert Canal, engineering units, three military aviation regiments, students of the Royal Military Academy and their instructors, as well as the 120,000 young recruits of the Recruitment Reserve (RR) who managed to retreat in complete improvisation towards the south. If we add up all these resources, it does seem conceivable to deploy more than 100,000 fighters into battle in the not-too-distant future. As soon as it was set up in Poitiers, the National Defence cabinet immediately went about reorganising the Belgian troops, actively seeking officers that matched the profile of those stranded in Tenby. Lieutenant Albert Guérisse, Jean's guiding light since their meeting amid the debacle at De Panne, was determined to head to Poitiers without delay to continue the fight. Lieutenant Georges Danloy did not hesitate to follow him, and, of course, Jean de Selys Longchamps needs no persuasion to go along with them. They did not know it yet, but the unwavering resolve of these three men, who could not bear the thought of surrender, would afford them the opportunity to pen some of the most epic pages in Belgian military history in the years to come.

Without further ado, the small group of Belgian officers made its way to Milford Haven, 80 miles west of Tenby, where they learned that ships were departing from there to the port of Brest. Barely 72 hours after taking every risk to reach Britain, Jean de Selys Longchamps was preparing with his companions to return to the continent to fight. What extraordinary and bewildering madness! This was a far cry from the cushy idleness and comfortable dilettantism that had characterised Jean's youth until that moment. While his surname and family's address book would likely have easily secured him a safe role within one of London's headquarters, the Belgian cavalier cared little for such safety: he was eager to fight for his country.

Milford Haven is a port with a long history. In 1914, a solid link was formed with Belgium when twenty-four fishing vessels and two steam trawlers left Ostend to take refuge there throughout the conflict. A monument still celebrates the friendship between the two cities today. However, in the early days of June 1940, Milford Haven was abuzz with the comings and goings of ships connecting France and England. On the one hand, there was the ongoing effort to repatriate British troops who were not trapped in the Dunkirk pocket (over 140,000 men), yet it also facilitated the transport of French troops who had survived the Battle of Flanders to rejoin the fight: from 1 to 12 June, no less than 70,000 soldiers would make their way back to France by ship via the port of Brest.

On 4 June, de Selys and the Belgian officers accompanying him boarded the *Batavia II* to Brest and from there proceeded to Poitiers, over 250 miles to the southeast. During the eighteen-day campaign, the swift German invasion forced the Belgian government to hastily relocate to Poitiers, which hosted the ministers and their fleeing administrations as of 23 May, meaning for a few weeks, Poitiers became the 'capital' of Belgium.

The Belgian officers hoped to receive clear instructions on their next assignments there, but the prevailing chaos was by no means conducive to any serene, clear or lasting decisions. What was decided one day was often reversed the next under the pressure of the relentless advance of Nazi troops and the numerous missteps of a beleaguered French government struggling to truly assist the Belgians.

The Belgian Minister of National Defence, Lieutenant General Henri Denis, in office since 1936, refused to abandon his faith. On 6 June, he attempted to rally the troops with a proclamation that was both grandiose and tinged with desperation, reflecting the prevailing disarray:

> Officers, Non-Commissioned Officers, and Soldiers of Belgium. After valiantly fighting the invader side by side with our Allies, the Belgian army was led to capitulation. Its leaders, its troops, its arms, its supplies have fallen into the hands of the enemy now occupying our country. Your wives, your children, your parents are under their control, crying out for those who will restore their freedom; your possessions are at the mercy of the occupier. In the face of such calamity, we must not wail or lament. We must stand tall, gather our energies, be determined to reclaim what has been taken from us. Thousands of Belgians fit to bear arms are currently in France. They will form new troops, numerous and powerfully armed, tasked with the glorious mission of liberating the Fatherland. Soldiers, know that you will be fighting for yourselves, for your families, for your religious, moral, and social heritage. All these treasures, many of which were won through long and arduous efforts sustained over many years, you will lose if Belgium remains in the enemy's hands. Only the resolve to continue the fight can restore them to you. Officers, non-commissioned officers, and soldiers, be worthy of those from 1914: you will cover yourselves in glory and be the saviors of Belgium.

When Denis spoke of being 'powerfully armed', it is unclear whether he truly believed this or if it was merely wishful thinking. The Belgians soon realised they had greatly overestimated the French quartermaster's ability to equip their troops effectively and transform them into credible opponents against the lightning-fast advances of the Wehrmacht divisions.

The promised cannons never arrived, while those that were delivered were taken back the same evening. The guns were so outdated (models from 1886 without shields) that they were unacceptable. Even more common equipment proved problematic: cartridges were provided, but of the wrong calibre. The Belgian forces moved from disillusionment to disillusionment, quickly becoming disheartened. Yet, the patriotic spirit remained strong, and plans continued to be made and assignments envisioned for those rallying to a cause that already seemed lost.

Soon, de Selys Longchamps and Guérisse received their orders, and their paths diverged for a few days. Jean was assigned to join 7th Motorcycle Regiment (7 MO) stationed in the south of France, near Montpellier.[3] This motorised cavalry regiment had been formed on 1 February 1940 to train the militiamen incorporated between January and April 1940 (the class of 1940). It was part of the Reinforcement and Training Troops (TRI) tasked with compensating for the losses suffered by frontline units. At the beginning of the eighteen-day campaign, the regiment boasts 92 officers, 193 non-commissioned officers, and 3,246 troops. It briefly settled in Hamme, south of Saint-Nicolas, but from 14 May, orders were received to move to France, where on 21 May it established quarters in Lunel and the surrounding villages, 15 miles northeast of Montpellier (Hérault department). A few short days later, the crushing announcement of the capitulation on 28 May cast a heavy shadow of doubt over what action to take next.

The days that followed were strained. Paul Reynaud, the French Council President, delivered an anti-Belgian tirade that rippled through the local populace, sparking incidents. Thankfully, the Belgian government's declared intent to continue the struggle alongside the Allies soothed tensions, and by the time Jean arrived in Montpellier, the situation had calmed down.

Albert Guérisse was assigned to the health service training centre in the Sables-d'Olonne region, along the Atlantic coast. However, by 15 June, the relentless advance of German troops put him at risk of capture, prompting a decision to flee towards the motorised division's gathering centre in the south of France, in Lunel, where his fellow escapee Jean de Selys Longchamps was now based.

However, bad news kept coming, and Monday, 17 June 1940 marked the definitive end of the first act of Hitler's armies' invasion, which had begun a month and seven days earlier: Marshal Pétain, who had just become the new head of the French government, announced in a broadcast message his intention to ask the Germans for armistice terms. Many soldiers interpreted his message as 'the armistice is signed' and immediately ceased fighting. Nonetheless, this changed little, as the armistice was ultimately signed on 22 June in the Compiègne Forest, with Adolf Hitler in attendance, seizing the moment to avenge the humiliation of 1918. After Belgium and the Netherlands, France had now been brought to its knees.

Stunned by this dire news, the Belgians once again faced the same dilemma they encountered on 28 May: surrender or flee? Those who had landed in Brest a few days earlier regretted having left England for this hellish impasse. Such misfortune! Yet, the small core of Belgian officers that reassembled did not hesitate for a moment: they had to find a way not to fall into enemy hands. And fast.

Among this group of indomitable spirits were Jean de Selys Longchamps, Albert Guérisse, Georges Danloy, Freddy Gréban de Saint-Germain, Jacques de Brabant, Paul Nicod, Victor Nicod, Jean 'Pipitje' Pieters, William (Billy) Janssens de Vaerebeke, and Jean Decloedt. The group decided to make for the nearby coast, heading for the port of Sète, some 18 miles away. There, part of the Czech soldiers who had survived the Battle of France were preparing to embark for England through a hastily arranged British operation, although it was far from the scale of Operation Dynamo at Dunkirk. In Sète, the operation resembled more of a massive scramble, notably lacking a codename, which was unusual for the military and indicative of the level of chaos and improvisation at play. However, it was effective: on 24 and 27 June, over 3,615 soldiers, mostly Czechs, and 315 civilians managed to board one of the thirty-nine ships in the makeshift armada.

Yet boarding was far from easy for de Selys and his companions. The docks at Sète were buzzing hives crowded with soldiers, and the air was filled with conversations in English, Czech, Polish, French, and Spanish. Demotivated and indifferent French policemen and officers, unsure of how to proceed since the armistice, provided nominal oversight. Aside from the Czech soldiers, elbowing one's way onto a boat was a real struggle. And by 'boat', we are not talking about a liner with cabins or even a somewhat modern military ship. In many cases, these were cargo ships that had just unloaded coal in Marseille and were ordered to Sète to pick up the escapees in their soot-filled holds.

After facing numerous rejections, the group of Belgians managed to persuade the captain of one of these coal ships to take them aboard, joining a significant contingent of Czech troops. On 24 June, they found themselves in the hold of the MV *Northmoor*, an English cargo ship, setting sail for Gibraltar.[4] The journey was gruelling, and the rationing of drinking water tested their endurance, especially since, upon reaching their destination on 27 or 28 June, the MV *Northmoor* anchored off the Rock of Gibraltar, waiting under a sweltering sun for permission to dock. The French author Marcel Jullian humorously described the appearance of Jean de Selys' group after this arduous journey:[5] 'Without their Belgian officer uniforms, they could have been mistaken for coal miners surviving a firedamp explosion.' The wait could have dragged on for endless

The Rock of Gibraltar as seen by Jean de Selys from the ship transporting him.

days had the Belgian officers not been miraculously welcomed aboard a French cargo, the SS *Rhin*, which was anchored nearby.

Once aboard, they encountered a colourful character: Lieutenant Claude Péri. Short, muscular, with piercing eyes, this Corsican exuded a powerful charisma, that of a man of adventure and cunning. Born in Hanoi, Indochina, in 1908, Péri boarded the *Rhin* at the end of April with an order from the French secret services in collaboration with the British Intelligence Service. On 9 May 1940, while the *Rhin* was in Las Palmas in the Canary Islands, Péri and a chief mechanic fixed plastic charges to the hull of the German cargo ship *Corrientes*, causing it significant damage. A few days later, on 17 June, while en route to Algeria, Péri heard the faltering voice of Marshal Pétain on the radio, announcing, '… we must cease fighting'. Stunned by the announcement, he decided to take control of the ship and steer it towards Gibraltar. This change of course did not sit well with everyone, leading to a brawl between crew members who wanted to continue the fight and those loyal to the new Vichy regime.

This series of events probably explains the strange, even electric atmosphere aboard the *Rhin* when the Belgians discovered the ship off Gibraltar. Yet they were unconcerned: their immediate priority was to rush to the showers to regain a semblance of humanity and dress more appropriately for their officer status. In the early evening, de Selys and his companions were welcomed by Péri in the officers' mess. The meal was excellent and well-lubricated, and tongues loosened. In a moment of frankness, Péri admitted that if he had welcomed the Belgians aboard, it was primarily because he was looking

On board the SS *Rhin* off Gibraltar. In the centre of the front row is Admiral Muselier. Jean de Selys is behind (second from right). Georges Danloy, wearing glasses, is recognisable on the left.

The inimitable Péri posing with Admiral Muselier and the Belgian officers. Jean de Selys is visible in the second row (second from right).

to assemble a new crew. He no longer trusted most of the men sailing with him. The evening's events proved him right, when a mechanical officer violently confronted him, leading to a brawl between the two men. The Belgians were stunned to witness what increasingly resembled a mutiny on a ship where tension seemed never-ending. Péri was violently struck on the forehead with some broken glass and bled profusely. Enraged, he ordered the mutineer to be put in irons. Guérisse, both shocked and fascinated by what he had just witnessed, tended to the wounded French lieutenant.

The following afternoon, when Péri welcomed Admiral Muselier aboard the *Rhin*, a large bandage covered the top of his head, giving him the appearance of a buccaneer. Admiral Émile Muselier warmly greeted the Belgian officers and posed with them on deck for a memorable photograph. Muselier's time in Gibraltar was drawing to a close, as on the evening of 30 June, after flying to England by seaplane, he was already in London to meet with General de Gaulle.[6]

Jean de Selys and his companions are unaware of it at the time, but they had just met the man who would become commander of the Free French Naval Forces and be named a Companion of the Liberation as early as 1 August 1941. It was Muselier who was credited with adopting the Cross of Lorraine to distinguish the ships of the Free French fleet from those of the Vichy navy, a symbolism extended to all branches of the armed forces. The fervent appeal made by Péri the previous night for the Belgians to join his crew persuaded three of them to stay on board to head to England with him. These were Jacques de Brabant, Jean 'Pipitje' Pieters, and Albert Guérisse, Jean de Selys' comrade from the very beginning. All were clearly charmed by the inimitable Lieutenant Claude Péri. This was evidently not the case for Jean de Selys, who did not extend his trust to Péri and decided not to remain with them.

For Guérisse, this marked the beginning of a saga that would count among the most epic experiences lived by a Belgian during the Second World War. Indeed, it is worth taking a moment to summarise the exploits of Albert Guérisse, as they splendidly illustrate the exceptional whirlwind of destinies experienced by this handful of Belgian officers who refused to bow down to the invader.[7]

A few days after leaving Gibraltar, the *Rhin* docked at Barry Docks in Wales, and Péri handed the ship over to the British. Thanks to his contacts with the Intelligence Service, he received assurance from the Admiralty that the ship and its crew would henceforth sail under the British flag. The *Rhin* was then armed and equipped for special missions along enemy coasts. It was renamed HMS *Fidelity* (D57) and became one of the first sea liaisons used by the SOE for France. The three Belgian officers on board were commissioned as naval officers, and thus, Lieutenant Albert Guérisse became Lieutenant Commander Patrick O'Leary of the Royal Naval Volunteer Reserve (RNVR). A pseudonym was necessary, as it was crucial that he not be identified as a Belgian citizen in case of capture, but rather as a British soldier to be treated as a prisoner of war. He was then attached to the Naval Intelligence Department, where he underwent six weeks of training to learn infiltration techniques in enemy territory: sabotage, camouflage, how to fake documents etc.

During a mission along the Roussillon coast in April 1941, O'Leary (Guérisse) was captured by the Vichy regime's coast guards. He was imprisoned near Nîmes, from where he managed to escape in July 1941 to reach Marseille. There, he assisted an SOE agent, Ian Garrow, in setting up an escape network for airmen downed above occupied territory. Now attached to MI9, Guérisse/O'Leary took command of the network in October 1941. Thanks to this network, also known as the Pat Line, a downed airman in France, Belgium, or Luxembourg could be repatriated to England via Spain in around twelve days. For the Allies, this network was invaluable as it took more than six months to train a pilot. No fewer than 600 British and American airmen returned safely to England via the Pat Line after their aircraft was shot down over occupied territory.

Albert Guérisse aka Patrick O'Leary, a true hero who became the most decorated Belgian officer of the Second World War.

On 2 March 1943, O'Leary was arrested again by the Germans in Toulouse following a betrayal within the network. Tortured by the Gestapo, he revealed nothing and was eventually deported to Mauthausen in October 1943, before being transferred to Natzweiler-Struthof (Alsace) in June 1944, and finally redirected to Dachau in September 1944. On 10 May 1945, he left the liberated Dachau camp for Paris, where he was welcomed by Miss Sylvia Cooper-Smith, a representative of MI9, who accompanied him to London and who he would marry in 1947 under his real name, Albert Guérisse.

Among the group of escapees who arrived in Gibraltar with Jean de Selys Longchamps, it is also important to highlight the fate of Lieutenant Georges Danloy,[8] affectionately nicknamed '*mon oncle*' (my uncle) by Jean de Selys. He, too, would make his way back to England, and a photograph taken in Tenby in September 1940 shows him alongside a few other Belgian officers who were his companions during the Sète-Gibraltar journey: Paul and Victor Nicod, Freddy Gréban de Saint-Germain, William Janssens de Vaerebeke, and Jean Decloedt. Danloy quickly took command of a platoon of Belgian riflemen and then a company. By 1942, he was promoted to captain and

Georges Danloy (fourth from right) in Tenby, September 1940.

joined 10th Inter-Allied Commando, where he commanded 4th Troop consisting of seven officers and 100 Belgian soldiers. His war name was George Chesty. After intense training in Abersoch in North Wales, his unit was deployed in Italy in 1943, then in Yugoslavia, on the island of Walcheren during the Battle of the Scheldt, and finally in Germany. In 1946, Danloy was promoted to lieutenant colonel and left a lasting mark on the history of Belgian commandos by creating the training centre at Marche-les-Dames before becoming the commander of the very first Belgian para-commando regiment created in 1951.

Jean de Selys Longchamps would never know what his companions from their harrowing journey, begun in the heart of the debacle of May 1940, would manage to achieve in the years that followed. Conversely, both Guérisse and Danloy would be posthumously exposed to the tales of aerial feats of the man they knew as a cavalry sub-lieutenant. Undoubtedly, this would earn Jean their deepest respect, recognising in him one of their own; that breed of man with an extra touch of soul, who decided to give life a little more than what was expected of them.

Before resuming the story of Jean de Selys Longchamps, let us also note the fate of two other Belgians who arrived with the group in Gibraltar at the end of June 1940, and who would also join the Royal Air Force, only to unfortunately meet the same tragic fate as Jean. Jean Decloedt would die at the controls of his brand-new Spitfire on 15 March 1942. His colour blindness had prevented him from joining a combat squadron, but he was active in a ferry unit. He had been trained at 61 OTU with Jean and was one of his roommates. Meanwhile, William 'Billy' Janssens de Vaerebeke would fall during an attack by two Messerschmitt 109s on 18 December 1942, while leading a formation of three Bristol Beaufighters from 235 Squadron over the Bay of Biscay.

Now, let us return to the story of Jean de Selys Longchamps, who finally received authorisation to disembark in Gibraltar on 2 July. The whimsical Claude Péri, commander of the SS *Rhin*, provided him with a document he did not hesitate to sign, proclaiming himself as 'commander of the French navy at Gibraltar'. A bold statement, but it worked. Jean even found himself in possession of a document stamped by the Naval Intelligence Centre of Gibraltar, granting its bearer access to any form of assistance needed. He could finally head to his next assignment. Tucked in one of the pockets of his uniform, Jean carefully kept a document he received in Montpellier on 22 June, just a few days before heading to Sète with Guérisse and the others. It was a marching order signed by Lieutenant General Albert Wibier (commander of the TRI, Reinforcement and Training Troops) instructing him to report to the commander of the Belgian flight school located in Oujda, Morocco. Indeed, an intriguing and promising destination that must surely have motivated de Selys after the setbacks of the recent weeks.

But what on earth was the Belgian flying school doing in Morocco?[9] On 12 May, the evacuation order to France was given in response to the swift advance of German troops. Four days later, the aircraft were parked at the Caen-Carpiquet airfield, awaiting transfer to Morocco, where the plan was to continue training student pilots in Oujda, close to the Algerian–Moroccan border. The choice of Morocco was dictated by two considerations. On the one hand, the quality of the local climate would allow for continuous training, uninterrupted by weather. On the other hand, Morocco brought the flying school closer to the Belgian Congo, where the possibility of its transfer was also being considered. The staff was transported by rail to Marseille, arriving on 25 May 1940.[10] The crossing then took place on board two cargo ships on 29 and 30 May, docking in Oran on 31 May. Arriving in Oujda in early June, the officers, instructors, and students discovered an airfield that was far from operational: the barracks had not yet been finished, and there were no sanitary facilities. And, most importantly, the planes, equipment, and vehicles had not yet arrived, being transported on a cargo ship sailing from Caen that would dock in Oran on 23 June, the day after the signing of the Franco–German armistice. This last event definitively disrupted the start-up of the Belgian flying school. Flights were soon forbidden by the French authorities under the agreements signed with the Germans, and profound boredom quickly affected the small Belgian colony, which felt truly trapped and forgotten by all. A project to evacuate to the Belgian Congo using seven SABENA SM73 trimotors, requisitioned in Algiers by the school's commander, General Tapproge, was also 'torpedoed' by the French, as was any attempt to embark for England.

This only served to infuriate the Belgians to the highest degree, prompting the most determined among them to defy the bans and try to reach England or the Congo at all costs. On 1 July 1940, fourteen airmen, including Jean Offenberg, mixed with the Polish pilots and embarked in Casablanca, duping French security agents, aboard the English cargo ship *Har Zion*, which reached Liverpool on 16 July.[11] On 3 July, another group of fifty-five students and pilots, led by Captain Robert Cajot, embarked on the *David Livingstone* and successfully reached Cardiff on 4 August. It was particularly brave to head for Britain at this time, as there was no indication the country would not soon experience the woes of a humiliating defeat like all its allies in the preceding weeks. Moreover, rumours circulated that the Royal Air Force did not accept foreign volunteers for diplomatic reasons. However, the Belgians could not care less: better to risk everything than to die of boredom. Captain Burniaux and Second Lieutenant Ceuppens headed, via Congo, to South Africa to enlist in the South African Air Force.

When Jean de Selys left Gibraltar for Oujda, supported by the British Admiralty, he had no idea of the chaos he was about to plunge into again. He might already have had a foretaste of it as he sailed towards Oran and his ship passed near Mers El Kébir, where, on 3 July, a fratricidal naval battle between the British and the French took place. The bulk of the French fleet was destroyed, and 1,295 sailors under Vichy command lost their lives. Nothing in the world seems to make sense anymore.

Finally arriving in Oujda, Jean discovered a unit in tatters and an atmosphere poisoned by defeatism, with the most determined aviators having already left. The majority of those that remained seem eager to return to Belgium at any cost, even if it meant surrendering to the Germans. Indiscipline and revolt were rampant in the ranks. There was truly nothing left to do there. 'An endless fall into a bottomless night, that's what hell is': Victor Hugo's words seem to perfectly match the exhausting succession of misfortunes that burden Jean de Selys' journey.

Fortunately, almost as soon as he had arrived, de Selys had to depart again after receiving a new marching order instructing him to present himself in Montpellier in execution of an order from HQ dated 10 July. The circus carried on.

Returning to France without falling into German hands was now possible since the establishment of the demarcation line on 25 June in the wake of the armistice. Spanning 1,000 miles, the line separated the German-occupied zone from the free zone, administered by the Vichy regime (referred to as the 'non-o' zone by the French). This concession to Marshal Pétain's government would only last until October 1943, but when Jean received his marching order, Montpellier was indeed in the free zone, meaning he could travel there without fear.

It must be remembered that in July 1940, the Belgian government, under Prime Minister Hubert Pierlot, was still operational in France and struggling to negotiate the return of 2 million Belgian refugees. Finance Minister Camille Gutt would not reach London until 8 August, and faced with increasing insecurity, Hubert Pierlot and Paul-Henri Spaak (the Foreign Affairs Minister) would also decide to leave France at the end of August, although they would not reach London until 22 October after an epic journey through Spain and Portugal. It would take more than five months after the invasion on 10 May for a legitimate Belgian government to finally establish itself on British soil.[12]

On 13 July, Jean embarked in Oran and headed for Marseille.[13] Somehow, he had learned that his brother François had been in a serious accident and was hospitalised in Pau. François was part of 7th Infantry Division's Cyclist Group that had retreated to the south of France after the disastrous May 1940 campaign, and a foolish road accident (where his bicycle collided with a military truck) caused a skull fracture that left him in a coma. Sensing that the assignment waiting for him in Montpellier would once again evaporate, Jean de Selys had no hesitation in deciding to visit his injured brother and immediately headed to Pau.

Jean was first seen on Wednesday, 17 July by the small Belgian contingent that had taken refuge in the town.[14] At last, good news followed for Jean: François had finally emerged from a lengthy coma lasting sixteen days. His brother's health was reassuring and Jean's stay in Pau opened a brief enchanted parenthesis in his life that had been in utter chaos since 10 May. In Pau, not only did he reunite with his brother, but also with Pauline, François' wife, who had come to his bedside. More surprisingly, he briefly rejoined his father Raymond, who spent 48 hours in Pau around 25 July. Seeing his loved ones again was priceless.

The Belgian colony that had settled in Pau welcomed Jean de Selys with open arms. Many were acquaintances from before the war. Jean frequently visited Villa Antoinette, where the Thys family and Louisette, whom he had escorted at Brussels' social events, were staying. Jean's presence was greatly appreciated, and the way he recounted his odyssey captivated his audience, who were impressed by his storytelling skills. Jean de Selys finally savoured moments of tranquility and simple pleasures, rediscovering the rich and complex taste of port, which he had not enjoyed for more than two months.

Jean was quite outspoken about his experience during the eighteen-day campaign. The words used by Louisette Thys in her personal journal are telling: 'He gave us a little idea of the complete rottenness encountered on all sides, he spoke of the complete disorder in which he fought.'

With great humour, Jean de Selys captioned his photograph and bitterly acknowledged his status as a 'tourist' given to him by orders and counter-orders.

The respite ended by mid-August. François, still convalescing, was finally able to travel and would return to Belgium, while the Belgian families exiled in Pau gradually did the same. In his conversations, Jean had clearly expressed his desire to continue the fight, and returning to Brussels was therefore not an option. He clearly regretted

Passport issued by the Belgian consulate in Marseille, 22 August 1940.

not having followed Guérisse, Danloy, and those others who were already in England, but he was not one to wallow in regret and instead took some time to evaluate the few options now available to him.

On 22 August, he obtained a passport from the Belgian consulate in Marseille, which allowed him to travel to North America, South America, and the Belgian Congo. The document also authorised him to transit through Algeria and Morocco. Clearly, de Selys did not want to close any doors at this stage.

During this period, Jean received mail via Countess Anne de Liedekerke, who resided in Pau at Castet de l'Array. This magnificent place, a couple of miles from the Spanish border, would serve as a refuge and passage for those looking to escape via the Pyrenees starting from the end of 1941. Those who stayed there could, like Jean, appreciate the very pretty sculptures created by the countess, who, in addition to a remarkable patriotic fibre, was a very gifted artist.

A letter received via the countess seems to particularly catch Jean's attention. It was written by Knight Alain de Theux de Montjardin, who lived in Congo. He was the eldest son of one of his mother Émilie's brothers. In his letter, Alain de Theux urged Jean to join him in Theuxville to assist in supervising the western district of the concession he was overseeing in Kivu. The letter was written on 10 July, but it must have taken some time to reach Jean's hands. He was sufficiently interested in the proposition that he used the document to obtain a departure authorisation for the Belgian Congo, issued by the Belgian consulate in Pau on 12 September.

Jean's adventurous spirit must have been tickled by an experience at the heart of this unknown distant colony. He must also have been quite disgusted by the dithering of his military hierarchy, which had been making him run around in circles since the debacle of 28 May. Perhaps he viewed leaving for Congo as fleeing, as opposed to his desire to fight and defend his homeland. It was a real dilemma. Jean seemed determined, however, and purchased a ticket from a travel agency in Marseille on 14 September, granting him 'Lisbon/Belgian Congo passage by steamer, as per possibility of departure'. In his letter, Alain de Theux specified that only two departures were possible from Lisbon: between the 5th and 10th and the 20th and 25th of each month.

Did Jean de Selys missed the opportunity to embark at the end of September due to lack of space on board, or did he change his mind? The fact is, he did not board any of the ships of the Portuguese National Navigation Company. Did the Battle of Britain, raging since July 1940, eventually convince him that the British were more determined than ever to continue the fight? Had he convinced himself that it was there, and nowhere else, that action was happening? Doubt had clearly crept into his thoughts.

For weeks, Jean's spirit had been consumed by hesitations, despondency, and frustrations, and his convictions had sometimes been terribly volatile. In an ironic twist of fate, Jean received a new order – this time would indeed be the last – dated 5 October 1940. It came from the Belgian High Commission set up in Vichy and ordered 'Second Lieutenant de Selys-LONGCHAMPS, Belgian Identity Card No. 860 837, to proceed to the departments of Bouches-du-Rhône, Haute-Garonne, Hautes and Basses-Pyrénées, with the mission to finalise the repatriation of Belgian refugees.' It specified that a Saroléa motorcycle and a Citroën car would be made available to him for the duration of the mission, from 10 to 30 October 1940.

This order seemed to come out of nowhere, but the name of its signatory – General Delvoie – lay the foundation for an interesting hypothesis. From his position, General Delvoie was a privileged observer of the growing tensions corroding the Vichy administration, where men with very different agendas clashed insidiously: collaborators, procrastinators, and, soon enough, resistants. There were signs of what appeared to be official or semi-official assistance for the escape and reception of Belgians wishing to join Great Britain. It is known today that Delvoie was part of the 'Resistance' movement: in the autumn of 1940, he was approached by an emissary sent by the Belgian consul general in Barcelona to organise an escape line to Great Britain via the Iberian Peninsula. This project materialised at the end of the year with Delvoie's deputy, cavalry captain Chevalier Frédéric de Selliers de Moranville, at the helm, giving birth to the Benoit network.[15] The connection between Jean de Selys and General Delvoie was, therefore, likely anything but coincidental, and this order, with a decidedly administrative tone, might have hidden a cover devised by Delvoie to allow de Selys to travel freely in preparation for his departure to England. It is also conceivable that contact with Delvoie was established via the military offices in Montpellier, which, from July 1940 to the end of 1942, played an active role in the escape of active and reserve military personnel, particularly airmen, to Spain.

Thus, Jean's demeanour during the summer of 1940, which might have seemed lethargic and paralysed by doubt and uncertainty, likely masked the actions of a man determined not to make peace with the Nazi monster.

On 6 November 1940, Jean de Selys boarded an Air France seaplane departing from Marignane to the hydro-base at the Agha basin in Algiers, where he transited before flying again to Casablanca, reaching it the next day. Once in Morocco, he headed to Tangier, where he stayed at the El Minzah Hotel. There, he interacted with the British Consul General, Alvary Gascoigne, who stamped his passport on 30 November with a transit permit to Gibraltar for onward travel to England. A Foreign Office telegram had already informed the Tangier consulate on 22 October to make this wondrous permit available to Jean de Selys, evidence that his journey this time was perfectly orchestrated and far from the improvised effort that had accompanied his first arrival in Gibraltar at the end of June in the holds of a coal ship. Jean de Selys was now in familiar territory: Alvary Gascoigne was a former cavalryman who had served in a dragoon regiment at the beginning of the First World War, and this no doubt created a bond between the two men.

On 30 November, Jean also visited the Belgian consulate in Tangier to add an authorisation to his passport allowing him to 'travel to all European countries', essential for entering Gibraltar. On 1 December, de Selys spent his last day in Tangier and conferred with retired Colonel W. Francis Ellis, who was now the press attaché at the British consulate. Perhaps he offered some advice for the next steps Jean would need to take with the British military bureaucracy? Or maybe he simply shared his joy in seeing a young man eager to return to combat?

On 2 December, more than five months after his first passage, Jean de Selys was back in Gibraltar. On the day of his arrival, at 5pm, he met Commander Berley, a staff officer of the Royal Navy. Everything was falling into place as planned. On 7 December, Jean boarded HMS *Argus* and sailed for Glasgow. The vessel was a Royal Navy aircraft carrier launched in 1918, but its small size and relatively slow speed limited its use as a warship, and by 1940 it was mainly used to develop aircraft carrier combat techniques and for sea pilot training. Its nickname – *Flatiron* – betrayed its minimal impact on the enemy. During this journey to Glasgow, the *Argus* was part of a convoy of seven ships. As the voyage progressed, other vessels joined them, and by 12 December there were no fewer than fourteen ships sailing together towards Scotland. On 14 December, the convoy arrived at the Clyde naval base in Glasgow, having suffered no attacks.

Jean de Selys' true adventure, the one that would give him wings, could now finally begin.

HMS *Argus* on which Jean embarked for Glasgow on 7 December: Britain had never been so close.

Chapter 7

The Sky is the Limit

(16 December 1940–7 March 1941)

On 16 December, de Selys Longchamps was already in London, experiencing the city in wartime attire. The Luftwaffe bombings had left an indelible mark on the capital, and the blackout plunged the city into utter darkness as soon as the sun set. Jean was no longer willing to waste time. For over six months, one can easily imagine his growing frustration, feeling like he had been running around in circles, engulfed by a profound sense of uselessness.

However, those long months of indecision had served one purpose: he now knew exactly what he wanted to do. Returning to the mire of Tenby was unthinkable for

The English capital was heavily hit by numerous Luftwaffe bombings before Jean arrived.

him. That was not where the action was. He had already invested so much time and hope in the hypothetical rebuilding of the Belgian army, but enough was enough; he would now proceed without it.

By December 1940, Jean was aware that the only real fight against Hitler was being waged by the British. It was, therefore, alongside them that he wished to fight.

English humour withstood all bombing raids.

Jean had heard of the incredible feats achieved by Royal Air Force pilots since the Battle of Britain had begun in July 1940. Although the battle had waned in intensity by the time he arrived in London, Luftwaffe bombings continued, as humorously evidenced by a French restaurant's menu Jean pasted in his photograph album: 'La Coquille remains open for dinner unless a bomb falls on the building.'

Jean soon learned that Belgian pilots had already distinguished themselves under the RAF roundels. Between 24 June and 5 August, no fewer than 124 aviators and student pilots had made their way to England. An agreement was quickly reached with the Air Ministry to allow these valuable resources to integrate into the RAF Volunteer Reserve, and twenty-nine of them were deemed sufficiently qualified to be directly placed into operational squadrons.[1]

Fifteen of them joined the fight in squadrons of Hawker Hurricanes, and the other fourteen bolstered the ranks of Coastal Command (coastal defence), where they served as pilots, observers, and even gunners on Bristol Blenheims.

At the end of the three most intense months of the Battle of Britain, the Belgians had already claimed twenty-one confirmed enemy aircraft shot down, plus six probable and three seriously damaged.

Maurice Buchin and Jacques Philippart were the first to open the Belgians' tally on 11 August, each downing a Ju 88 bomber with their Hurricane from 213 Squadron. Both would lose their lives in flight shortly thereafter: Buchin on 15 August, Philippart on 25 August. Philippart, however, managed to write one of the most legendary pages in the history of Belgian pilots by downing six German aircraft in twelve days (plus one probable victory). Quite remarkable.

The attrition rate was frightening; the average lifespan of a pilot at that time was only four weeks. No wonder young aviators struggled to gain experience. The youngest Belgian pilot to lose his life was Roger Émile de Cannart d'Hamale, who was killed in combat by Messerschmitt 109s on 1 November 1940; he was barely 21 years old. In the preceding weeks, he had emerged unscathed from two major incidents: a parachute jump to escape his damaged aircraft and a belly landing due to fuel shortage. Sadly, luck turned against him on the third misfortune.

It is worth noting that many Belgian pilots who refused to lay down their arms and made their way to England in 1940 to continue the fight were condemned in absentia for desertion by the Belgian High Command.[2] As incredible as it may seem, it was not until 1948 that these pilots were formally acquitted of their 'crimes'. It is staggering when one recalls that some of them were killed serving the Allies before this condemnation was lifted. In a context where pilots were precious but scarce assets, Jean de Selys Longchamps' desire to join the Royal Air Force could only find a favourable response when he opened up to Lieutenant Colonel Aviator Louis Wouters,[3] the former military attaché at the Belgian embassy in London since September 1939.

From June 1940, he had been working to rebuild the Belgian military aviation in England. Wouters, aged 48 in 1940, was an experienced military man. He had started the First World War as a cavalry officer but was detached to the aviation company as an observer in August 1915, where he witnessed the fledgling beginnings of Belgian

Colonel Louis Wouters (left) played a major role in integrating Belgian pilots into the Royal Air Force.

military aviation. In London, even before a Belgian government was established, he tirelessly endeavoured to put Belgian military aviation at the service of the Allied cause.

Wouters and his deputy, Captain Léo (Léon) De Soomer, literally pestered every British decision-maker, even going as far as Anthony Eden, the Secretary of State for War, to plead their case. It was anything but simple, as the British were preoccupied by countless other priorities, and it took a treasure trove of patience and tenacity to move matters forward. But the Wouters/De Soomer duo excelled in diplomacy and succeeded in convincing the British to create spaces within the RAF for Belgian aviators.

When he met de Selys at 107 Eaton Square, the headquarters of the Belgian military mission in London, Wouters was delighted: this cavalry officer clearly has the grit and temperament to become a pilot and bolster the Belgian ranks, which were already in dire need after the gruelling Battle of Britain.

There was just one downside that Jean carefully avoided discussing with Wouters: by December 1940, Jean was 28 years old and already too old to become a student pilot in Fighter Command's pipeline. No matter: he decided to falsify his documents to make himself younger. An 'administrative detail' was certainly not going to thwart the pilot's destiny now beckoning him!

Jean de Selys was not the only Belgian to counterfeit his identity documents: Lucien Leboutte went even further by managing to hide his 42 years to join a night fighter squadron. Once the war was over, Leboutte would become the first Chief of Staff of the Belgian military aviation, proving that one can take liberties with regulations and still have a distinguished career.

Before joining the Royal Air Force Volunteer Reserve, Jean de Selys still had two obligations to fulfil. The first was obvious – to pass the medical examination, which was particularly demanding for aircrew, and which he did with ease. The second was more cumbersome: convincing MI5 agents that his profile was 'clean' and he was not a spy. It was in a former girls' school in London called Patriotic School that the routes taken by newcomers to Britain were dissected by agents on the lookout for inconsistencies and grey areas. Fortunately for Jean, the story of his long and tortuous journey from De Panne to Glasgow was deemed reliable, as it did not hinder his march forward.

In a letter to Sam Heapy (the English jockey Jean knew before the war, who also went into exile in Britain) written at the end of December, Jean was full of zeal as he outlined his journey and confided to Sam: 'Now, I'm doing fantastic training in London's clubs waiting for my turn at the RAF.'

Thus, on Thursday, 16 January 1941, Jean de Selys Longchamps presented himself at Odiham Air Base, located 50 miles southwest of London in Hampshire (Hants). It was here that the very first Franco-Belgian flying school was established on 28 October 1940. The school was set up in a rush to address the massive influx of French and

Belgian aviators and aviator candidates, most of which shared the same handicap: their level of English was too poor to join RAF schools. Therefore, Odiham's school had a dual purpose: to teach its students operational English and to train them in flying. It was an ambitious programme.

The French and Belgian Flying Training School (FBFTS) fell under 22 Group of the Training Command, and the Odiham base, where it was located, hosted fighter squadrons during the Battle of Britain. 609 Squadron, which Jean would later join, had even used it on several occasions.

Jean de Selys in RAF uniform at Odiham in early 1941.

The school was headed by Wing Commander Wynn, with Flight Lieutenant (F/LT) Davies serving as his deputy in charge of the French and Belgian instructors.[4] The school's strength lay in embodying the most demanding English standards in training through excellent instructors who shared the same nationality as their students. On the Belgian side, were Henri 'Moustique' Gonay, Léon Prévot, Giovanni Dieu, Jacques d'Ursel, Carlos Goethals, Georges Van Cromphout, and Robert Cajot. Remember that it was under Cajot's initiative that fifty-five student pilots had left Oujda in early July for Britain, just before Jean had headed to Morocco. They would finally have the opportunity to meet, especially since Cajot had taken command of the Belgian section. The French were supervised by Captain Henry de Rancourt de Mimérand, a future Companion of the Liberation. Alongside the instructors, there were also, of course, English teachers who would instil the solid basics of Shakespeare's language, tailored to the operational needs of the Royal Air Force.

The presence of French and Belgian instructors was a boon for the student pilots, as the school's curriculum was very demanding and conducted under stringent British military discipline. Some were indeed upset by the severity the English command imposed. It is true that the English were particularly irritated by some aviators who had excessively inflated their flight hours to accelerate their progression to combat. Those small adjustments to reality caused accidents, and the British were uncompromising: here, everyone started from scratch based on English standards.

The school's programme was based on the Empire Air Training Scheme (EATS) that the RAF imposed on its dominions who had an air force (South Africa, Australia, Canada, and New Zealand) to ensure coherence and quality of training throughout the Empire. Its ambition was to successfully train pilots in eighteen to twenty-four

The student pilot de Selys had not yet earned his Wings but already has the look of an RAF pilot.

months by putting them through four stages: the Initial Training School (eight weeks), the Elementary Flying Training School (ten weeks), the Service Flying Training School (sixteen weeks) at the end of which the pilot received his Wings, and finally, joining the Operational Training Unit (four to six weeks), which completed the pilot's preparation before transferring to an operational squadron. Any failure in the tests that concluded each stage was definitively eliminatory.

That, of course, was the theory, but as the war had progressed, the programme Jean would experience at Odiham compressed the first two stages into fourteen weeks, in addition to adding the linguistic component that obviously did not exist in the dominions. This would put the dilettante student Jean had often been in the past under pressure and force him to roll up his sleeves. However, it would take significantly more to discourage him, and he was determined to become a pilot, at all costs.

Although de Selys joined Odiham in mid-January, he did not actually get into an airplane until 8 March. The English classes occupied his first few weeks, and he also became acquainted with the imposing syllabus that would constitute his pilot training.[5] The entire programme was structured around what the British called 'airmanship': the acquisition and development of all the skills and knowledge that every pilot must master. Some were directly related to flying (theories of flight, controls and operations, aerial navigation), others to peripheral elements (communication, Morse code, weather) and some even covered more technical notions (aircraft structure, engine, armament). It was all very comprehensive. Even when he started flying, Jean's days continued to alternate between practical lessons, theoretical classes, and language courses, leaving him very little free time.

This was the price to pay to stand a chance of obtaining the Holy Grail: the Wings of a Royal Air Force pilot. At this stage of his training, this objective remained quite distant and unattainable, but to keep his spirits up and constantly remind himself of the ultimate goal, Jean pinned an RAF pilot's wing badge on his room's desk lamp. It was at this desk, occasionally glancing at the pair of Wings proudly surrounding the royal crown, that he briefly kept a personal journal, which provides some insight into his feelings and state of mind.

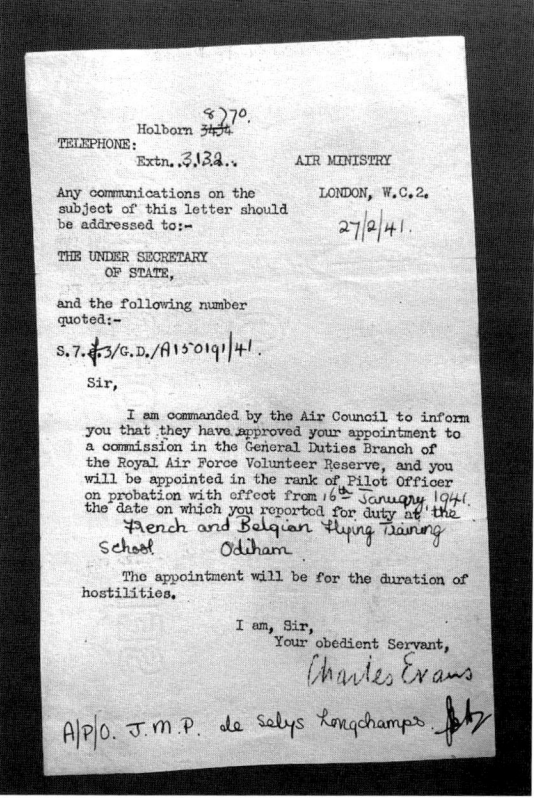

Confirmation from the Air Ministry of Jean de Selys' incorporation into the RAF Volunteer Reserve (VR) as a pilot officer.

The days were long and full, leaving Jean with little opportunity to visit the neighbouring village for a drink at the pub with the other students. Yet, Odiham did not lack charm, boasting an inn dating back to the sixteenth century, and even a cinema, the Regal, which had opened in 1938. Often, before the film started, an officer would stand in front of the screen to comment on the national and international military situation. Invariably, his conclusion left no doubt to the other clientele: the final victory against the forces of evil was assured. Always a boost for morale. To get to town, de Selys and his friends managed to obtain a car, nicknamed 'Prudence'.

London also was not too far away, and Jean sometimes made a trip there on Sunday, the students' only day off. This was an opportunity to pick up the two Belgian newspapers published in England (which Jean found 'pretty pathetic') and especially to hunt for news from home in Belgian restaurants – at Gaston's, Rose's, or Maria's – and to savour a delicious 'steak-frites' that brought back so many good memories. But even when they were not on duty, the Belgian officers maintained their sense of duty. Thus, on Sunday, 2 February, Baron Jean de Selys Longchamps and his friend

Leave in London was very popular with Jean de Selys as it gave him a chance to fish for news from home.

Rodolphe de Grunne, a close friend of Jean, convalescing after being wounded in combat. He is accompanied by his sister, the Countess de Bousies.

Count Rodolphe de Hemricourt de Grunne distinguished themselves by fighting a fire started by incendiary bombs that had struck the roof of a London church. Rodolphe 'Dolfo' de Grunne was no longer a student but a seasoned pilot with three victories to his name in the RAF and ten more earned during the Spanish Civil War. In May 1940, he had been part of 1st Squadron of the Belgian military aeronautics (the one that sported the famous 'thistle' on its Hurricanes, already visible on the plane of the 1914–1918 ace, Willy Coppens). On 18 August, 'Dolfo' had bailed out of his burning Hurricane, seriously burned. When he distinguished himself with de Selys on a church roof, Rodolphe de Grunne did not know he would disappear in combat a few months later. The wheel of fate that dictated a hellish pace to the life of RAF pilots never stopped turning.

It is striking to note how quickly Jean was able to reconnect with the multiple networks beginning to weave through the small Belgian community that had taken refuge in Britain. In letters to Sam Heapy sent in early 1941, he wrote long lists of mutual acquaintances, detailing their fates – they were sometimes dead, missing, prisoners, or part of the Belgian forces serving Great Britain – and he seemed to know everything, or almost. He was, of course, aware that Edé, his younger brother, was a prisoner in a camp in Germany. A royalist at heart, he had also formed an opinion on King Leopold III's stance in May 1940: 'It's clear he did absolutely right, and nothing can be held against him. On the contrary. He was simply magnificent.' No doubt, his convictions had already led to some very animated discussions with Belgians who did not share his views on this highly contentious issue.

Chapter 8

'Maggie'

(8 March–13 May 1941)

The 8 March 1941 is forever linked to the very first entry in Jean de Selys Longchamps' brand new Pilot's Flying Logbook. Its sky-blue cover bears the words 'ROYAL AIR FORCE' and 'PILOT'S FLYING LOG BOOK' above the name of its holder, neatly written, 'de SELYS LONGCHAMPS'. Only later, once he had earned his Wings, would Jean add 'P/O' (Pilot/Officer) and later his other ranks. Since receiving his logbook, Jean had been eager to start filling it out. How many times had he already flipped through its blank pages, imagining the flights he would soon record?

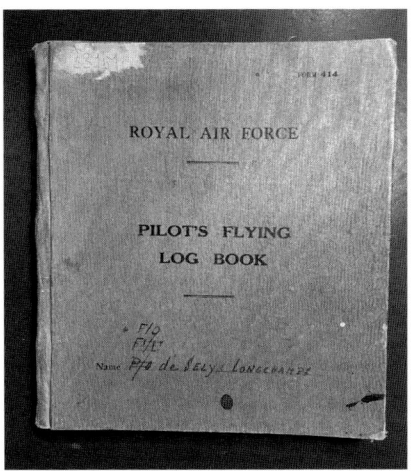

Cover of Jean de Selys' logbook.

Thus, on a Saturday, the long-awaited moment finally arrived: the Miles Magister with serial number T9912 had the honour of becoming the first ride of the cavalier aspiring to be an aviator. At Odiham base, there were eighteen training aircraft of the same type. Affectionately nicknamed 'Maggie' by the student pilots, the Miles Magister was the RAF's very first monoplane training aircraft. It offered a more modern alternative to the de Havilland Tiger Moth, a biplane the RAF used until 1952, and the Belgians until 1957. Unlike the Tiger Moth, 'Maggie' boasted wheel brakes, flaps for added lift, and a tailwheel. According to its pilots, it was a pleasant aircraft to fly, propelled by a small 130 horsepower engine (a Gipsy Major identical to the Tiger Moth's) enabling it to reach speeds of up to roughly 145mph.

Accompanying de Selys on his first ascent to the sky was an experienced instructor with a predestined name: Giovanni Dieu ('Dieu' meaning 'God' in French). Born in Châtelineau, east of Charleroi, in 1907, Dieu was 34 years old when he became Jean de Selys' designated instructor at Odiham (Jean would do all but five of his dual-control flights with him). P/O Dieu began his career in the Belgian military aviation in 1927.

The Miles Magister, nicknamed 'Maggie' by pilots, in which Jean de Selys would take his first steps as a pilot.

In May 1940, he was a first-class aviation sergeant and belonged to 3rd Aviation Regiment. After the eighteen-day campaign, Dieu arrived in Britain on 23 June, participated in the Battle of Britain with 236 Squadron flying Bristol Blenheims, and then became an instructor at Odiham in October 1940.

Not without apprehension, de Selys slipped into the rear seat of the two-seater, while Dieu took the front. The cockpit was narrow and very basic, almost spartan.

The very minimalist cockpit of the Miles Magister was designed for the student pilots to focus on the essentials and familiarise themselves with basic instruments and controls.

Barely six gauges populated the dashboard to allow students to focus on the essential instruments: engine oil pressure, engine RPM, speed, artificial horizon, altimeter, and turn and slip indicator. At the top left, there was also the ignition magneto to start the Gipsy Major. On the left side, the throttle lever, carburettor adjustment, and flaps control. On the right side, a compass and the trim control. Finally, a tube that looked like a curious mix between a funnel and a vacuum cleaner hose was visible in the upper centre of the dashboard: it was through this acoustic tube the instructor could shout – literally – his instructions to the student during flight.

'Maggie' was not very comfortable – both instructor and pilot sat on their parachutes – but this was almost instantly forgotten, as the adrenaline quickly took over and the startup process captured all their attention.

The first flight of the Jean de Selys/Giovanni Dieu tandem lasted fifty-five minutes over the Hampshire countryside. It was anything but touristic, however, as evidenced by the first entry in Jean's logbook (the flight allowed them to cover the first four basic stages of the training programme). Once this initial flight had been completed, the countdown had already begun: the first real test for the student pilots was indeed imminent. The goal was to let them go solo after 10 to 12 hours of flight in double-

Jean's first instructor, Giovanni Dieu, is on the right. In the centre are Jacques d'Ursel and Henri Gonay (in the foreground). On the left is Léon Prévot.

command flights at most, those who did not rise to this challenge were set aside, and they were numerous: on average, between a quarter and a third of RAF student pilots failed to pass this first milestone and were redirected towards other roles (navigators, gunners etc.).

However, it would certainly take more to intimidate Jean de Selys. On 11 March, he undertook two more flights with his instructor. On 13 March, they flew together three times. On 19 March, another two flights. The exercises followed one another without respite, and when he was not flying, de Selys studied on the ground, sometimes dressed in his old Guides' uniform. The days were long and exhausting.

Then came D-Day: Friday, 21 March. On this day, de Selys would take off four times. Twice with Giovanni Dieu, once with Léon Prévot for a final test with the Chief Flying Instructor of the Belgian students, before finally, the moment arrived for him to perform his first solo flight after just under 9 hours of dual-command flight. This meant that de Selys was therefore well within the timeframe allowed, but he still needed to succeed in this first outing alone at the controls.

A solo release is a significant experience in a pilot's life. For the first time, no one is sitting in front of you, giving a never-before-seen and terribly impressive perspective on the front of the aircraft. No one is there to guide you and keep you in line. You are alone in the air, overwhelmed by an incredible sensation of freedom accompanied by a good dose of stress.

After the usual cockpit checks and the engine startup, de Selys gradually opened the throttle, and his Miles Magister, with serial number T9764, slowly left its parking spot

The very first double page of Jean de Selys' logbook records his first flight and first solo.

to align with the runway. Jean had been informed of the wind's force and direction, confirmed by the orientation of the Belgian and French flags he could see fluttering in the distance near the base's buildings. He ensured the tailwheel was straight. The aircraft accelerated, propelled by the now familiar sound of the Gipsy Major, leveraging each of its 130 horsepower to gradually ascend into the sky.

All of Jean's aircraft movements were scrutinised from the edge of the runway by Giovanni Dieu and Léon Prévot, and perhaps even by some fellow student pilots like Henri Marchal. The solo flight lasted twenty minutes, during which Jean performed a series of required exercises in the sky over Odiham. At the controls of his aircraft, Jean felt sensations that today's pilots no longer know in their modern cockpits:

One of the 'Maggies' at the Odiham school. The Belgian flag can be seen flying in the background.

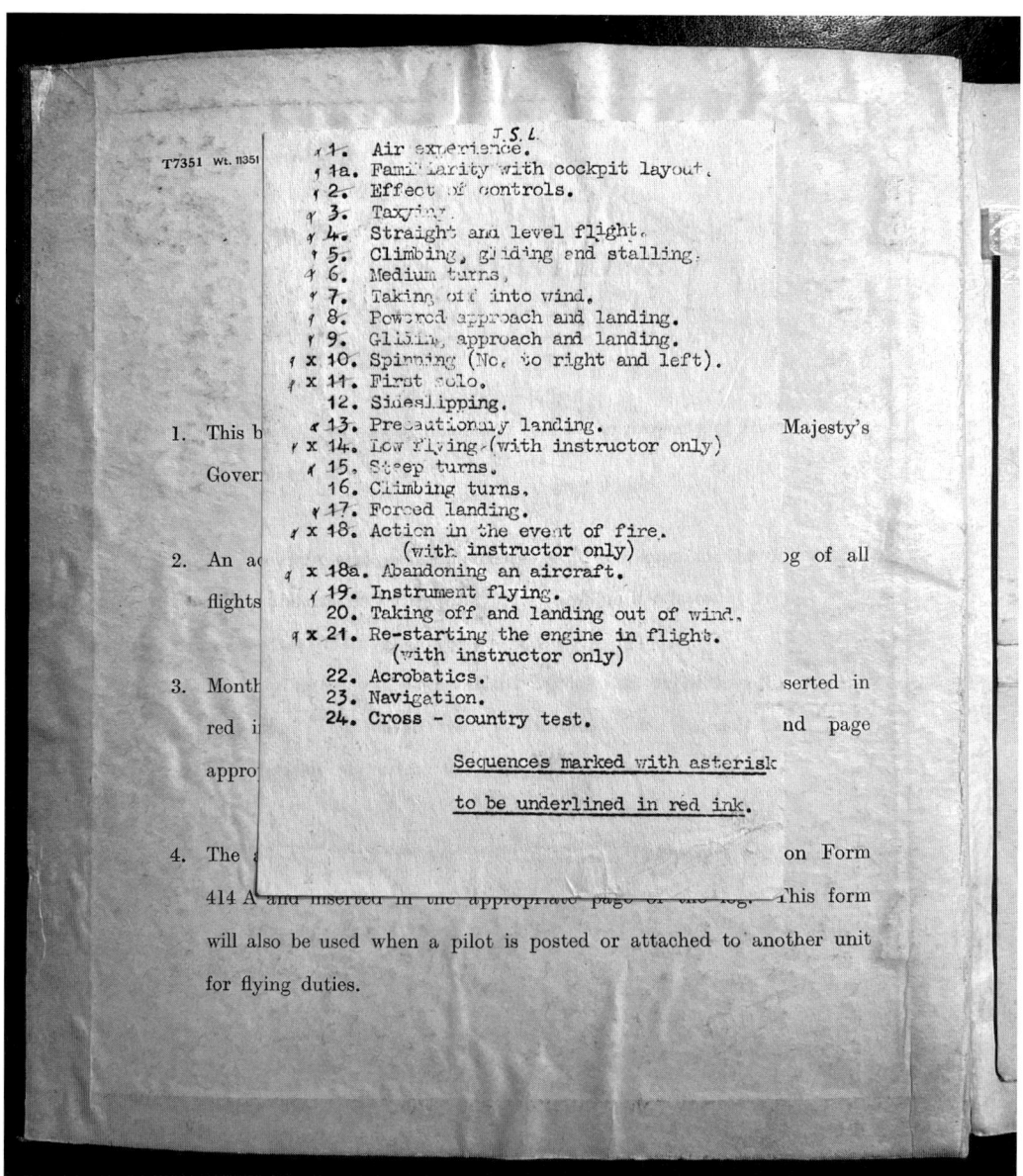

Jean de Selys pasted into his logbook the captions of the twenty-four training sequences he had to master as part of his training at Odiham.

even if their speed is significantly higher (a SIAI Marchetti SF. 260, the current training aircraft of the Belgian Air Force, can reach a speed of 275mph, twice that of a 'Maggie'). Flying in an open cockpit allows the pilot to feel the wind whipping his face and thus truly appreciate the aircraft's speed. It is an exhilarating sensation that must have reminded de Selys of the long straight lines he galloped along on Belgian racecourses before the war. At the end of the twenty minutes of flight, Jean landed the plane, feeling liberated. The test was obviously successful.

In March, Jean completed twenty-eight flights to reach a total of 17 hours and 25 minutes, including 5 hours and 15 minutes solo.

On 26 March, Jean received a promotion: he was commissioned as a lieutenant 'for the duration of the war'. For de Selys, who regularly railed against the Belgian government in London and held some of its leaders in very low esteem, the commissioning letter signed by Camille Gutt (Minister of National Defence) must have been heartwarming. It was an encouragement for him to continue his efforts to live up to his new rank.

April saw the pace of training intensify even further, and de Selys relentlessly multiplied his flying hours: 15 hours and 30 minutes in dual-command, 22 hours and 10 minutes solo. The in-flight exercises became more and more demanding and varied: tight turns, medium turns, dives, spins, forced landing simulation, approach and landing in glide with the engine at idle, low-altitude flight, navigation, acrobatics… The entire repertoire was repeated until it was mastered perfectly.

The few photographs from his time in Odiham that Jean had carefully preserved in his album reflect a sense of fulfillment that seemed to have inhabited him. One photograph, in particular, captures the attention: his gaze is full of mischief, and his smile is complicit. Everything in his face radiates a certain form of serenity and the

Jean wearing his Pattern 1930 flight suit with a fur collar and scarf – it was cold in the open cockpit of the 'Maggie' – which gives him a bit of a First World War pilot look.

sensation that he might have finally found his path. He found above the clouds of Hampshire, pushing his limits further each day. The long succession of the previous difficult months – De Panne, Tenby, Poitiers, Montpellier, Sète, Gibraltar, Oujda – and the many moments of astonishment they provoked gradually gave way to much more positive experiences.

'The real place of birth is that in which one has taken a first intelligent glance at oneself', wrote French author Marguerite Yourcenar. For Jean, this place could have been Odiham, where he finally shed the miasma of a spoiled child's life and truly found himself by rising into the air. The past few months had been a redemptive fall for him. The transformation that began in the darkened atmosphere of May 1940 continued with a flying helmet on his head, and it was in the skies of Hampshire that he stopped being a ne'er-do-well to truly become Jean de Selys Longchamps.

That said, make no mistake: the war, occupied Belgium, the distance from his loved ones, and the slim survival chances promised to a future fighter pilot tormented Jean, as evidenced by the poignant text he wrote in his personal journal on Friday, 11 April 1941, Good Friday. Writing clearly allowed him to release the deep-seated pain trapped in someone who knew he was living on borrowed time:

Why am I sad this Good Friday?
Do I sense more strongly that I will never again see my loved ones here below? Perhaps also because today I contemplate death without worry. It will be for me not an end that I dread, but, if it can catch me in flight, even better in combat, the final point as I wish it, of an era of my existence where I believed I lived as I thought I should.

I write this page tonight so that papa and mama know I've been graced to end this life, whose youth had given them some worry, in a way I'm sure they'd approve of. I have lived nearly thirty years without worrying about the duties I had to fulfil. Through atavism and education alone, it was given to me not to harm those around me. I hardly tried to do any good; the war forced me to think of others; I did it as best as I could.

I thank my parents for instilling in me the sense of honour, the love for my Country and my King, the faith in the Catholic doctrine.

I thank the officers of my original regiment for instilling in me the respect for my rank and the duties it entails.

I thank my parents and educators again for helping me to be the Christian I am. It is thanks to them that I have been able to give the war I am fighting the character I want it to have: a struggle for the preservation of the Roman Catholic Church in my country.

> To all those who have made me who I am today, I offer my life for what they have given me so that what I received from them can be given to those who will follow me. I do not see death as an escape, as an easy solution to a life that is sometimes so difficult to lead straight and clear.
>
> But if death must come, I wish it to be useful for something great and beautiful, so that it may redeem a little of what my youth had of pettiness and dullness.

When he wrote this text, resonating with painful premonitions, Jean de Selys Longchamps did not know he had only 857 days left to live…

Jean was happy at Odiham. Giovanni Dieu was a smiling and benevolent instructor. Only pilots can understand the nature of the relationship that forms with their first instructor and the deep respect the student has for him. An unalterable bond, a subtle mix of veneration and admiration, are established with the one who teaches you to fly. It is unlikely you will forget your first love, but nothing in the memory of it will approach the affection and gratitude forged over many hours of flight with your very first instructor. Initially, the way the instructor masters the aircraft leaves the student intimidated and fearing he will never be able to replicate what his instructor accomplishes. Such a level of mastery and control is almost daunting for the young student pilot. But bit by bit, it comes along, and the student begins to approach his master. In less than two months in the skies of Odiham and its surroundings, Giovanni Dieu took a prominent place in the pantheon of people who would shape the aviator Jean de Selys Longchamps.

The pace remained intense until the end of the training, averaging two flights per day, in addition to 4 hours of classes and 2 hours of daily study. Jean de Selys Longchamps had never been so studious, and his teachers from the Maredsous College would struggle to recognise their once troublesome student.

As part of his training, Jean also spent 6 hours in the Link Trainer flight simulator, nicknamed 'Blue Box' by the student pilots. Compared to modern simulators, the Link Trainer looked more like a soapbox than a high-tech system, but for its time, it was surprisingly effective.[1] Edwin Albert Link, an aviation enthusiast without the money to indulge his passion, had built an ingenious flight simulator using bellows, pumps, and valves used for organ manufacturing, his family's business specialty. His invention effectively simulated instrument-only flights without visibility, disturbances due to various weather conditions, and a range of different malfunctions.

When he left Odiham at the end of April, having passed all the imposed tests – including an Odiham-Luton-Odiham navigation cross-country – with an overall assessment that earned him an 'average' rating and qualified him for the next stage, Jean's logbook now displayed a total of 55 hours and 10 minutes of flight.

Jean at the controls of the Link Trainer, the most advanced flight simulator of the time.

The Franco-Belgian school at Odiham would close its doors on 31 May 1941, barely a month after Jean de Selys' class had departed. The base was only about 37 miles from the coast and was ultimately deemed too exposed to house a flight school. However, Odiham base remained operational and would play a significant role in the Dieppe Raid (Operation Jubilee) in August 1942 and even more so in the preparations for the D-Day landings on 6 June 1944 (Operation Overlord). From June 1941 onwards, most Belgian student pilots would henceforth be trained at other bases in England and sometimes even in Canada.

Chapter 9

Wings of Desire

(14 May–28 September 1941)

Wednesday, 14 May 1941 marked a pivotal moment as Baron Jean de Selys Longchamps joined the Tern Hill RAF Station and his new unit – 5 Service Flying Training School (SFTS) – with a very specific goal in mind: to earn his RAF pilot's Wings. If all went well, de Selys could be promoted to Flying Officer at the end of the sixteen weeks this final stage of training was expected to last, before his assignment to an Operational Training Unit (OTU), the last hurdle before joining a fighter squadron. If Jean continued his current trajectory, he could hope to be combat-ready in six months. But that was far from a done deal, as the training that began set a very high bar, and the challenge was not just to pass the tests, but also to demonstrate to the instructors that you had the qualities to become a fighter pilot. At this stage of training, the threat of being redirected to a bomber or transport pilot role was still very much present: for those dreaming of piloting a Spitfire, it goes without saying that this was a highly undesirable option. The twenty-one Belgians accompanying de Selys in his class dreamed only of Fighter Command: Jean Ester, Louis Flohimont, André Cantillon, Albert Herreman, Jean Van Leerberghe, André Lambotte, Arnold José Blairon, Antoon Claesen, Louis Hansez, Guy De Patoul, André Lemaire, Robert Alexandre, Henri Van Moffaert, Léon Harmel, Henri Goblet, Louis Peeters, Maurice Raes, Édouard Feyten, Henri Marchal, Jean Decloedt, and Raymond Lallemant.

If the programme awaiting the student pilots was terribly demanding, the new aircraft that would accompany their progression was no less so.

The Miles Master, designed by the same manufacturer as the Miles 'Maggie' Magister within the Reading factory (Berkshire), was a fast, elegant, and aggressive beast. If the Miles Magister that Jean piloted at Odiham could be compared to a rather nonchalant Shetland pony, the Miles Master was a racehorse that needed to be mastered. The horseman in de Selys would appreciate the analogy. The Master had been a part of the RAF since 1939, reflecting the desire to bridge the ever-widening performance

Group photograph of the fifty pilots who were part of the 5 SFTS. Jean is in the front row, fourth from the left. He would add crosses over time next to the names of his comrades who were lost in action.

gap between training aircraft and modern fighters like the Hawker Hurricane or Supermarine Spitfire.

To familiarise students with what a real fighter plane was, the Master was a two-seater monoplane that almost entirely resembled a 'big one': a closed cockpit, retractable landing gear, a three-blade variable-pitch propeller, landing flaps, twin .303 machine guns (identical to those of the Hurricane and Spitfire), and was powered by a Rolls-Royce Merlin Kestrel engine of more than 700 horsepower. Its performance was eloquent: it could fly at 250mph, climb to 28,000 feet and had a range of 390 miles. It was day and night when compared to the 'Maggie': the Master flew over 125mph faster and climbed 10,000 feet higher. It was also significantly longer and four times heavier. In short, it was a marvel of an aircraft to pilot, but it only revealed itself to those who were not intimidated by it.

The complexity of the Miles Master's dashboard clearly reflected the intention to bring the training aircraft up to the level of the fighters destined for the best students.

The Miles Master was a demanding aircraft that ideally prepared student pilots for conversion to Hurricanes and Spitfires.

From the six gauges populating the Magister's dashboard, one moved to twenty-three, plus a plethora of buttons, switches, and levers. The dashboard design was inspired by what the RAF called the 'selective scan': the idea was to centre the pilot's gaze on the artificial horizon and allow him to scan the other instruments at regular intervals with a quick glance. This was essential when the pilot needed to fly through clouds or with low visibility. Finally, the Master's control column had stopped resembling – literally – a broomstick, as it did on the 'Maggie', and instead faithfully mirrored that of the Hurricane and Spitfires, machine gun control included.

No. 5 Service Flying Training School had about 100 Miles Masters at the Tern Hill base. That number might seem impressive, but Jean de Selys Longchamps' class counted no fewer than fifty pilots. Between the planes that were broken, being repaired, and those that were destroyed (accidents, sometimes fatal, were numerous), it was barely enough to vigorously conduct the training of so many student pilots, who were each required to fly over 70 hours in just a few weeks.

After joining RAF Tern Hill, over 170 miles away from Odiham, de Selys was able to explore a new region of England, the heart of Shropshire, in the West Midlands. Trips to London on a whim were out of the question: the nearest cities now were Birmingham (43 miles south), Liverpool, or Manchester (55 miles north). In his journal, de Selys bitterly complained, 'London seems to be at the end of the world'. The airbase was

In his room at Tern Hill, Jean pinned RAF pilot wings to his radio. Thus, he always had in sight the goal he promised to achieve at the end of his pilot training. He captioned the photograph in his album: 'My hopes! My tools'.

created in 1916 before being closed and then reopened in the mid-1930s. A variety of RAF squadrons, Canadians from the RCAF, and even Poles had succeeded one another before 5 Service Flying Training School settled there on 19 November 1940, with its Miles Masters and a few Hawker Hurricanes.

The decision to establish a pilot school at Tern Hill may have been related to the fact that everything around the base's environment encouraged the student pilots' concentration.[1] What struck the newcomers was that the site was uninviting, and that the airfield was located in the middle of the countryside of one of England's most rural counties, far from inhabited areas. When the RAF took back possession of the site in the 1930s, they had a hard time controlling the large colonies of rabbits that had taken over the place. Jean de Selys failed to hide his gloom when he described Tern Hill and talked about an 'incredibly lost dump' and a 'horizon where factory chimneys take the place of palm trees'. To keep the students busy when the weather was too bad to fly, and to cope with food shortages, some of them turned to gardening and established vegetable patches.

At the end of May, the weather at Tern Hill was dreadful. On 31 May, his birthday – he was 29 – Jean recalled that just a year before he had left De Panne to reach Britain for the first time. But this memory failed to cheer him up. Downcast, he noted in his journal: 'forced inaction for more than a week. Fog, rain, one accident after another, leave us whole days to hope. And then nothing. Flights suspended.' Doubt set in: 'My Wings, a mirage I chase like a child and which men and things seem to push further away whenever I think I'm getting closer.'

Before the weather started to deteriorate, Jean had nevertheless been able to kick off his training on the Miles Master. Five days after his arrival, on 19 May, he conducted his first thirty-minute flight in a dual command with a French instructor, Wing Officer Eugène Signeux, in the rear seat. Originally from Melun, Signeux was a former Air Force pilot instructor who had arrived in England on 20 June 1940. On 21 May, they flew together twice more and by 26 May, four flights had been scheduled: two more flights with Signeux, a brief test with an English instructor (Flight Officer Brown), and, after only 4 hours of flying on the Master, de Selys was already put to the test of his first solo flight. Aboard the aircraft registered T8841, he flew for thirty minutes alone at the controls of an aircraft that was famous for being demanding due to its

Smiling broadly, Jean de Selys proved to be a diligent student.

power-to-weight ratio that had nothing in common with what the students had known until then. To say that flying solo on a Master was an adrenaline-filled experience would certainly be considered an understatement. But evidently, Jean de Selys was a gifted student, and he once again passed the test with flying colours.

But beyond the dreadful weather, what primarily dampened Jean's spirits was the announcement of the death of his friend, Count Rodolphe de Hemricourt de Grunne, with whom he had fought the fire on the roof of a London church on 2 February. On 21 May, during a raid over northern France, de Grunne's Spitfire from 609 Squadron had been hit and he was forced to bail out over the Channel. Despite Air Sea Rescue's efforts, his body was never found. It was not the first time Jean learned of the death of a close friend in combat, but over the months, the rate of disappearances continued to accelerate. Heavy-hearted, de Selys added too many little white crosses next to names in his photograph album, a sign of the frightening brevity of RAF pilots' life expectancy in 1941.

Facing Tern Hill base, the only sign of outside life was a pub, the Stormy Petrel, which welcomed student pilots eager to drown their stress, boredom, or sadness in beer, whisky, or gin. The pub's name was inspired by the Storm Petrel bird, known for landing on fishing boats when a storm is brewing. Surrounded by an aura of mystery, superstition, and legendary beliefs, the bird's name is also sometimes used to describe those labeled as troublemakers. Essentially, the pub's name fitted its colourful clientele of budding fighter pilots to a tee. However, their modest salaries imposed a degree of moderation. Yet, when circumstances demanded, they knew how to party, and if they suffered from a severe hangover the next day, the more daring among them knew that hiding in a cockpit for five minutes with an oxygen mask could quickly revive them, making them ready to conquer the skies once more.

Grounded by the weather until the end of the first week of June, and undermined by flagging morale, de Selys revealed an unexpected poetic streak when describing the gloomy surrounding atmosphere: 'artificial flowers, spring's old dust, make love in the English manner on the mess table' or 'rare sunsets… casting shadows and half-shadows amid black clouds of smoke and soot.'

Flights resumed at a steady pace, beginning on Friday, 6 June. Wake-up at 5am, bed by 10:30pm, up to 5 hours of flying per day, and 'ground school' for the remaining time. When the weather was fair, there was hardly any room for melancholy. In June, de Selys completed twenty flights, including eleven solos. His solo flights grew longer, and on 27 June, he undertook a cross-country navigation flight lasting one hour and fifty minutes; his longest solo flight to date.

The French instructor had now been succeeded by an English instructor, Pilot Officer Pile, with whom Jean would fly sixteen times.

The flight programme (around sixty hours) provided by Service Flying Training School was divided into two cycles: two-thirds of the hours were devoted to mastering the Miles Master, repeating exercises learned at Odiham on a faster and more demanding aircraft. The final third was dedicated to much more difficult exercises validated solo (formation flying navigation, low altitude flights, and instrument night flights).

When flights were in full swing, and the base was bustling with activity, one of the major challenges was navigating through the intense traffic due to constant landings and take offs. Another issue for young pilots was the retractable landing gear. A loud horn sounded in the cockpit if the pilot forgot to lower the gear while throttling down. 'Belly landings' were taken very seriously by the RAF, and students were threatened with court-martial if they landed on the belly without a proven technical issue being the cause.

As the programme intensified, accidents multiplied. Some student pilots decided to quit mid-training, realising that what they were being prepared for was not for them.

Low altitude flights were thrilling but put nerves to the test. Quick sanctions followed: those flying too low were penalised, and those not focused enough lost their lives, adding to the KIFA (Killed In a Flying Accident) statistics.

The most dreaded challenge, however, was undoubtedly night flying. In the darkness, many pilots struggled to judge their distance from the ground. For practice, instructors

With a fleet of over 100 aircraft and increasingly challenging flight programmes, Tern Hill was the scene of numerous accidents.

took a small group of pilots to a nearby field where columns of paraffin pots were lit as runway markers. For safety reasons, no more than two planes flew at the same time. They repeatedly took off, flew a circuit, and landed. It was crucial to adjust the magnetic compass before taking off to successfully find the makeshift runway in the middle of the night for landing. In the pitch-black countryside, the pilots could see nothing but their instruments. The first circuit was flown by the instructor, and the student then completed two circuits under supervision. The same procedure followed the next day, plus a solo flight and three landings. A few nights later, the routine was repeated, but this time the student performed six landings. Jean de Selys conducted his night flights on 18, 19 and 26 July, and his night vision was deemed 'above average'. He totals 4 hours and 40 minutes of night flying, including 1 hour and 35 minutes solo.

Just before his first night flights, Jean de Selys also experienced a highlight of his training: his first try in a real fighter, the Hawker Hurricane! With this aircraft, he had truly moved up a notch: a Rolls-Royce Merlin engine of over 1,000 horsepower propelled him to nearly 340mph. It might not be a Spitfire, but it was clearly a real war machine. The Hurricane is credited with 55% of confirmed aerial victories during the war, establishing it as the most effective Allied fighter.

With the Hawker Hurricane, Jean de Selys experienced the thrill of a true fighter.

Curiously, when well-mastered, it proved easier to pilot and safer than the Miles Master. For student pilots, the first challenge came from the Hurricane being a single seater and was therefore impossible to explore with the comforting presence of an instructor in the cockpit. This entailed significant groundwork before the first flight to familiarise oneself with all cockpit routines by 'chair flying': spending considerable ground time in the cockpit to become acquainted with all instruments, controls, and procedures. Jean de Selys flew solo in the Hurricane for the first time on 14 July, the French National Day, which the twenty-three French pilots in his class celebrated in style. Like all pilots discovering the Hurricane, Jean had to deal with the aircraft's long nose, which obstructed visibility during take off and landing. When the plane was on the ground, pilots often had to lean out of the cockpit to ensure there was no obstacle ahead. Retracting the landing gear was another challenge, requiring a hand switch on the control stick to operate the lever. Beyond these tricky details, it was a magnificent plane that propelled Jean into another world, allowing him to grasp what he was so passionately and determinedly training for. During his first solo in the Hurricane, Jean surpassed the 100-hour flight mark since his first take off at Odiham just four months earlier. Time had well and truly flown.

Baron de Selys Longchamps undertook eleven flights in the Hurricane at Tern Hill, totaling 9 hours and 50 minutes. In July, he seamlessly transitioned from the

Jean de Selys is seated in the cockpit of a Hurricane, and the pride radiating from his face and smile is evident: the serious business had truly begun.

Master to the Hurricane and also completed ten hours of ground-based training in the Link Trainer.

On 21 July, a ceremony for Belgian National Day took place in London, where nine Belgian aviators received the War Cross from Camille Gutt, the Belgian Minister of Defence. A few compatriots based at Tern Hill attend, although Raymond Lallemant decided not to go and it is likely that Jean de Selys also stayed at Tern Hill. He despised Paul-Henri Spaak, who headed the Belgian government in London. In a text written in his notebook in April 1941, he recounted a conversation with the Prime Minister during which Jean felt 'a tension of contempt' as he shook his hand. 'I looked him in the eyes. I think he must have sensed what I was thinking.' Jean, an unreserved royalist, was very critical of this government, which had taken many missteps since the capitulation on 28 May 1940.

Jean's training had accelerated significantly. Initially scheduled to last sixteen weeks, it took only twelve and ended in early August. The final days were not the least strenuous, as beyond the numerous highly demanding flight tests throughout the training, students also had to pass theoretical exams (navigation, flight theory, armament etc.) organised at the end of the cycle. As one might expect, most students

Success in theoretical exams was essential, and Jean de Selys discovered an unexpected scholarly temperament.

had rather neglected this aspect of their training, and the week before saw a slight panic spread through the dormitories, which suddenly became studious to make up for lost time. No doubt, the Stormy Petrel was considerably calmer during these few days. But the effort was worth it, as passing those theoretical exams was mandatory to earn the coveted 'Wings'.

Jean de Selys Longchamps excelled in both practical and theoretical tests, earning an official stamp in his logbook from the commander of 5 SFTS, which stated that his piloting skills were judged 'above the average' after 74 hours and 40 minutes of flying in both the Miles Master and Hawker Hurricane.

On 6 August 1941, he received his Wings and was promoted to the rank of pilot officer. The former second lieutenant from 1st Guides had successfully turned himself into an aviator in less than seven months. The testimony of his classmate, Raymond 'Cheval' Lallemant, shed further light: 'He was a born horseman, a go-getter. That's what allowed him to become an aviator despite his age. (…) Learning to fly at 29 is a bit late, but I believe that through his determination and motivation, he compensated for what could have been seen as a disadvantage due to late training.'[2]

Jean de Selys' training at Tern Hill ended somewhat abruptly. Traditionally, the wing presentation involved a grand ceremony with a high-ranking RAF officer proudly pinning the Wings on the chests of the new pilots. However, as confirmed by the Operation Record Book of the unit and the biography of Jacques-Henri Schloesing, a French pilot certified alongside Jean, none of this happened on 6 August: 'The instructors concluded the course and without any further ceremony, handed out the diplomas.' There was no time to waste with bells and whistles as pilots were urgently needed in squadrons engaging daily with the Luftwaffe.

This was probably of no concern to Jean de Selys, as the main goal lay elsewhere: his excellent results opened the doors to a fighter conversion unit. He was about to start his operational conversion on a Spitfire!

Glad to leave Tern Hill behind, de Selys moved to Heston base (Middlesex) on 14 August 1941 to join 61 OTU (Operational Transformation Unit). Heston had been around since 1929 and its location was sure to delight Jean, being around 12.5 miles from London. RAF Station Heston no

Jean had successfully earned his RAF pilot wings and entrusted a professional photographer to immortalise his new look in a uniform adorned with the prestigious badge.

After a ruthless selection, Jean joined 61 OTU in Heston with about sixty other pilots eager to join a squadron. He is in the second row, eleventh from the left.

longer exists, but 4 miles away, a monument of commercial aviation emerged in 1929 that still operates today: Heathrow International Airport. In the 1930s, Heston was a favoured airfield, and Neville Chamberlain regularly used it when travelling to Germany for the Munich Agreement negotiations in 1938. The RAF would later develop aerial photographic reconnaissance techniques there and establish 1 Photographic Reconnaissance Unit. Jean's unit, 61 OTU, had been active there since June 1941.

The experience awaiting Jean at Heston bore little resemblance to the training he had received at Odiham and Tern Hill: this was a true fighter school. The goal was to ensure an operational conversion on the Spitfire and to teach young pilots flight and combat tactics, essentially transforming young aviators into warriors. Once OTU training was complete, in just a few weeks the pilot would be transferred to a fighter squadron and thrown into a war where aviators struggled to survive more than a few weeks. It would then be a matter for them to instinctively master the piloting to focus on the essentials: tactics.

The training was extraordinarily intense, aiming for the pilot to be operational immediately after joining a squadron. The enemy showed no mercy to new pilots; from the first sortie, they had to save their own lives at all costs to continue gaining experience and improving their survival chances.

At Heston, as soon as the weather allowed, they flew. Over and over again. The experience gained with the Hurricane was invaluable for Jean, as the Spitfire was also a single-seater aircraft that would be piloted solo from the start.

So, it was back to 'cockpit drills' on the ground where, for more than 3 hours in a Spitfire placed on solid trestles to manoeuvre its landing gear, the young pilot would learn all the subtleties of the dashboard and controls, the retraction and extension of the landing gear, the operation of flaps, etc. The startup routine was memorised using the acronym BTFCPPUR: Brakes, Trim, Flaps, Contact, Pressure, Petrol, Undercarriage locked, and Radiator. Everything was repeated ad nauseam to become almost Pavlovian. Any negligence or a reaction time that was too slow could quickly become a hazard in flight or cost the pilot a victory.

Things moved very, very quickly for de Selys. Arriving on 14 August, he flew in a DH.89 Dominie on 19 August. The Dominie was a small twin-engine used by the RAF for personnel transport and radio navigation training. For de Selys, it was just an aerial reconnaissance of the area to familiarise himself with his new playground. The next day, a 15-minute double-command flight on a Miles Magister completed his familiarisation with Heston's procedures. And by Thursday, 21 August, exactly a week after his arrival, the time had already come for his very first 40-minute flight in a Spitfire. That same day, Jean would fly another two 60-minute sessions in this extraordinary aircraft. Many pilots said that on the first flight, it was not you who flew

With the Spitfire, Jean met the best in modern fighter aircraft.

the Spit, but rather it was the Spit that carried you. Even coming from a Hurricane, discovering its capabilities came as a serious shock.

The Spitfire was designed in the mid-1930s by Reginald J. Mitchell, who sadly died in 1937, a year after the prototype's first flight, and thus missed out on the extraordinary destiny of his creation. By the time Jean de Selys discovered it, the plane was powered by a Rolls-Royce Merlin engine of 1,440 horsepower, allowing it to exceed 370mph and climb to over 19,500 feet in 7 and a half minutes. It was a masterpiece of harmony and power. Pilots lacked the words to describe the aircraft, which stood out for the smoothness of its controls and its extraordinary responsiveness. It was extremely manoeuverable and lighter to pilot than a Hurricane.

When he took control for the first time, de Selys noted the same flaw observed with the Hurricane: a very long nose that complicated forward visibility. The first time you landed the Spit was almost a moment of great solitude as the runway was more guessed at than seen. You held your breath until the wheels made contact with the ground and it was clear the landing had been successful. It took some getting used to, but beyond that, the aircraft was a dream. As soon as the engine started with a thunderous noise and the exhaust pipes on the side of the engine spat out long blue flames wrapped in black smoke, the plane impressed with the power it radiated, giving the pilot a feeling that anything was possible at the controls. When Jean moved his hand just a fraction of an inch on the throttle, the engine was unleashed, encouraging the pilot to become bolder.

Jean enjoyed himself, but that did not prevent him from occasionally feeling blue. On 19 September, he recorded in his diary that he had listened to a BBC radio programme featuring parents speaking to their children who were refugees, separated by a great distance. These mundane but emotionally charged conversations made Jean nostalgic, and he lamented, 'if only I could hear my own parents just once', concluding pessimistically he had, 'one in a thousand chance of being able to hear them again.'

The flight programme was a treat for the future fighters: formation flying in pairs, four-ships, twelve-ships, cloud flying, acrobatics, low-altitude flying at nearly 310mph, air-to-ground and air-to-air shooting (filmed by the camera gun to be analysed later with the instructor), rapid climbs to 18,000 feet… Not to mention, of course, aerial combat (dogfights). While pilots obviously could not hear their machine guns' detonation, everything else about the engagement was hyper-realistic: tight turns that churned the stomach, brutal manoeuvres that buffeted the body with G-forces, high-speed changes in direction or altitude that constantly threatened blackouts, dives when one feared you would never emerge alive as the ground approached at a dizzying speed, a neck that nearly twisted off from scanning the sky 360 degrees looking for the enemy, the vital need to always remember not to fly straight for more than thirty seconds in a combat zone… Everything was designed to make training sessions exciting and realistic, but also terribly demanding. Yet, it was only a foretaste of what would become the daily lot of all these pilots once they arrived in their squadrons.

In such a context of very high performance, it is needless to say that incidents, and even accidents, were not uncommon. For instance, on 28 August, Belgian pilot André Lambotte, who was one of the eleven Belgians at 61 OTU, caused an accident when landing his Spitfire.[3] Due to the notorious visibility issue, he failed to see a Miles Master taxiing on the grass and literally landed on top of it. Both occupants of the Miles Master were killed, and Lambotte was seriously injured. In an incredible twist of fate, once recovered, Lambotte resumed his training but was killed under the same circumstances when a Spitfire landed on his aircraft on 6 November 1941, killing him instantly.

Fortunately, in the evening, within the smoky and noisy atmosphere of the mess, the young pilots could relax and boost their morale by sharing news of the exploits of pilots shining in the fighter squadrons and writing the RAF's legend. Soon, they themselves would be the ones about whom future pilot students would talk enviously, without doubt.

One topic the students extensively practised during their time at OTU was the use of the radio. On patrol, the aircraft were in constant contact with ground control, which directed them towards their targets, as well as with the other aircraft in the formation. Consequently, they needed to acquire a good technique to instantly understand the messages received and be able to send the same clear and direct messages in return. The Link Trainer was often used to work on speech clarity for radiotelephony.

During the month and a half that Jean de Selys spent at Heston, he flew a great deal: fifteen flights in Spitfires in August (17 hours) and twenty-eight flights in September (33 hours 15 minutes). It must be said that at 61 OTU, they flew every day, including Sundays.

On 12 September 1941, Jean noted in his personal diary that he had asked the Belgian pilot Jean Offenberg,[4] a respected ace with seven victories already to his credit, to intercede on his behalf with his CO (Commanding Officer) so he could join the prestigious 609 Squadron. As he wrote down his hopes, Jean did not know at the time that his wish would be granted by the end of September.

Chapter 10

'Tally Ho!'

(28 September 1941–26 April 1942)

The efforts of Baron Jean de Selys Longchamps had finally paid off. Since joining the pilot training programme at Odiham ten months earlier, he had dedicated himself fully and revealed a serious and diligent student within, more eager to impress his instructors with his abilities than with his antics. This marked a first for the mischief-maker, who had always leaned more towards being carefree rather than industrious. The reward matched his investment, and, on 30 September 1941, he achieved a double milestone by tying his fate as a fighter pilot to two legends of the Royal Air Force: a mythical airfield and a squadron that everyone talks about.

The airfield he joined – Biggin Hill, located on one of the highest points of Kent – had indeed become one of the symbols of the RAF's valour during the Battle of Britain. Situated less than 18.5 miles south of the capital, Biggin Hill was at the forefront of the Luftwaffe's assaults on London: the airfield was bombed nine times between August 1940 and January 1941. Winston Churchill, who passed by Biggin Hill airbase when travelling from his private residence at Chartwell to his headquarters in London, had a particular affection for the airfield, calling it the 'strongest link' in the chain of RAF bases protecting the English capital. Biggin Hill was one of the eight principal sectors of 11 Group, Fighter Command, which was led with sharp insight by Air Vice-Marshal Keith Park during the Blitz. The Hurricanes and Spitfires based there claimed 340 victories during the Battle of Britain albeit with a heavy toll: fifty-four of their pilots lost their lives in combat. To Jean, Biggin Hill had an entirely different aura than Tern Hill, that was for sure!

The other RAF legend with which Jean de Selys would forever be linked with was, of course, 'Six-O-

The crest of the famous 609 (West Riding) Squadron.

Nine', 609 (West Riding) Squadron,[1] where he was about to take his first steps in an operational unit. Here too, was an icon that had shone brightly since the beginning of the conflict, becoming the first squadron equipped with Spitfires to reach 100 confirmed victories. Initially, 609 was an auxiliary squadron, a regional reserve squadron officially titled 'West Riding of Yorkshire'. Practically, this meant that in peacetime, the pilots flew only on weekends and on extended summer camps. By the end of 1938, as the threat of war loomed closer, 609 was attached to Fighter Command but was only equipped with Spitfires in August 1939 (previously, the squadron flew outdated Hawker Hinds, biplane light bombers). 609 Squadron quickly distinguished itself, paying a high price in the process: during the nine weeks from Dunkirk in support of Operation Dynamo to the start of the Battle of Britain, 609 lost nine pilots in combat. Among those nine aviators, seven were former auxiliary pilots (the squadron had twelve

These six Belgian pilots of 609 Squadron (left to right: Louis Van Arenbergh, Jean de Selys, François de Spirlet, Jean Offenberg, Christian Ortmans, and Raymond Lallemant) exude great enthusiasm. Only Raymond Lallemant would still be alive at the end of 1945.

initially) who were outmatched by the highly experienced pilots of the Luftwaffe. But over the months, 609 professionalised, and the newcomers significantly bolstered its two flights. The squadron's resilience was remarkable: according to RAF standards, a squadron would be 'in the line' (on the front line) for a consecutive period of one month to six weeks. Sometimes, units were even hastily relieved after just a week or ten days when the trauma of clashing with the enemy and the subsequent losses were deemed too significant. The Battle of Britain, however, shook RAF doctrines, and when Jean arrived at Biggin Hill in September 1941, 609 had been on the front line continuously since late May 1940, over sixteen months! It was a source of pride within the squadron, and it was said that 609 had one of the best victory/loss ratios of the entire Fighter Command. Another characteristic of 609 Squadron was its extraordinary 'Belgitude'.

By the end of September 1941, when Jean joined the squadron, it counted no less than twelve Belgian pilots in its ranks: Roger Malengreau, François de Spirlet, Vicky Ortmans, Robert Wilmet, Count Ivan du Monceau de Bergendal, José Muller, Louis Van Arenbergh, Jean Offenberg, Giovanni Dieu (Jean's first instructor), and Christian Ortmans. Three other Belgians had already left for another squadron (Eugène 'Strop' Seghers, Willy Van Lierde, and Baudouin de Hemptinne), one was missing in action (Alex Nitelet), and one had unfortunately died in combat (Rodolphe de Grunne). Such a concentration of Belgian pilots was exceptional for the time (the 'Belgian' Squadrons, 350 Squadron and 349 Squadron, would only be created in November 1941 and January 1943, respectively) and this affinity for the black/yellow/red colours would continue throughout the conflict, as no fewer than fifty-five Belgian pilots would don 609's colours, earning a third of the prestigious DFC (Distinguished Flying Cross) awards the squadron would boast by the end of the conflict.[2]

Among the operational Belgian pilots in 609 when de Selys arrived, Jean 'Le Pyker' Offenberg was undoubtedly the most experienced. He had joined on 17 June 1941, already boasting 230 operational flights with 145 Squadron, which he had joined on 17 August 1940. His nickname, 'Le Pyker', was a phonetic interpretation by the English of his Brussels nickname, 'Le Peï' or 'Peïke' (usually translated as 'guy' or 'mate'). His assigned Spitfire carried the fuselage codes PR-M ('M for Monkey'). On 7 July 1941, he added a Messerschmitt 109 to his tally, which he downed without firing a single shot. Plunging into a dizzying dive in pursuit of the German fighter, which he shadowed closely at a quarter mile, Offenberg had pulled up at the very last moment to avoid crashing into the sea. During the resulting climb, he momentarily blacked out, but when he regained his vision, he saw that the German he was chasing had crashed into the Channel in a 'tremendous splash'. It was his first victory with 609, his seventh overall. A month before Jean's arrival, 'Le Pyker' was promoted to flight lieutenant and given command of one of the squadron's two flights. On 9 September,

Within the 609, Jean Offenberg was unanimously respected. He was a remarkable pilot and an exceptional human being.

he was decorated with the DFC by Air Vice-Marshal Douglas. Jean Offenberg was a pilot who was appreciated and respected by all, whose skill at the controls of a fighter was matched only by his extraordinary modesty. A great man indeed.

To reach Biggin Hill, Jean de Selys shared his ride with Raymond 'Cheval' Lallemant.[3] Lallemant's account sheds light on Jean's personality:

He was a gentleman, a very stylish guy, who had a big heart, a true friend. (…) We travelled together to join the squadron. At that time, I was a sergeant while Jean was already an officer. So I went with Jean and it happened that during the farewell celebrations at the school, I had lost my RAF wedge cap, I was annoyed, and as we were crossing London to go to Biggin Hill, at some point, we saw a tailor's shop. Jean stopped and I thought to myself 'why is he stopping?' He entered the shop and fetched me a 'Cap', so that I didn't arrive at the squadron bareheaded, in violation of the rules.

When they arrived at Biggin Hill, the two friends were welcomed by Jean Offenberg himself. They were surprised by the many traces of bombings still present on the base: it seemed that wherever he looked, there was not a single building intact. Mechanics bustled away in makeshift hangars, and 609's dispersal, in front of which the squadron and Belgian flags fluttered, was housed in a shack where pilots spent most of their day when not flying. One wall of the main room hosted a large board – the Operations Board – which detailed the composition of the two flights and their programme for the day. The other walls were adorned with pin-up photographs; portraits of the squadron's illustrious former members challenging the newcomers to do as well as them, and silhouettes of enemy aircraft that were essential to memorize, as one often had only a split second to decide whether they were 'friend or foe?' and stay alive. Often, the inside of the dispersal was filled with the melody of records being played on an old gramophone. Given the size of the French-speaking contingent, Maurice Chevalier, Jean Sablon, or Charles Trenet were regularly heard. Maurice Choron, a French pilot who was an instructor in Corsica, regularly added Tino Rossi to 609's very Frenchy playlist. The French influence could also be found in the songs that became hits during the alcohol-fuelled evenings the squadron allowed itself to help relieve pressure. Thus, '*Gentille alouette*' and '*Les chevaliers de la table ronde*' were joyously sung by all pilots, even the British, late into the night. In conversations with their new squadron mates, Jean and Raymond began to understand why Belgians were so massively present within 609 Squadron. It was the former Squadron Leader – Michael Lister Robinson – who left 609 at the end of July (to take command of the Biggin Hill Wing) who was behind the impressive vein of Belgian pilots.[4] Robinson had been injured in France in a flying accident on 9 May 1940, just hours before the Nazi invasion. In the days that followed, amidst the total chaos gradually paralysing France, he was evacuated from one hospital to another as the Germans advanced, eventually finding himself in Pau. Clad only in a hospital gown and still recovering, his options were severely limited. It was then he encountered a stranded Belgian detachment in Pau, which took him under its wing. Dressed in the blue uniform of the Aéronautique Militaire Belge, he was sent to Bordeaux from where he was evacuated to England. Once recovered, he on 16 August he was assigned to 601 Squadron, with whom he fought in the Battle of Britain, distinguishing himself with several victories. After a brief stint with 238 Squadron, he took command of 609 on 4 October 1940. He used this opportunity to formally request the Air Ministry for his squadron to create a flight of Belgian pilots. He clearly had not forgotten what he owed to the Belgian people and would have multiple opportunities to prove it even more concretely. When Vicky Ortmans was shot down over the Channel while escorting Blenheim bombers on 19 August, piloting his Spitfire, Robinson circled for a long time above the crash site to protect his Belgian No. 2 who had fallen into the sea and to clearly indicate his location to the fast Air Sea Rescue launch coming to his aid. Robinson stayed on site until the very limit of his fuel reserves, only just managing to reach the nearest airfield – Manston – where he eventually landed on the belly of a Spitfire on its last legs.

By the time Jean de Selys and Raymond Lallemant arrived at Biggin Hill, Squadron Leader George Kemp Gilroy,[5] a 27-year-old Scotsman from Edinburgh, known by the nickname 'Sheep' due to his pre-war profession as a sheep farmer, was leading 609. He was an ace with an impressive record: inaugurated early with a shared victory over a Heinkel 111 bomber on 28 October 1939 – the first Luftwaffe aircraft to crash on British soil. Gilroy had entrusted the command of his two flights to two Belgians: François de Spirlet (A Flight) and Jean Offenberg (B Flight), with Jean assigned to B Flight. François de Spirlet was another ace of 609 with two victories (two Messerschmitt 109s) and a dramatic experience of parachuting over the Channel after his engine was damaged by a German fighter off Dover. Two days later, De Spirlet was back at the squadron, ready to fight again.

Speaking of parachuting over the Channel, another Belgian from 609 – Victor 'Vicky' Ortmans – had done it twice. His exploits on 19 August have already been mentioned, during which Squadron Leader Robinson watched over him until the last drop of fuel, but just over a month later, on 27 September, Ortmans experienced the same misfortune – he was even rescued by the same team. Incredulously, they greeted him aboard with a 'What?! You again?' to which Ortmans quipped back, 'Yes, yes! Me, two lives!' Adding to these misadventures, he had also belly-landed on a beach near Lydd on 30 September 1940, after an epic fight with a 109. When he did manage to stay in the air, however, Vicky Ortmans, also from Liège, was a formidable pilot with more than five victories to his name, plus two shared. He was also one of 609's merry pranksters, always ready to tap dance on pianos or billiard tables, invariably provoking the ire of their owners or the base authorities. Lastly, unique to Vicky was the presence in the squadron of his brother Christian, who joined him at the end of August 1941. Thus, there were two Ortmans on 609's Operations Board.

Billy de Goat, the mascot of the 609.

This brief overview of 609 Squadron's leading figures would be incomplete without introducing the squadron's extraordinary mascot, William 'Billy' de Goat.[6] This charming young British Toggenburg goat became a real personality at Biggin Hill. He was adored by all and the pilots' darling. Billy entered the squadron at the end of June 1941 and, unsurprisingly, it was the inimitable Vicky Ortmans who was responsible for his arrival at the Royal Air Force. Ortmans received Billy as a gift from Biddie, the landlady of the Old Inn – a pub housed in a cottage on the outskirts of Biggin Hill – which was the favourite hangout of the Belgian pilots. Biddie, from Belgium, spoke French, had a radio for news from Belgium, and her wine cellar was renowned: the perfect mix for her to become a sort of second mother to these young men who risked their lives daily, far away from their loved ones. As his horns grow over the months, Billy gained an increasingly prominent place within the squadron, even ascending to the rank of Honorary Air Commodore and being awarded a Distinguished Service Order (DSO).

Billy de Goat would even feature in an article by the famous American author John Steinbeck[7] and would accompany 609 on all its assignments until the end of the war. But as charming as he was, Billy remained a goat, and his gluttonous antics did not go unnoticed wherever he went, much to the dismay of the bases' officials hosting 609. For instance, at a party (Billy was, of course, invited to all festivities), left unsupervised

Jean de Selys posing here with Spit, the 609's mascot dog.

for a moment, he consumed 200 sandwiches, three cakes, a sheet of music, and drank half a bowl of punch before joyfully cavorting among the dancers! Billy de Goat shared 609 Squadron with a much calmer mate, a dog named Spit. Over the months, Jean grew fond of the pup, and one of the most well-known photographs of Pilot Officer de Selys immortalised them together.

For the first time since starting at the Franco-Belgian school in Odiham, de Selys did not need to familiarise himself with a new aircraft. Thanks to the training received at 61 OTU, Jean already had over 50 hours of flight time in a Spitfire, which would once again be his mount. Only the version equipping 609 Squadron – the Mk V, the latest service model – was different. The aircraft was more powerful and faster than the versions he has previously flown, but this did not stop him from getting straight

Jean teasing Spit in the squadron's dispersal area.

to work – he flew on 1 October – and absorbing the invaluable lessons his highly experienced new squadron mates would offer.

In October, Jean flew extensively: more than thirty-two outings, totaling 31 hours 40 minutes (including a short night flight of 35 minutes). The focus was on learning formation flying (seven flights were dedicated to this), dogfights (four flights), shooting (air-to-air, air-sea), acrobatics, and navigation.

On 13 October, Baron de Selys had the opportunity to prove he was a strong recruit for 609. During a dogfight exercise against another Belgian who had arrived with him, Louis Van Arenbergh, Jean clearly dominated the encounters. However, an incident occurred when Van Arenbergh's Spitfire's propeller touched Jean's right wing, severing his aileron and a piece of wing. Jean's Spit plummeted abruptly by 5,900 feet. He did

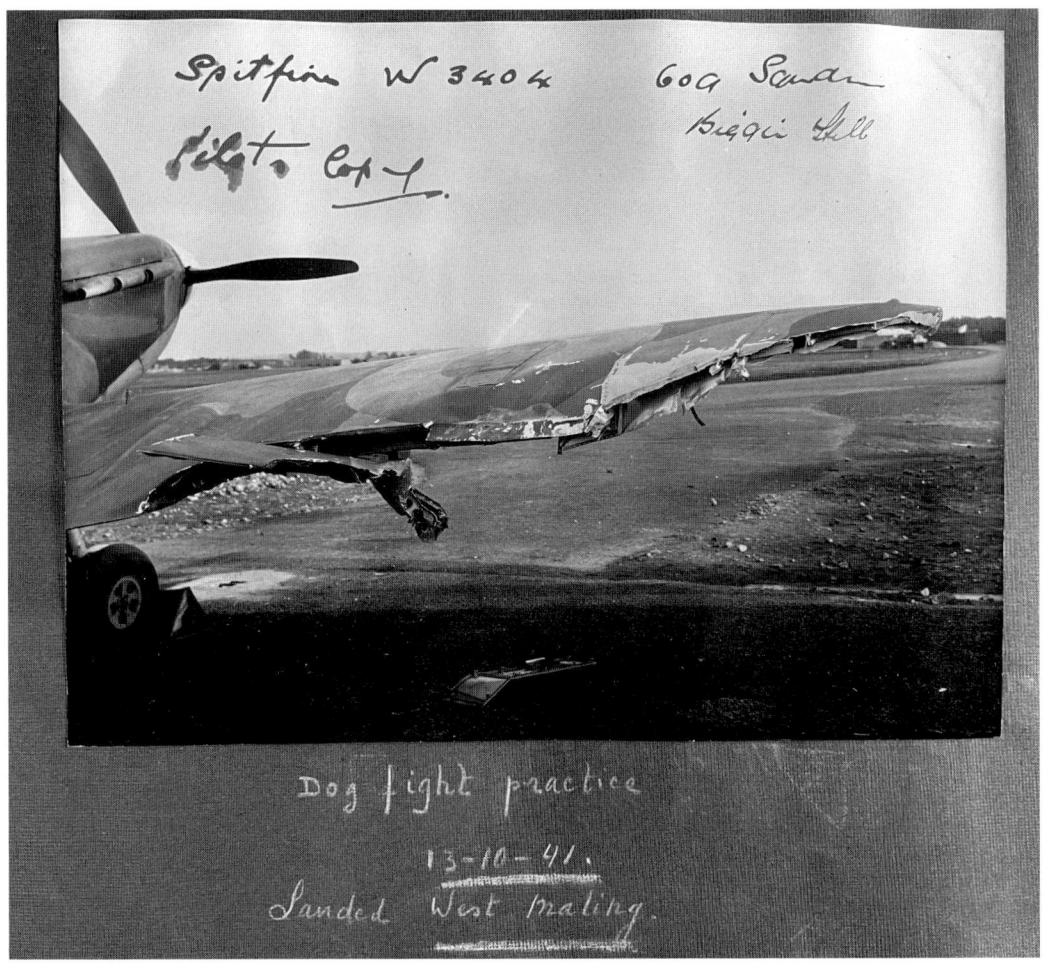

The damage was significant on Jean de Selys' plane after his mid-air collision with Van Arenbergh.

not panic, however, and decided not to abandon his aircraft. Following ground control instructions, he headed towards West Malling, where, after two attempts, he achieved a perfect landing with a severely damaged Spitfire. The aircraft was saved, earning Jean a commendation in his logbook from the group captain commanding Biggin Hill base: 'Landed his badly damaged aircraft safely thus showing great presence of mind, skill, and courage.' This was ideal for gaining credibility within the squadron.

Conversely, this accident contributed to escalating statistics 609 could well do without: the squadron had just experienced four accidents in 80 hours of flight, while its previous 'record' was one accident in 90 hours. The pilots were clearly fatigued.

To unwind, they regularly met at the White Hart or at Biddie's. They also occasionally travelled to London, which was very close. For transportation, the Belgians even obtained a vehicle, a large Ford Estate, as a gift from their government. Promptly nicknamed 'Belgian Barouche', this legendary vehicle, which was refuelled for free at all RAF gas stations and in which pilots piled in beyond reason, would be involved in all the good times that would pepper the squadron's life.

As the month progressed, the first harbingers of winter started to appear – what Frank 'Ziegly' Ziegler (the squadron's intelligence officer) called the 'winter bullshit season' – and from 20 October, all pilots had to report to the dispersal at the beginning of the day to sign documents warning them daily of various dangers and flight restrictions imposed by the weather.

On 21 October, a very dark day unfolded as 609 lost two of its pilots, an occurrence not yet seen in 1941 in a single day. Sergeant 'Goldie' Palmer and the Belgian Vicky Ortmans were both participating in a 'Rodeo' (the new term adopted by the RAF for 'Sweep' – a massive fighter sortie – which pilots would struggle to adopt). It was a significant operation involving eighteen squadrons divided into five wings. Upon reaching the Pas-de-Calais, the 'Rodeo' was engaged by the Luftwaffe's JG2 and JG26 squadrons, the latter with its star pilot, ace Adolf Galland. It was 609's first major encounter with the JG26's new fighter, the Focke-Wulf 190, which immediately proved to be a far more formidable opponent than the Messerschmitt 109.

Ortmans was shot down near Le Touquet; his aircraft seen crashing into the sea once again. It was the third time in two months he ended a flight in the Channel. Despite all efforts to find him, Vicky Ortmans was declared missing. His brother Christian, who was part of the same 'Rodeo' and on his first operational sortie, was devastated. Losing a squadron mate was profoundly upsetting, but it was surely worse when it was your own brother.

Jean de Selys embarked on his first war operation on 26 October. Piloting Spitfire AD352, he took off at 11am to join a 'Sweep' in the triangle of Hardelot – Saint-Omer – Gravelines with 401 Squadron and 72 Squadron. The operation lasted 1 hour and 50 minutes and unfolded without incident for him, though one aircraft from 72 Squadron was shot down.

Before take off, he was introduced to the ritual established by Frank 'Ziegly' Ziegler, ensuring pilots carried no documents (letters, notebooks etc.) that might compromise their identity and that of their loved ones if they had to abandon their aircraft over enemy territory. Ziegly also handed each pilot a wallet with currencies of the countries they would fly over, aiding any potential evasion.

Jean de Selys headed out on an operation again the next day at 11:25am for a new 'Sweep' lasting 1 hour and 30 minutes, taking him again towards Gravelines and Saint-Omer, and over Nieuport. It was the very first time Jean had flown over Belgium as a pilot and the first time he had seen his country since his departure from De Panne on 31 May 1940. It must have felt like forever. He could not help but think about his family, just 20 minutes flight away, yet the distance between them seemed insurmountable. Would he ever have the chance to fly over them? The 'Sweep', however, which was meant to be a cakewalk for the newcomers, turned serious when the British formations encountered unexpected opposition. Five pilots from 401 Squadron would not return to Biggin Hill.

It is worth nothing that overflights of France and Belgium by Belgian pilots might have seemed obvious in hindsight, but at the beginning of 1941, operations over the continent were strictly prohibited for Belgian pilots due to fears of capture by the enemy and potential reprisals against their families. Dissatisfied with this, Jean Offenberg and Baudouin de Hemptinne campaigned at the London HQ to lift this ban, and achieved success on 21 January 1941.

On 27 October, Jean took off again at 2:25pm for an escort operation of two Air Sea Rescue boats searching for pilots who had fallen into the sea. It was almost more thrilling than the 'Sweeps', as 609 encountered several groups of Messerschmidt 109s and Focke-Wulf 190s. Squadron Leader 'Sheep' Gilroy added two more victories to his tally.

On 31 October, he undertook his final operation of the month, during which 609 was involved in a cover operation over the Hawkinge base, the closest RAF aerodrome to occupied France. The operation proceeded without a hitch, and 609 Squadron ended the month with three confirmed kills, one probable, and three enemy aircraft damaged. The month had been rather calm, heralding the forced slowdown that autumn, and soon winter, would impose. Even the experienced Jean Offenberg only flew seven operational sorties that month, opening fire only once. Far from the Hollywood image suggesting each sortie involved dizzying dogfights with seemingly unlimited ammunition, the reality was much more mundane: many operations proceeded without any engagement, and a vast majority of pilots went through the conflict without claiming a single victory. During the Battle of Britain, a period of high-intensity aerial combat, 61% of RAF pilots achieved no victories, 39% achieved at least one, and only 8% became aces (claiming more than five aerial victories).[8] An interesting study by Merle Olmsted goes further,[9] revealing that among the 5,000 American fighter pilots engaged over Europe in 1944 and 1945, a third participated in no aerial combat at all! Only 172 of these pilots (3.44%) downed at least one opponent, and just 42 became aces. Aerial combat was not as frequent as one might have thought, but this does not diminish the extreme lethality of operations that placed the lives of fighter pilots in great peril with each sortie, as the recent loss of the experienced Vicky Ortmans bitterly reminded everyone.

November was particularly 'gloomy' due to shorter days and the winter weather hindering flights with its mix of fog and low cloud cover. What especially dampens the spirits of 609 pilots, however was the dreaded confirmation of their imminent

One of the last photographs taken at Biggin Hill in November 1941. From left to right: de Spirlet, Van Arenbergh, Ortmans, Barnham, de Selys, Greenfield, Rigler, Van Schaick, Lallemant, Smith, Nash, Atkinson, Galloway, Evans, and Laing (and, of course, the mascot Spit).

departure for Digby, where the squadron would be sent for rest. The pilots felt they were at their peak, a subjective assessment, and fatigue was noticeable among those most exposed. Remember that the squadron had been on the front line for eighteen months by this stage, yet 609's performance remained excellent: since arriving at Biggin Hill in February, it has accumulated fifty-one victories, nineteen probables, and forty-one enemy aircraft damaged for 'only' fifteen MIA (Missing In Action). In its last eighteen days at Biggin Hill, 609 claimed four victories and two probables, so it was difficult to deny they were not on top of their game!

On 2 November, air raid sirens shattered London's tranquility for the first time in ninety-five days. Jean de Selys undertook five new operations on 7, 8 (twice), 9, and 18 November. Each time, the operations sent him over Nord-Pas-de-Calais, except for the second flight on 8 November, which involved an operation over the Channel searching for six missing pilots from 401 Squadron (only one man would be found). Jean was eager to claim his first victory, and after his last 'Sweep' on 18 November, during which 609 escorted eight aircraft sent to bomb the Hesdin distillery, he noted in his logbook: 'Last chance for this year!' He knew the squadron's departure for Digby, scheduled for 21 November, would deprive him of further opportunities to encounter 'Jerries' for a while. When Jean Offenberg learned of the squadron's move to Digby, he exclaimed: 'There will be no fighting there. They might as well have sent us to Australia or the Belgian Congo!'

A few days before their departure for Digby, 609 Squadron was officially presented by Air Commodore Harald Peake with its insignia, approved by King George VI. The insignia prominently features the squadron's fighter squadron DNA: two hunting horns topped by a white rose (honouring Yorkshire) and the motto 'TALLY HO!' (rooted in the famous 'taïaut!', shouted by hunters upon spotting their prey). To celebrate the occasion, 609 officers were invited by Peake to the Savoy Hotel in London, near Trafalgar Square, where they dined in the prestigious Pinafore Room alongside Camille Gutt and Trafford Leigh-Mallory, commander of 11 Group of Fighter Command.

Toasts to King George VI and the King of the Belgians abounded. The evening was memorable, and the pilots of 609 wanted to conclude it spectacularly by attempting to steal the statue of Kaspar the Cat, one of the Savoy's treasures. The statue of Kaspar was used to ward off the bad luck associated with a table of thirteen diners: in such cases, Kaspar would become the fourteenth guest, taking his place at the table with a napkin tied around his neck, facing his own plate with cutlery identical to those of

Minister Camille Gutt visiting the 609. He personally piloted the Stampe biplane he used to meet 'his' pilots.

the other guests. The pilots vied in cunning to steal this legendary statue, but needless to say, Kaspar's disappearance would cause quite a stir later on.

As planned, on Friday, 21 November 1941, Jean took off from Biggin Hill to join his rest base at Digby, about 12 miles from Lincoln. Nottingham was 44 miles away, and Sheffield was over 60 miles. Although it was just a brief 35-minute flight, the pilots of 609 were about to enter a completely different world: leaving Biggin Hill was painful, more so than they had anticipated. To the fog and dreary days would now be added an environment 609 would find increasingly inhospitable.

The RAF Station at Digby, part of 12 Group, had hosted Canadian squadrons with far more orthodox profiles than the turbulent 609 since February 1941. Upon their arrival, 609's pilots came with the assurance of those who had made a formidable name for themselves against the Luftwaffe, perhaps displaying a bit of arrogance and, above all, a more relaxed discipline than that prevailing on a base infinitely less exposed to the tensions of war than Biggin Hill. Until their departure from Digby four months later, tensions between the base authorities and the troublemakers of 609 Squadron would only increase.

At Digby, Jean shared a rather uncomfortable cabin with Jean Offenberg. The place was spartan: a few suitcases, two uniforms in a wardrobe, toiletries on a table, some personal photographs, and flying boots under the camp beds. The bare minimum. Once settled, Jean followed up with some reconnaissance flights of the area, as was traditional, to familiarise himself with his new environment. He also practised 'dusky touches' (landings at twilight), as 609 Squadron intended to take advantage of its winter stay to perfect its night flying skills.

With activities significantly slowed down, Jean found time to write to Sam Heapy and his wife. He recounted his beginnings at 609, lamented the cowardice of Luftwaffe pilots ('too cowardly to engage in combat unless they are at least three times more numerous') while being very pleased to have finally seen action ('for more than two months, I've been able to enjoy myself and start making those bastards pay for what they've done to us'). Jean again expressed his passion for the great affair of his life – horse racing – and in an unexpected burst of optimism, wrote: 'As soon as the war is over, if I'm still alive, I'll put my Spitfire in the garage… and long live the little horses! Sam, old boy, we'll gallop again on the Stockel track on cold mornings with frozen fingers.'

Billy de Goat, the mascot, arrived at Digby on the 21st and would soon make his presence known to the sticklers running the base. Indeed, 609's mascot staged a raid in one of the offices, eagerly devouring the base's Christmas cards and a third of the files… A notable entrance. The 'Belgian Barouche' also made the trip, and the pilots were glad of it, as the first decent pub – the Musician's Arms – was 4 miles away. The base provided a vehicle for the pilots, but its designated driver refused to drive after dark. Soon, the 'Belgian Barouche' drew the ire of Digby authorities, who deemed it a waste of the base's precious fuel. The 609 guys did not care, but their frustration with the endless nitpicking grew daily.

Despite difficult weather (including fog and violent winds), Jean de Selys completed twenty-seven flights in December, including five in a 'Maggie' similar to the one flown at Odiham. Not bad for a supposed rest period! However, the pressure really eased off, as absolutely no enemy contact was reported throughout the month.

There was, however, a lot of coming and going within the squadron. Each RAF squadron had to provide a quota of pilots to reinforce units in the Middle East and Asia (where Japan had entered the war after the Pearl Harbor raid on 7 December). Belgian pilots were not affected by these quotas, leaving little leeway for the squadron leader to identify 'transferable' pilots. Five English pilots left 609, including one who had just arrived. To compensate for these departures, nine newcomers arrived (eight sergeants and one officer). Consequently, a significant training and leveling-up programme was run, leading some to jokingly call the new squadron '609 OTU'. Van Arenbergh, who had collided with Jean on 12 October, was transferred to the CFS (Central Flying School) after completing no operations with 609. Even after joining a squadron, relentless selection continued.

Night flights increased, and pilots who were comfortable with such exercises – including Jean de Selys – were involved in 'searchlight cooperation' operations. During these operations, pilots interacted with anti-aircraft defence units, especially those operating powerful 'searchlight guns' scanning the sky for enemy aircraft. The British military had just developed a new VHF radar system – the Searchlight Control, SLC, phonetically nicknamed 'Elsie' – which accurately guided the searchlight it was connected to. With a traditional searchlight, the probability of successfully tracking a target was barely 1%, but with 'Elsie', this rose to 90%. 609 Squadron pilots collaborated on the system's development in 'real conditions'. Jean was involved in three of these operations, totaling 3 hours and 20 minutes of night flight.

On 16 December, Ivan du Monceau faced off against a Typhoon – 609's future aircraft – in a friendly dogfight and came away unimpressed, asserting that his Spit climbed faster, turned faster, and dived faster. Not very reassuring.

Three days later, on Friday, 19 December, the most improbable news spread through Digby: Vicky Ortmans was alive! A letter sent from a German POW camp and passed on by the Red Cross, signed Vicky Ogilvie (he used a Canadian pilot's surname so as not to endanger his family), confirmed, after multiple verifications, that it was indeed Vicky Ortmans. Months later, it would be confirmed that during his fight on 21 October, he was wounded by an explosive shell in the left shoulder but had managed to bail out over the Channel. He spent two days and one night in his dinghy before being picked up by the Germans and was sent to Saint-Omer for treatment. He was then transferred to Stalag Luft III, from where he would finally be liberated in May 1945. Vicky Ortmans claimed to have downed two Focke-Wulf 190s in his last fight.

Learning that Vicky was alive brought joy to everyone, especially his brother Christian, who thought he had lost his hero. Coincidentally, a massive party was already planned for that evening, and by 9:30pm, the 400 attendees had already consumed the planned 550 litres of beer. Fortunately, once the barrels were empty, the men could still dance until the early hours, and the guys from 609 certainly did not hold back.

As Christmas approached, the atmosphere became more festive; the 22nd, a clay shooting competition was organised and won by François de Spirlet. In the evening, a few officers from 609 crashed a party of the Women's Auxiliary Air Force (WAAF) and, as usual, caused a bit of a ruckus. On 25 December, the pilots were invited to dine by Lady Londesborough at nearby Blankney Hall. Jean de Selys' networking was to thank for this invitation as along with a few others, he regularly rode Lady Londesborough's horses, thus establishing close ties with her. Blankney Hall had become a real refuge for the pilots, who were always happy to escape the austerity of the Digby base.

In terms of aerial activity, the year ended spectacularly on 28 December with a record 19 hours of night flying, mainly as part of cooperation with anti-aircraft units, which amused the pilots greatly.

In late December, Jean sent a 609 Squadron Christmas card to Sam Heapy and his wife, including a photograph of himself in the cockpit of a Hurricane, taken at Tern Hill. On the back of the photograph, Jean wrote, 'Training - Hurricane. July 1941. A bit like a thoroughbred!' The card's message was optimistic: 'Christmas '42 in Brussels! And what a celebration it will be! Keep your courage and optimism. We are about to start the good year - the year of victory.'

From 29 December until the end of the year, nearly uninterrupted fog enveloped Digby, and 609 Squadron's final act of the year was a New Year's Eve party where the pilots drank a rum punch prepared by the officers' mess until the early hours. The hangover the next day was legendary, sending everyone to bed by 9pm on the first day of 1942.

On 2 January, 'Sheep' Gilroy, the squadron's CO, received a letter from the Savoy demanding the return of Kaspar's statue. 609 complied, mainly because Air Commodore Peake was also losing patience, being embarrassed each time he visited the Savoy.

A few days later, 609 was thrilled to receive a visit from Alex Nitelet, who had been presumed missing since 9 August 1941 after his plane was shot down near Boulogne. The Belgian had not only survived but also managed to return to England.[10] He shared his story of being seriously injured upon crash-landing, being flipped over, and then

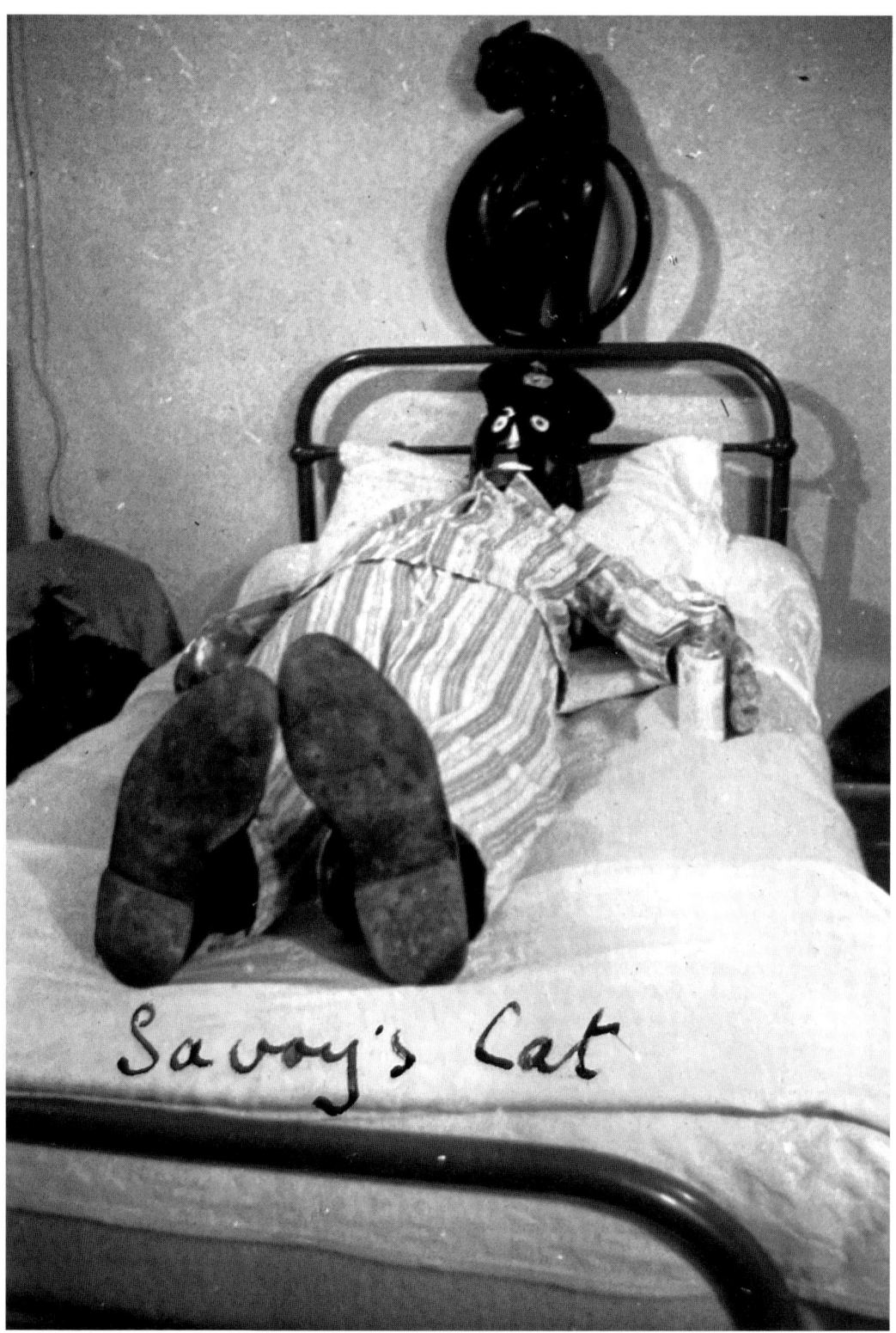

Kaspar the cat, the Savoy Hotel's cat statue kidnapped by the 609 gang, in its 'place of detention'.

Jean simply wrote the caption 'Three Friends' for this beautiful photograph capturing a moment of relaxation at Digby (Offenberg, de Selys, de Spirlet).

rescued by a local farmer before the Germans could capture him. After recuperating, an escape network helped him journey through Paris, Tours, Toulouse, and Marseille, then on foot over the Pyrenees, through Barcelona, Madrid, Gibraltar, and finally to Plymouth, where he arrived on 24 December 1941, five months after his crash. In Marseille, he met a Belgian leading an escape network, known as Pat O'Leary, who was none other than Albert Guérisse, Jean's former companion in adventure after the May 1940 debacle. Nitelet, now prevented from returning to 609 due to problems with his vision, would go back to France to become a radio operator for Pat O'Leary.

January's weather was particularly bad, with snow significantly disrupting flight plans. Jean's logbook entries are notably sparse: only seven flying days for a total of 11 hours and 40 minutes, the least he had flown since joining the RAF.

At the start of the year, 609 Squadron's Operations Record Book (ORB) details the order of battle for B Flight, to which Jean belonged: Jean Offenberg (flight leader), Roger Malengreau, Thomas 'Tommy' Rigler, John Van Schaick, Peter Nash, Bruce

An unusual view of a Spitfire in the snow, a scene unfortunately too common at Digby, where the winter was desperately long.

Osborn, George 'Russ/Reg' Dickson, Charles 'Mac' McConnell, H. Patterson, William 'Bill' Stock, and Alfred Moore.

On 15 January, two of these pilots narrowly escaped disaster, when 'Tommy' Rigler and Christian Ortmans embarked on a 'Rhubarb' operation over Holland. They departed from Hampstead aerodrome, refuelling for a 110-mile flight. Near the coast, they attacked two Flak ships but Rigler was wounded by gunfire. Despite his injuries, he made another pass only to find his guns no longer worked, so with two Messerschmitt 110s approaching, they broke off the engagement. Rigler landed at Martlesham, bleeding profusely from shrapnel wounds.

To make the most of the pilots' time while they were grounded by poor weather, they were sent to advanced training courses. Jean attended navigation and air gunnery courses on 17 and 21 January, respectively, though pilots were generally unimpressed, deeming them a 'waste of time'. They were, however, more interested in a session on 20 January that presented flight evaluation results of captured German aircraft and offered concrete recommendations on combat tactics. Many questions revolved around the Typhoon, which they would soon fly, and its capabilities against Luftwaffe fighters.

Meanwhile, 22 January witnessed a tragedy that shook 609, when Jean 'Le Pyker' Offenberg died in a collision with another Spitfire. Returning from a formation flying training session with Robert 'Balbo' Roelandt, they were unexpectedly attacked by

On 26 January, Jean Offenberg's body was carried by his comrades to his final resting place. Jean, visibly very affected, is second from left.

Sergeant Godfrey De Renzi of 92 Squadron, resulting in a collision. Offenberg's plane dived vertically, preventing him from bailing out, and he died on impact. De Renzi, whose surprise attack caused the accident, also perished in the crash. Offenberg's death deprived him of a promising career; his superiors saw him as wing commander material.

On 26 January, the squadron mourned Offenberg's death. His coffin, draped in English and Belgian flags and carrying his officer's cap, Wings, and decorations, was carried by eight comrades, including Jean, to his burial in Scopwick cemetery. The snowfall during the ceremony added to the desolation, but a brief clearing and the appearance of the sun offered a solemn tribute to the ace. Despite the tragedy, operations continued. Jean flew two operations, including a night flight, on the evening of Offenberg's funeral.

By the end of January, 609 had trained twelve pilots in operational night flying. February began quietly, with Digby covered in snow and ice, and on 2 February, 609 engaged in a spirited snowball fight with the neighbouring 92 Squadron. Jean resumed flying on 6 February, undertaking four flights, including a convoy protection patrol where he fired at a Luftwaffe Dornier 217 bomber for the first time. Despite expending all his ammunition, he achieved no result, but the convoy remained unharmed. The following day, Jean and Lallemant, eager for action, participated in another operation. The frustration from the previous day's unsuccessful engagement and the enforced inactivity of recent weeks drove them hard. However, their 'Sea Sweep' operation ended up being frustrating as they encountered only British aircraft, but the pilots rejoiced at the return of 'Tommy' Rigler from the hospital after his epic 'Rhubarb' operation in January. On 9 February, he was back in the squadron, and Jean greeted him playfully, saying, 'What about a Rhubarb, Tommy?' The Englishman assured him he was ready to go again without hesitation, but admitted attacking Flak ships was a very bad idea.

On 12 February, 609 Squadron was on alert, and eleven aircraft, including Jean de Selys', took off in the early afternoon for Biggin Hill. They were to participate in a significant 'Sea Sweep' operation, the details of which were kept secret. Ultimately, 609 Squadron's aircrafts took off but were not engaged in the operation. The pilots learned only the next day, much to their regret, that the operation involved blocking the route of three battleships - the *Scharnhorst*, *Gneisenau*, and *Prinz Eugen* - and a heavy German cruiser that had forced their way through the Channel to return to Germany from Brest.

On 15 February, Jean de Selys wrote a letter to Jean Offenberg's uncle who lived in Argentina, informing him of his nephew's death. Jean found his address in Buenos Aires among Offenberg's papers. The death of 'Le Pyker' deeply affected Jean, who had been his roommate since their arrival at Digby. In his letter, Jean wrote:

> I don't know if you were closely acquainted with your nephew. Jean was the most magnificent, the greatest among us. Having joined the RAF in August 1940 as a Pilot Officer, he was, less than a year later, a Flight Lieutenant and a leader in combat. Often, it was he who led the entire squadron in operations. In May 1941, His Majesty King George awarded him the D.F.C. for his brilliant conduct, exceptional courage that allowed him to claim six certain victories and five probables, and on 21 July 1941, the minister awarded him the Belgian Croix de Guerre, in the name of the King.
>
> I cannot express what Jean meant to us all. He was a very pure and beautiful symbol, a constant example, an inexhaustible source of hope, faith in the future, in our future, in the future of our country, our King, everything dear to us. Without fully realising his quality, we felt he radiated moral support during moments of discouragement, weariness, an unwavering and unshakable support during combat. His presence brought so much freshness and purity to the troubled and

violent hours we lived! His death was a terrible shock to us. We felt with dismay the inevitability of Providence. His time was marked. It rang at a time when we were happy to see him finally taking the rest he had long deserved. If his death surprised us, it certainly did not surprise him. Perhaps you know how much Jean was a believer. The only consolation given to us, and I think it will be yours too, is to think that he finally has Peace, infinitely more precious than any that could have been given to him in this world.

We buried him piously in a small cemetery in the English countryside. We retain the imprint he left on us, too profound not to continue his work among us. Having had the happiness of living in the squadron with him, having him as a leader and even more as a friend, I gathered everything that belonged to him. Following a written wish, his belongings were handed over to an English family who loved him dearly and where he spent most of his leaves, who will take care of them until the day it will be possible to return them to his parents.

A long-awaited event then took place on 17 February: 609 Squadron left its quarters at Digby to move into a residence near the base, Ashby Hall. The residence was not in great condition and was particularly cold, but the pilots did not care less: they had finally regained their independence and were freed from the constraints that Digby's authorities had been inventing to complicate their lives. The property's park became the scene of epic hunting parties, where the most dedicated hunters turned out to be 'Bob' Wilmet, 'Mony' Van Lierde, and, of course, Jean de Selys, who reconnected with the pleasures he had experienced with his father. The 'Belgian Barouche' and 'Caroline', a small Morris Eight belonging to Vicky Ortmans, were used to get to the base, located less than 1.2 miles away, and to transport meals prepared at Digby's mess.

The arrival at Ashby Hall had an immediate positive impact on morale, as on 18 February, Ivan du Monceau shot down a Dornier 217, making it the first bomber destroyed by Squadron 609 since 1940.

Billy de Goat joined the pilots at Ashby Hall on 22 February, also escaping the authoritarian pall that had settled over RAF Station Digby.

By the end of the month, Jean de Selys had accumulated 30 hours and 55 minutes of flight during twenty-eight sorties. In his logbook, he proudly noted that in his first year as a Royal Air Force pilot (from 3 August 1941 to 3 July 1942), he had already accumulated 312.05 hours of flight, including 253 hours solo.

March started with the same poor weather, and no flights were conducted in the first week. The pilots took advantage of the forced inactivity to enjoy ice skating, which they practised on the frozen lake of Ashby Hall. On 5 March, Billy de Goat was thrilled to have a new companion to keep him company after one of 609 Squadron kidnapped a white goat belonging to a nearby regiment of Welsh Fusiliers. On 6 March, the pilots attended an exhibition of German equipment and were particularly impressed with the quality of the radio equipment.

Fortunately, the weather finally cleared up on Sunday, 8 March. 609 Squadron and 402 Squadron headed to West Malling to participate in an 'Offensive Sweep'. The two squadrons took off from the Kent airfield at 3:35pm with a 'rear support wing' operation along a Dunkirk-Calais line, from which they were to cover Boston bombers returning from a raid on Comines. A formation of about twelve Focke-Wulf 190s was spotted by 609 Squadron, and a series of dogfights ensued. Jean de Selys, responding to the call sign 'Red 3', lined up a German fighter in his sights but, due to a regrettable reflex after weeks of shooting practice, accidentally pressed the button of his camera gun instead of his cannons. Instead of firing, he ended up taking a 'jolly little picture' of a Focke-Wulf, as 609 Squadron's ORB sarcastically notes after the operation. This was the kind of mishap that occurred when men were away from combat for too long and only engaged in mock dogfights.

Jean was furious at missing this first victory that was within his grasp. However, he did not have time to dwell on it, as he was soon involved in a swirling dogfight with three Focke-Wulf 190s, deftly transitioning from the hunted to the hunter, though he never managed to get into a good firing position. Shortly afterwards, he took over from another Spitfire pursuing an enemy aircraft and fired two short bursts from less than 1,300 feet away. Unfortunately, he had to break off the engagement because of engine trouble. Luckily, he managed to make it back to England without being attacked by the two enemy fighters that flew over him without noticing: a stroke of luck. Running low on fuel, Jean landed at Manston and in the debriefing he gave after the flight, his testimony contributed to the validation of a victory claimed by Ivan du Monceau. The rest of the squadron also claimed two 'probables' (du Monceau and Dieu) and damaged two enemy aircraft (Gilroy and Morai). It was a prolific day for the Belgians of 609 Squadron, a day Jean would have loved to fully participate in.

Over the course of the month, Jean was 'scrambled' three times. He was now accustomed to the drill, knowing it was a race against time to take to the air as quickly as possible to intercept the enemy before they reached their target. The two pilots put on alert were already wearing their full flying equipment and waiting for a potential alarm signal in the dispersal. This could be excruciatingly long, as the alert may never come, especially in a less threatened area like Digby. So, they needed to kill time, which could seem to stretch indefinitely, by reading, playing cards and napping, but when the alarm sounded, it was time to snap out of the torpor in a fraction of a second and rush to their aircraft, around which two mechanics were already waiting for their pilot, like grooms preparing to welcome a rider about to go fox hunting. One of the mechanics

The Spitfire with which Jean made a forced landing returning from a night mission on 26 March.

was perched on the left wing, assisting the pilot with his harness. The other mechanic was already activating the starter battery that would kick the engine into gear once the pilot had performed a few cockpit manipulations and hit the starter.

Once all essential checks (pressures, temperatures, and controls) were completed, the aircraft could start taxiing towards the runway, with the two mechanics having removed the chocks that kept the plane in its parking spot. Once airborne, ground control provided a heading, and the challenge was to get there as quickly as possible. Unfortunately, the vast majority of 'scrambles' from Digby led to nothing, and the two pilots returned, the rush of adrenaline being replaced by the bitter feeling of having wasted their time again.

On 26 March, upon returning from a night flight, Jean damaged his most regularly used Spitfire – serial number W3705 – during landing. The incident was due to the poor positioning of one of the runway markers, and he was not held responsible. Jean was unharmed, but the plane required repairs.

Despite the disastrous weather during the first week, March ultimately allowed Jean to add 27 hours and 20 minutes of flight to his logbook.

The month ended spectacularly with the end of the rest period at Digby and the long-awaited departure for Duxford, which finally took place on 30 March. But first, the end of this prolonged stay in Lincolnshire had to be celebrated, and a massive 'party' with seventy guests was organised at Ashby Hall. A few days before the party, the pilots sought charitable souls who could supply them with festive drinks, and Jean, always well-connected, secured a few bottles through the Belgian headquarters in London. Jean had also been promoted for this 'farewell party': he was now 609's drinks officer, responsible for storing the most precious beverages in his room. The pilots were so eager for this party that they managed to delay the departure for Duxford by two days.

Once at Duxford, 609 Squadron's activity scaled up significantly. The main reason for the squadron's deployment to this important Cambridgeshire base was the RAF's desire to rapidly make operational the very first Wing entirely made up of squadrons equipped with Hawker Typhoons. Three squadrons were involved: 56 (whose conversion was already done and temporarily based at Snailwell, 18.5 miles away), 266 'Rhodesian', and of course, 609.

609's facilities at Duxford were very average: their offices were in a wooden barrack next to a hangar where continuous Typhoon engine tests were conducted. As a result, the ambient noise often hindered conversations, and everything was covered in dust. But nothing could dampen the immense satisfaction of having left Digby, so everyone adapted and was happy to resume a role worthy of the name. However, the very first Typhoon was only received by 609 Squadron on 18 April, and so the Spit remained the pilots' main tool of work in this particularly busy April.

The weather was good, and operations multiplied. The first one assigned to de Selys and Dickson was to escort the 'Duxford Exhibition Circus' belonging to the Air Fighting Development Unit (AFDU), composed of a Heinkel 111 bomber and a captured Messerschmitt 110 fighter in perfect flying condition. They were convoyed to North Luffenham, and the 1-hour flight offered Jean an extraordinary opportunity to observe these aircraft for even better recognition in combat. Mischievously, Jean noted a surprising 'Protection He 111 & Me 110' to describe the operation in his logbook.

Jean was eager to return to combat, and after a request for a 'Rhubarb' operation was denied on the 3rd, he and Wilmet received the green light the next day. The target was Fécamp, but the operation was cut short as the cloud cover was deemed insufficient, and they had to turn back. It was another missed opportunity that would have been a morale booster for Jean, who had just learned with great sadness of the death of a Belgian RAF member, Captain Baron René Lunden, a navigator on a Boston bomber from 23 Squadron that crashed on landing at Tangmere. As attempts were made to extract him from the wreckage of his aircraft, heavily damaged by Flak, he said to one of his surviving crew members (Léon Terlinden),[11] 'Oh, I know I'm going to die. Tell my mother that I died believing in God.' Jean knew René Lunden well and was devastated to attend the funeral a few days later.

On 5 April, for the first time since 1940, the two flights of 609 Squadron were separated, with 'A' being sent to Coltishall, and 'B' remaining at Duxford.

'Sheep' Gilroy had the opportunity to test a Typhoon on 10 April and was impressed. The aircraft was so fast that he found himself over North Weald (30 miles north of Duxford) without realising it, and although he found the aircraft easy to manoeuvre, it was a bit tricky on take-off.

Between 11 and 25 April, the two flights of 609 Squadron operated together eight times from West Malling as part of offensive operations led by 11 Group. Jean participated in four of them. The first, on 12 April, gave de Selys the opportunity to fly again with his favourite Spit, W3705, which was now back from repair. The operation went smoothly, although Jean ended up alone in the 'Blue Section' as both his leader and wingmen had to turn back. The second operation (13 April), taking them from north of Le Touquet to Cap Gris-Nez, was even calmer, and at 21,000 feet, 609 Squadron saw no enemy aircraft.

The third 'Offensive Sweep' planned for 15 April was much more eventful. Jean, flying as 'Blue 3', was led by Malengreau, with Roelandt (who quickly aborted the operation due to oxygen issues) and Blanco as wingmen. The 'Blue Section', flying the highest, was attacked by a formation of about twelve Focke-Wulf 190s from two directions. A 190 repeatedly tried to lure 'Blue 3' away from its formation and make him an easy target for Luftwaffe planes lurking higher in the sky. Each time Jean pretended to follow, the German fighter changed direction to further separate him from his formation. But de Selys did not fall for it and managed to shake off the nuisance. Later, two Messerschmitt 109s dived with the sun behind them on 'Blue Section', but when the Spitfires turned to engage, the German fighters refused combat. The day was particularly successful for CO 'Sheep' Gilroy, who added a tenth victory to his tally.

The last 'Offensive Sweep' of April Jean de Selys participated in was the most epic. The three sections – Yellow, Red, and Blue – of 609 Squadron were sent on a cover operation for six Bostons raiding Abbeville. Nos. 411 and 412 squadrons also participated in the operation. 'Blue Leader' (Malengreau) lost contact with the formation while observing aircraft silhouettes shimmering in the sun. He decided to patrol with the rest of his section (de Selys, Innes, and Rigler) along the coast, between Le Tréport and Le Crotoy, waiting for the bombers to return. Six 190s dived on them, sparking a hair-raising dogfight. Briefly, an enemy fighter was seen attacking Innes' plane, which was then lost from view. Malengreau engaged with another, and a third surprised Jean by opening fire from below the Belgian's Spitfire. Too late to avoid the tracer bullets multiplying in front of his plane, an explosive shell hit him, causing a flash on the cockpit side when a fragment lodged in the fuel tank. At the same time, another fragment wounded Jean's right knee. Concerned about the state of his aircraft and the extent of his injury, de Selys sent out several 'maydays' that went unheard. Fortunately, he quickly realised he would be able to make it back to West Malling – it was not yet time for him to end up 'in the drink', as RAF pilots say when crashing into the Channel. The fourth member of 'Blue Section', Tommy Rigler, was engaged by three Messerschmitt 109s and shot one down. Upon returning to base, the disappearance of Sergeant Innes, a Rhodesian pilot, was confirmed. 609 Squadron had not lost a pilot in combat since 15 November 1941. In its account of the day's operations, the squadron's Operations Record Book specifies what all pilots now felt: the tactics that were effective against the Messerschmitt 109s had become completely obsolete against the formidable Focke-Wulf 190.

From 26 April, opportunities for 609 Squadron to participate in major operations were significantly limited, as only about eight Spitfires were operational, a consequence of the aircraft's age and damage sustained in recent operations. Fortunately, the transition to the Typhoon was accelerating, and twelve such aircraft were now available to the pilots.

On Monday, 27 April 1942, Jean de Selys flew his first flight in a Typhoon, registered R7628, lasting 25 minutes. From 28 April, 609 Squadron ceased to be an operational day squadron with its Spitfires but, curiously, remained operational for night flights. Jean would fly sixteen more times in a Spitfire before the end of May, but the Typhoon gradually became the main tool for 609 pilots.

On 29 April, Jean concluded a Typhoon flight by performing a loop that ended at an altitude of 5,000 feet, earning him a reprimand. A new rule would now prevent pilots from performing such manoeuvres below 8,000 feet. On the evening of 29 April, Jean was part of a formation of six Spitfires put on alert and taking off at 11:35pm for a 1 hour and 35-minute moonlit flight. The assigned altitude – between 11,500 and 14,500 feet – was too high, and they did not encounter the enemy, who flew lower and was engaged by planes from 266 Squadron. Once back at Duxford, the pilots remained on alert until 4:15am.

Jean de Selys wrapped up the month with an additional 37 hours and 5 minutes of flight time, including 3 hours and 25 minutes at the controls of a Typhoon in just three days. Little did he know that this fighter he was just getting to know would be the aircraft with which his name would be forever associated.

Chapter 11

'Tiffy', the Plane of a Lifetime

(27 April 1942–19 January 1943)

At the beginning of May, the squadron adorned with the white rose already boasted fifteen Typhoons and a remainder of thirteen Spitfire Mk Vs. To enable a comfortable transition to the Typhoon, 609 was spared from operations, allowing it to focus entirely on training flights. This was clearly not a luxury, as the 'Tiffy' was a formidable machine that had already revealed some major flaws to the pilots of 56 Squadron, who had been flying the 'beast' since September 1941. The squadron itself was accustomed to pioneering, as it was the first to fly the Hurricane back in 1938.

To understand the teething troubles hindering the aircraft's development, it is necessary to revisit its inception.[1] In 1938, the Air Ministry issued a specification for a successor to the Hurricane, with the requirements significantly inspired by a series of conversations held as early as 1937 between Air Commodore R.H. Verney and Sydney Camm, Hawker's chief engineer, who was already responsible for the Fury and Hurricane. Guided by Verney's insights and vision, Camm set his team to work before the official tender was announced, giving Hawker's project a decisive edge over its competitors (Supermarine, Gloster, Westland, and Bristol), who started their designs seven months late. Thus, it was no surprise when Hawker clinched the deal with its 'Typhoon' project, to the dismay of its competitors, who were disgruntled by a highly questionable selection process.

Sydney Camm was a conservative engineer, and there are many structural similarities between the Hurricane and the Typhoon. Many observers, upon discovering the new Hawker aircraft, saw it as an 'enlarged Hurricane', significantly so, as the Typhoon was much heavier (5 tons empty weight compared to 3 for its predecessor), longer, taller, and with a greater wingspan and wing area. It was entirely made of metal and featured Hawker's typical tubular structure for the front part and a monocoque element for the rear. Its massive wings were in one piece (except for their tips) and it was equipped with a particularly robust landing gear. What truly bestowed the Typhoon with its impressive beastly nature, however, was undoubtedly its firepower (four 20mm cannons fed by 140 rounds each) and, above all, its formidable Napier

Sabre engine, producing 2,000 horsepower (500 more than the Hurricane or Spit). This bulky and complex engine would prove long and difficult to refine and would cause a lot of trouble for pilots and maintenance teams. It quickly revealed a nasty tendency to catch fire upon starting (if it would start at all), necessitating a mechanic to always be on hand with an extinguisher during startup procedures. The engine was also capricious in flight – it might stall unexpectedly – and it was not uncommon for it to spray oil on the windshield. Finally, it became a mechanic's nightmare due to its extraordinary maintenance requirements: its twenty-four cylinders and forty-eight spark plugs required constant attention, not to mention a service every twenty flight hours, making the aircraft's operational availability extremely tight.

Objectively, it must be acknowledged that the Typhoon's development was significantly disrupted by the outbreak of war and by the Battle of Britain in particular, which concentrated all production efforts on the already operational fighters, the Hurricane and Spitfire. While the first Typhoon prototype took its maiden flight on 24 February 1940, less than two months before the German invasion of Belgium, the second flight did not occur until 3 May 1941, well after the Battle of Britain had ended. Further proof of the scarcity of resources allocated to the Typhoon is that the first service models were not equipped with the four 20mm cannons and had to make do with .303 machine guns like the Spitfires. Of the fifteen Typhoons available to 609 Squadron in May 1942, only four were Mk Ib models fitted with cannons. It is clear that when it began its squadron service, the aircraft and its engine's development was far from complete.

Consequently, when they received their Typhoons, the pilots of 56 Squadron unwillingly became test pilots and were soon exposed to other vices of the aircraft. Many started complaining of headaches and nausea without the problem's source being identified. Only with the investigation report following a fatal crash on 11 November 1941 – when a Typhoon crashed to the ground after a 3,000-feet dive – was it finally understood that the pilot had lost consciousness due to carbon monoxide poisoning from the engine. The cockpit's sealing was far from optimal, and the issue was never fully resolved. Despite adding ventilation louvers in the cockpit and modifying the exhaust pipes on the sides of the engine hood, the problem persisted, and the only effective solution was that pilots had to wear their oxygen masks from engine start to complete shutdown.

In January 1942, B Flight of 266 Squadron received its first Typhoons and joined 56 Squadron at Duxford to continue the aircraft's development. When 609 Squadron received its Typhoons starting April 1942, not a single operation had yet been flown by a Typhoon, indicative of the myriad problems slowing its implementation. In fact, the first significant wartime operation involving Typhoons would not take place until

The Typhoon registered PR-G of the 609 Squadron CO (here with Paul Richey at the controls).

mid-August 1942, eleven months after their arrival at 56 Squadron. To say doubts were beginning to emerge about the aircraft's true potential is an understatement.

This aura of suspicion was significantly reinforced by the pilots' feedback who, once they had more or less tamed the aircraft, described disappointing performances. They noted that the engine lost power above 4,500m (14,800 feet). The climb rate was unimpressive, and the aircraft's manoeuvrability raised concerns: in dogfighting, the Spitfire proved to be much more agile, outmanoeuvering the Typhoon in just a couple of turns. From the cockpit, forward visibility was less than ideal due to the thick canopy frames. The question quickly arose: was the Typhoon the fighter truly capable of gaining the upper hand over the formidable Focke-Wulf 190 that the RAF desperately needed?

For Jean de Selys and the pilots of 609, as for all the pilots of other squadrons before them, the transition from Spitfire to Typhoon was particularly challenging. For aviators accustomed to a light and agile aircraft, their new steed was anything but easy to handle. In addition to all the problems listed, all squadrons observed landing gear failures due to rough landings. Fortunately, despite its flaws, the Typhoon was robust, and forced landings generally went relatively well, except at sea, where the large radiator housed under the engine acted like a scoop and accelerated the aircraft's immersion in the water.

Beyond the aircraft's massive and intimidating aspect, what struck the pilots most before the engine even started was related to cockpit access: on the Typhoon, this was done via a side door, one on the left of the cockpit (which was sealed) and another

View of the Hawker Typhoon cockpit.

on the right that opened like a car door and was equipped with a window that could be lowered and raised using a crank reminiscent of an automobile. Pilots reported that the doors vibrated annoyingly throughout the flight and opening the windows made the cockpit extremely noisy, rendering the radio inaudible. The cockpit was larger than what they were used to, and ergonomic efforts were made whereby the flap and landing gear controls were placed to the pilot's left, near the throttle lever.

Portrait of Jean de Selys, May 1942.

In mid-April, Jean wrote to Sam Heapy, informing him that he had received news from the de Selys family in Belgium. Although the news was somewhat vague, it seemed that 'everyone is more or less well'. He learned that Edé had attempted to escape from his prisoner camp but had been recaptured. In his letter, Jean reflects on the death of René Lunden ('a magnificent guy') which fuelled his desire to fight ('another one to avenge. And they will pay dearly for it'.).

The month of May saw 609 starting with its lowest total of available pilots, barely nineteen (seven pilots below the standard). Fortunately, from the 12th, three new pilots, each with over 1,000 flying hours, joined the squadron. The experience of these pilots (bearing in mind that Jean only totalled 370.5 flying hours at the beginning of May, and, despite his age, thus remained a 'very young' pilot) highlighted the fact that the RAF was aware of the difficulties presented by the Typhoon. Only pilots considered above average were now assigned to Typhoon-equipped squadrons. Among the three newcomers were two Belgian pilots: Raymond Dopéré and Jean 'Le canard' (the duck) Creteur. Both had been approached by 350 Squadron, the first 100% Belgian squadron, but they preferred to join 609, which was highly regarded within Fighter Command. Dopéré was a true survivor, who had suffered mistreatment in Spanish prisons during his escape to England.

Throughout May, training exercises increased (formation flying, interception, air shooting, ground attack, cooperation with the army etc.) without any major issues for the 'Junior Typhoon Squadron' until Friday, 29 May, when Jean de Selys experienced the biggest scare of his flying career. While performing an aerobatics training flight in the Typhoon registered PR-X, which was fitted with new motor parts from Napier

Jean de Selys at the controls of the PR-M. On the left door, one can see the monogram of Leopold III that the very royalist de Selys insisted on placing on his plane.

Camille Gutt visiting, posing with the Belgian pilots of the squadron, from left to right: Lallemant, Ortmans, de Selys, Blanco, de Spirlet, Dopéré, Malengreau, and Van Lierde.

industries, his engine suddenly caught fire, forcing him to parachute out. It was the very first time a pilot had successfully bailed out of a Typhoon in flight. A visibly shaken Jean de Selys was picked up by a group of pilots at his landing spot, where the 'Home Guard' took care of him. Upon their return to the Duxford mess, thirty-two pints of beer were arranged on a table to form a large '609' as a bit of comfort after an emotionally charged day. Everyone in 609 knew the Napier Sabre engine was unpredictable, but seeing one of their own involved in such an unexpected incident cast a new shadow of doubt over an aircraft that increasingly looked like a 'death trap'.

The month ended with the farewell party of Squadron Leader George Kemp 'Sheep' Gilroy, who reluctantly handed over the reins of 609 to his successor, Paul Richey, who had arrived a few days earlier. Gilroy had led the squadron for ten months and participated in forty-seven of the fifty-four operations conducted under his command, securing four victories. For his last evening, he adhered to the ritual that 609 pilots, never short of whimsical ideas when it came to partying, had established since the beginning of the month: after climbing a human pyramid, the pilot had to leave a footprint on the 20-feet-high ceiling of the Duxford mess antechamber. A perilous task and the source of much laughter.

For 26-year-old Paul Richey, his arrival marked a return to 609, with whom he had previously led A Flight from April to August 1941, shortly before Jean de Selys' arrival.[2] This Londoner had made an early name for himself by downing a German aircraft before the invasion on 10 May. During the campaign in France, he had fought boldly and bailed out twice from his damaged aircraft (on 11 and 15 May) before making a forced landing on 19 May after a fierce dogfight with a group of Luftwaffe planes, during which he shot down three with his Hurricane. His injuries forced him to be repatriated to England, where his convalescence prevented him from participating in the Battle of Britain as a pilot. However, he had still contributed to the RAF's resistance by serving on the ground as a 'Fighter Controller' at Middle Wallop before returning to squadron service to continue the fight.

June began with a new significant problem adding to the already long list of 'gremlins' plaguing the Typhoon, when two aircraft from 56 Squadron were shot down

Paul Richey back with the 609. He is seen here during his first tenure with the squadron surrounded by Squadron Leader Robinson and Belgian pilot Nitelet.

by Spitfires who had mistaken their Typhoons for Focke-Wulf 190s! One pilot was injured, and the other was killed. This confusion would be repeated several times in the coming months and would not only concern Allied aviators: English operators of coastal anti-aircraft batteries also struggled to identify Typhoons and targeted them as enemy fighters. Reports indicated that even the Germans had been fooled by this striking resemblance. Various marking alternatives were thus considered to avoid confusion, the ultimate decision being to paint four black stripes separated by white stripes under each wing by early November 1942. These markings may be confused with the invasion stripes painted on all Allied aircraft during the Normandy landings, but this anti-friendly fire marking predates them. However, as we will see later, these underwing stripes were not a panacea, and incidents would continue to occur until the end of the war, with American pilots arriving later in the European skies being among those who mistakenly identified the Typhoon as the Fw.190.

On a more optimistic note, the visit to Duxford by Prince George, Duke of Kent, on 9 June 1942, witnessed a near-miracle, when a formation of thirty-five Typhoons from 56, 266, and 609 squadrons flew over the base, astonishing those who thought launching so many aircraft simultaneously was impossible due to the chronic issues afflicting the machine. This feat was repeated the next day – this time with Jean de Selys – in the presence of Air Marshal Sholto Douglas and Air Vice-Marshal Richard Saul. Many feared this XXL formation gave the High Command a skewed view of the true operational level of the Typhoon Wing. Old habits die hard, however, and 10 June was also marked by Remy Van Lierde's forced landing, an opportunity for him to appreciate the aircraft's solidity in such situations and fortunately to escape unharmed.

Unfortunately, the accident that occurred on 26 June was far more tragic.[3] A 100% Belgian formation of four Typhoons (led by François de Spirlet with 'Cheval' Lallemant as the left winger and Christian Ortmans on the right, followed directly by Bob Wilmet) was taxiing for take off. As the planes picked up speed, wing to wing, the left tyre of François de Spirlet's aircraft burst, abruptly veering his Typhoon into Raymond Lallemant's. Due to the high speed and proximity of the aircraft, a catastrophic collision was inevitable, and François de Spirlet died instantly. Lallemant emerged from the accident in shock, claiming he would never fly again. Paul Richey, the squadron's new CO, showed tremendous qualities of psychology by encouraging him to fly again the next day in an identical formation, leading with Lallemant as his left winger. This test had the desired effect, as Lallemant overcame a mountain of apprehensions and eventually regained his confidence. With the death of François de Spirlet, who was universally liked, the pilots of 609 had lost one of their best. His funeral, on Sunday, 28 June, was yet another day of great sorrow, as 609 had already seen too many, and yet everyone knew it would not be the last.

François de Spirlet, one of the best assets of the 609 Squadron, would lose his life in a take off collision with 'Cheval' Lallemant's Typhoon.

Jean resting near the dispersal area. A lot of tension accumulated during flights on the unpredictable Typhoon.

By the end of that grim month of June, 609 Squadron counted eleven Belgian pilots, ten English, two Canadians, one French, and one Rhodesian. When July arrived, 609 was finally officially declared operational on Friday, 3 July, although no operations occurred before 19 July. In the meantime, for Jean and his fellow pilots, training continued in flight as well as on the ground, as 'dinghy drills' were regularly organised in a pool near the base so that pilots became familiar with their life rafts. The pilots, prevented by the endless operational pause from releasing their testosterone, devised increasingly 'physical' parties. Once night fell, different squadrons at Duxford (266 being clearly the preferred adversary of 609) challenged each other in more or less good-natured contests: relay races between pint drinkers, rugby matches with a log from the open fire, and even outright brawls, where punches flew. The next day, bruises were visible on bodies and faces, but the men proudly displayed them as trophies, swearing to do it all over again as soon as possible.

On 12 July, Jean de Selys and Peter Raw, while calmly walking on the base, narrowly avoided cannon fire accidentally triggered by a Typhoon during landing. No one quite understood what had happened, but it was a close call to what could have been a particularly foolish accident. On 21 July 1942, Belgium's National Day, a decree by the Belgian ministers in council confirmed Jean de Selys' promotion to the rank of

Jean de Selys and Ivan du Monceau (photograph taken on Belgian National Day, 21 July 1942).

Self-portrait of Jean, whose seriousness echoes the difficult period the 609 was going through: the beginnings on the Typhoon were far from what the pilots had dreamed of.

reserve captain of aeronautics. The same day, Jean and a group of 609 pilots attended a military parade of Belgian forces at the Chelsea Barracks in London. The day was very festive, marked by a sumptuous lunch offered by the Belgian government at the Rembrandt Hotel followed by an evening reception at Grosvenor House, where all Belgians present in England seem to have been gathered.

Just when it seemed the lengthy list of the Typhoon's vices was fully known, an accident involving a Typhoon from 257 Squadron occurred on 25 July when the aircraft crashed under mysterious circumstances after apparently breaking up in flight. Two similar incidents would also happen in August and it would take many more accidents and several months to understand that this time, the aircraft's tail was to blame. We will return to this later, as this structural weakness of the Typhoon, despite the implementation of reinforcements, was one of the hypotheses that might explain the fatal crash of Jean de Selys Longchamps a little over a year later.

At the end of July, Jean participated in his first operation in a Typhoon. On the 28th, he took part in a 'Channel Sweep' during which he followed a circuit 'Duxford – Gravelines – Ostend – Duxford'. His last operation before this was on 25 April, more than three months earlier. This latest operation proceeded without incident, and to the pilots' great disappointment, no enemy was spotted.

Paul Richey, behind the panel with crossed arms, surrounded by the 609 members. Jean holds a young puppy in his arms. On the far right, leaning on the wing, is Frank Ziegler, the intelligence officer, and the pilots' confidant.

On 30 July, de Selys embarked on another operation ('Offensive Sweep' involving the entire Wing) over Gravelines and Calais, once again without enemy contact. However, an incident occurred on the return when a Spitfire attacked a Typhoon from 56 Squadron and shot it down effortlessly. The plane fell into the Channel, but fortunately, the pilot, a Norwegian, managed to bail out and parachute to safety. Ironically, the Spitfire pilot was Norwegian too; the epitome of 'friendly fire'!

The mediocre weather of July extended into August, during which 609 Squadron took part in nine offensive operations, with enemy aircraft spotted on only three occasions. On Thursday, 6 August, Jean de Selys Longchamps was promoted to flying officer (equivalent to lieutenant in the Aéronautique Militaire Belge). Although he was not involved in the fiasco of Operation Jubilee (the failed raid on Dieppe on 19 August 1942, in which thirty-four Typhoons from the Duxford Wing participated), he was engaged in various operations where, as usual, the enemy remained frustratingly invisible. His only scare came at dawn on 25 August, during a 'dawn patrol' where he intercepted an aircraft that turned out to be an RAF Lockheed Hudson, which, unsurprisingly by now, fired a burst of 500 rounds towards Jean. The gunner from the light bomber's dorsal turret had once again mistaken the Typhoon for a Luftwaffe fighter. Fortunately, the fire was inaccurate, and Jean returned unharmed.

August 1942 also witnessed the very first victory claimed by a Typhoon when, on 9 August, an aircraft from 266 Squadron shot down a Ju 88 bomber. Good news concerning the Typhoon was too rare not to mark this as a red-letter day.

On 20 August, Jean wrote a very touching letter intended for Sybille, François' daughter, who had been born a year earlier, on 28 August 1941. Jean had, of course, never seen her, but he was thinking of her on her first birthday, and the text surprises with its delicacy:

> This letter, little Sybille, will arrive too late. Your birthday will have passed, and I wasn't there. Yet I thought of it. And you can be proud, little one, that your charm already has such an influence! I know you are beautiful. I have only an imperfect image of you. You are more the fruit of my imagination made of memory and hope. I believe your eyes are blue, your nose is button-shaped, and you have the same cute little hands your brother had at your age. (…) You were born to play with flowers, songs, laughter, and gentleness. And one day, perhaps for a future birthday, I will bring you a big blue bird (…) I wish you, in 20 years, many more love letters. Remember, when reading them, the old, very old grumpy uncle who wrote you the first one.

Whenever Jean picked up the pen (which he handled quite elegantly), he revealed a great sensitivity that might have surprised most of those around him. After all, beneath his stubborn exterior, he was actually quite a gentle soul.

The month of August ended with a significant mark of confidence bestowed upon Jean de Selys when he was chosen to become acting commander of B Flight due to Flight Lieutenant Beamont's injury (from a trivial fall) and Roger Malengreau's imminent departure for a well-deserved rest. It was a heavy responsibility placed on a pilot who, by the end of August, had logged just 486 hours and 50 minutes of flight time in his logbook, including one entry for 103 hours in a Typhoon.

September arrived with a decisive turning point in the operational life of the Typhoon. Drawing on the experience accumulated over the first two months of the aircraft's operational life, Paul Richey, CO of 609 Squadron, wrote an operations report for his superiors, taking the opportunity to throw a substantial wrench in the works. In it, he argued the Typhoon was unsuitable for large-scale Wing operations at high altitude.

A swarm of Typhoons preparing to depart on a mission. Under Paul Richey's leadership (whose plane is seen at the far right), the doctrine of the aircraft's use was beginning to take shape (18 September 1942).

Such operations to date had all proven their ineffectiveness and were even dangerous. Richey recommended dismantling the Duxford Wing and dispersing its squadrons closer to the country's southern coast to fully exploit the Typhoon's undeniable low-altitude potential. Richey's conviction was to dedicate Tiffies to intercepting Fw.190s which were increasingly conducting low-altitude bombing raids below radar detection thresholds. Outpaced, the Spitfires were unable to hinder such raids. Richey's advocacy resonated with what many pilots had already observed: although designed as a pure fighter, the Typhoon was clearly inferior to the Fw.190 at high altitude, but became truly formidable at low altitude, where it was over 30mph faster than the Luftwaffe fighter. Once caught, the Focke-Wulf had little chance of escape, and if it decided to climb, it remained an easy target for a Typhoon unleashing the 2,000 horsepower of its Napier Sabre. Meanwhile, in tight turns, the Fw.190 stalled more quickly than the Tiffy. In all scenarios, low altitude was the Typhoon's preferred domain. Paul Richey's solid arguments hit their mark, and the decision was made to move 609 to Biggin Hill as quickly as possible.

On 18 September, the CO of 609 wrote on the dispersal's blackboard a large 'Tally Ho! Gone away!' The Air Ministry had acted swiftly to dissolve Duxford's Typhoon Wing, and on that day the squadron would fly to Biggin Hill. Leaving Duxford was bittersweet, as life there had been pleasant – the mess cuisine, courtesy of its Belgian chef, was a real treat – but the opportunity to return to Biggin Hill was far more exciting. The 'White Rose' Squadron found its old quarters, which had aged – the previous 'tenants' were hardly careful – but surprisingly remained as they were. Pilots were astonished to find in the crew room, where they stored their flight gear, hooks under which the names of pilots who were part of 609 in November 1941, just before the departure to Digby, were still written. It was profoundly moving, as they also found the names of those who had left the squadron, as well as those who had since lost their lives. Eight pilots, including Jean de Selys, found their names under a hook: five Belgians, two English, and one Canadian. It was indicative of a squadron's life, rhythmically enduring through the relentless pace of transfers and human losses.

On 22 September, Paul Richey gave a detailed briefing to all his pilots to explain their new role. He stated it would primarily be defensive, with patrols organised along coastal sectors at very low altitudes to increase the chances of stopping high-speed enemy aircraft coming in under radar detection fields. The planes would operate within a zone ranging from 2 to 6 miles off the coast. To improve responsiveness, planes would regularly operate from bases closest to the coast (Manston, Lympne, and Hawkinge), and while Richey clarified that 609 might still participate in 'Sweeps', it would now be with four-aircraft formations dedicated to 'rear support'.

In the following weeks, various patrol formations, up to twelve aircraft, were tested in all weather conditions, but while 609 flew very intensively, results were slow to come, and there always seemed to be something disrupting the smooth conduct and effectiveness of operations.

While other squadrons were not lacking in action – 133 Squadron, also based at Duxford, an 'Eagle Squadron' of American volunteers, lost eleven of its twelve pilots in an operation on 26 September – 609 Squadron seemed cursed, unable to secure any victories. Flying at very low altitude over water in poor weather conditions was extremely challenging for the pilots, who had only limited confidence in their engines and knew that ditching would be extremely risky due to the radiator likely turning the Typhoon into a submarine upon contact with water. Yet, if Typhoons were battling against bad weather, they were also fighting against British anti-aircraft batteries along the coast. The 'friendly fire' from 'Ack Ack' (Anti-Aircraft Command or Ack Ack Command) had indeed been authorised to fire on all aircraft approaching below 1,000 feet. This significantly complicated the task for 609 Squadron pilots, who often operated under the clouds at this altitude. On 6 October, Jean de Selys, patrolling the Hastings-Dungeness area, became the target of 'friendly' battery fire, which fortunately caused no damage.

The tension accumulated during these flights was substantial: pilots had to constantly monitor engine temperature, tirelessly scan the sky for intruders, beware of Ack

Visit of two prominent figures to the 609: General Van Strydonck and Colonel Wouters are received with great pomp by the squadron.

Ack batteries, view all Spitfires with great suspicion, avoid getting too close to cliffs, maintain a safe distance from barrage balloons (the 'silver elephants', as the population nicknamed them) and the 1-mile-long steel cables connecting them to the ground. All this stress, however, seemed for naught: coastal patrols in October – up to fifteen a day – only spotted enemy aircraft on two occasions, without a single shot being fired.

Fortunately, October was also punctuated by some lighter moments. On 7 October, 609 Squadron received a visit from General Van Strydonck de Burkel, a veteran of 1st Guides, whom Jean had likely encountered in Tenby in early June 1940 and who was now the inspector general of the Belgian forces, and Colonel Wouters. Weather conditions prohibited any flying, but fortunately, a magnificent lunch was served in the mess, and the pilots honoured their visitors by joyously singing their repertoire of French songs. On the 9th, Jean received his 'second stripe', formalising on his uniform the role of acting flight lieutenant he had been occupying since the end of August. The same day, 609 also saw two Belgians, Roger Malengreau and Bob Wilmet, both

Jean in discussion with Paul Richey during the visit of Van Strydonck and Wouters.

part of the first Belgian contingent to join the squadron in April 1941, leave for other assignments. Yet the Typhoon troubles were never far away, and de Selys was dismayed to see 'his' brand new Typhoon Mk Ib, registered PR-M, belly land with Flight Lieutenant Atkinson at the controls on Monday, 18 October. Fortunately, it would be as good as new once it had passed through the hands of the repair shop artists, who were beginning to get used to repairing damaged Typhoons.

The 19th also marked a change in CO for 609, when Paul Richey, who had led the squadron for just four months, left to take command of a Hurricane squadron in India, managing to convince Christian Ortmans to accompany him. This was yet another demonstration of Richey's persuasive power, as it also required convincing the Belgian government, which was reluctant to have its pilots assigned to units outside of England. Christian Ortmans would thus become the first Belgian to fight Japanese pilots. Unfortunately, he would be killed on 1 April 1943 as he descended by parachute after leaving his stricken Hurricane. He was shot by Australian soldiers who believed they were dealing with a Japanese pilot. For Jean, Paul Richey's departure was certainly a new cause for melancholy, as he had formed strong bonds with him, even agreeing to become godfather to Richey's daughter.

'Tiffy', the Plane of a Lifetime 151

Jean at the christening of Paul Richey's daughter, for whom he was the godfather (February 1942).

Paul Richey's successor was Roland 'Bee' Beamont,[4] who, at 22, became the youngest squadron leader of 609. Despite his youth, Beamont was an experienced pilot, having emerged from the Battle of France with one victory (a Dornier 17) and ending the Battle of Britain with five more Luftwaffe aircraft to his name (a Ju 88, two Messerschmitt 110s, a Do 17, and a Messerschmitt 109). He received the Distinguished Flying Cross (DFC) at just 21 and when his 'tour of duty' ended, and he was due for rest in December 1941, he declined the opportunity to become aide-de-camp to Air Marshal Leigh-Mallory, preferring an option that would allow him to continue flying. Thus, with his 800 hours flying a Hurricane, he then became a test pilot for Hawker, the manufacturer of… the Typhoon. Beamont was involved in various development programmes for the aircraft and gained extensive knowledge of the strengths and weaknesses of Hawker's latest creation. His first experience ended with an emergency landing, but flight after flight, Beamont began to appreciate the Tiffy.

Roland 'Bee' Beamont in October 1942.

When he returned to a squadron in July 1942, he naturally joined a unit equipped with Typhoons (56 Squadron at Duxford), and by the time he arrived at 609 in October, 'Bee' Beamont was probably the pilot with the best mastery of the aircraft and the most intimate understanding of its real capabilities in the entire Royal Air Force. This unparalleled experience would play a decisive role in the fate of the Typhoon, about which doubts were increasingly being raised. During an important meeting he attended at Fighter Command HQ, Beamont realised that the future of the Typhoon was clearly threatened, as it was considered significantly inferior to the Spitfire and unsuitable for the needs of the RAF. Despite most likely being the youngest officer present at the meeting, Beamont confidently spoke up to defend his firm belief: condemning the Typhoon would be a mistake as it was vastly superior to the Spitfire for all low-altitude operations. None of his counterparts had flown a Typhoon, and Beamont drew on his extensive flight hours in the aircraft to support his argument. He left the meeting with a free rein to demonstrate with 609 the validity of his vision and to define a completely new doctrine of use. If the Typhoon continued its operational life until the end of the conflict, it was surely thanks to Roland 'Bee' Beamont.

However, it was a close call for Beamont to have the opportunity to plead the case of the Typhoon. When he arrived at 609, Bee was a newlywed: his wife was part of the WAAF and had landed him in a court martial in late 1941 because he had flown with her aboard his Hurricane. Beamont owed the leniency of the military authorities only to his outstanding service records. No doubt this is the kind of escapade that would appeal to Jean de Selys and the other spirited pilots of 609: without a doubt, their new CO boasted quite a pedigree, despite his youth. He was exactly the kind of guy you wanted to go into battle with.

On 21 and 22 October, 609's dispersal turned into a film set when a team from the RAF's Film Production Unit arrived at Biggin Hill to shoot a report on the life of a fighter squadron called *Between Friends: a Brief Visit to a Fighter Station*. The film lasted about 10 minutes and is still viewable on YouTube,[5] providing a rare testimony from a handful of pilots, whose acting skills are inversely proportional to their piloting abilities. The film is somewhat naive and clumsy, but it remains very moving to see these young men feign nonchalance while risking their lives on every flight. Proof of this is the pilot, Roy Payne, who is seen playing the clarinet in the film and who would make a belly landing eight days later, fortunately emerging unscathed. More sadly, Raymond Dopéré, the Belgian pilot who joined 609 the previous May and is briefly introduced in the film, lost his life the day after shooting took place in a flight accident due to poor visibility. Finally, the presence of Jean de Selys on screen in this film, the only existing trace of his voice, makes the document extraordinarily precious and deeply touching. It should be noted that this film was not broadcast during the

Jean de Selys proudly posing on his Typhoon, a challenging plane that only revealed itself to pilots who managed to tame it.

war as it contains scenes of Typhoon take offs that were on the RAF's 'secret list', prohibiting its distribution. This was being overly paranoid, however, as a Typhoon had already been shot down over France and examined at leisure by the Germans.

At the end of October, Jean de Selys was detached for a month to the Central Gunnery School (CGS) at Sutton Bridge, also known more explicitly as the Air Firing School (akin to an early version of 'Top Gun'). The Sutton Bridge base was located 38 miles southeast of Digby, stirring mixed memories for de Selys, and was 6 miles from the coast, facilitating shooting exercises over the sea. Initially, the CGS was solely focused on bomber gunners, but the Battle of Britain highlighted a significant gap in fighter pilots' training, who were well-versed in flying, but noticeably weak in their mastery of aerial shooting and 'deflection shooting' (predicting the movement of a moving target for accurate firing). The creation of a fighter wing within the CGS is credited to RAF ace Adolph 'Sailor' Malan from South Africa, who distinguished himself during the Battle of Britain with an impressive tally of twenty-seven victories, seven shared victories, three probables, and sixteen damaged enemy aircraft. He knew his stuff in air combat, having devised the 'Ten Rules of Air Fighting' displayed in nearly every squadron.

The student body – consisting of ten fighter pilots and thirty-two gunners – regularly participated in combined exercises where school Spitfires would engage Vickers Wellington bombers. They also practised air-to-air shooting at towed targets using a Miles Master or a Westland Lysander. The planes participating in the exercise were equipped with ammunition that had a specific colour for each of the pilots, allowing for a precise analysis of impacts on the target and the correct attribution of hits at the end of the exercise. Ground-attack shooting was also on the curriculum. Lastly, the gun camera mounted on the Spitfires' wings allowed for post-operation analysis of combat sequences (between fighters or against bombers) with instructors.

Despite the challenging winter weather that hindered flight schedules, Jean still managed to log 32 hours and 10 minutes in Spitfires and 40 minutes in a Miles Master during his stay at Sutton Bridge for the 'Number 15 course'. Mid-course, the school's head had to rally the pilots, whose engagement was lacking, with a warning that 50% might not meet the success criteria if the trend continued, a caution which seemed to spur their enthusiasm. Jean finished the course with average grades and was not identified as a potential shooting instructor, which he likely was not aiming for anyway as it seems he attended this training somewhat reluctantly (in his final report, his laziness was deemed a 'bad example' by his instructor, who criticised his 'lack of interest, except for clay shooting and air-to-air target shooting'). The frustration of the preceding months, during which the Typhoon's potential had not been met, weighed heavily on him, especially with the loss of Belgian pilots Offenberg, de Spirlet, and Dopéré in the last ten months. There is little doubt he viewed this detour to the Air Firing School as a waste of time, likely making no effort to hide his feelings.

Upon his return to 609 Squadron, Jean quickly realised much had changed in just a month. The squadron had moved from Biggin Hill to Manston,[6] closer to the English Channel, and he was delighted to learn that the new operational doctrine advocated by 'Bee' Beamont had not only been implemented but was yielding more than encouraging results. Beamont had initiated low-altitude night raids with one or two aircraft, utilising the Typhoon's power and the pilots' acumen to great effect.

Furthermore, by 5 December, a probable victory over a Fw.190 was credited to Alan 'Babe' Haddon, which was somewhat ironic as he had initially vowed never to fly the 'big bastard' Typhoon upon his first encounter with the craft. Another particularly heartening piece of news shared with Jean was that in November, the Typhoon fleet of 609 Squadron had achieved over 1,000 flight hours with just one engine change, setting a new reliability record for the aircraft. The Typhoon finally seemed to be on the right path, and Jean would soon have the opportunity to see this for himself.

On 13 December, the first 'Rhubarb' operations carried out by Typhoons of 609 Squadron were launched, and Jean participated in the very first one, alongside another

Typhoon taxiing on the Manston runway.

Belgian, Joseph Renier. Taking off from Manston at 10:50am, their mission was to attempt to destroy trains within the Bruges – Ghent – Courtrai triangle. After crossing the coast near the town of Le Coq, they spotted a German train on the Ostend – Bruges line. Renier was not in a position to attack, but de Selys did not miss his chance, hitting the locomotive with a burst of 20mm shells. The convoy halted, and the engine vanished under a thick cloud of smoke. In a bold move, Jean then strafed about fifty German soldiers who were trying to escape from the halted train, flying so low that his wing snagged several yards of telegraph wires, which he inadvertently brought back to Manston as an unexpected trophy. Indeed, mechanics found pieces of wire tangled in his wing and radiator, and a bullet impact on his wing indicated the Germans had fired back despite the apparent chaos. For a first attempt, it was a masterstroke, and Jean's record was credited with a locomotive (Cat B) and convoy damage. A British newspaper article, which Jean proudly pasted into his logbook, recounted the feat. Finally, some action!

The next day, Jean de Selys was back on patrol and spotted a lifeboat with six castaways. After relaying their coordinates to the Air Sea Rescue, he circled the area until a Walrus rescue seaplane landed. The rough seas, however, made the operation difficult, and the plane returned to Dover with only three survivors aboard, who turned out to be German sailors! Jean, true to his caustic humour, wondered: 'What's the point of shooting at German soldiers if we're going to save German sailors the next day?'

15 December turned out to be the most fruitful day for 609 Squadron in over a year. Jean led a 'Rhubarb' operation alongside Polish pilot Tadeusz Turek, who had been featured in the *Between Friends* documentary filmed in late October (he is the one seen bringing tea). They headed towards Belgium under a very low ceiling (200 feet), and the planes split up as they crossed the coast. Jean encountered Flak as he approached Ostend but soon spotted a barge transport moving along the Yser Canal, which he decided to attack. After four passes, de Selys left the convoy in flames, adding a tugboat (Cat III) to his tally. His No. 2 had a slightly luckier run, encountering two locomotives, which he destroyed. Hit by Flak, Turek made it back to Manston with minor injuries and significant engine trouble. In another 'Rhubarb', 'Bee' Beamont and Evans destroyed three more locomotives. And in a third 'Rhubarb', 'Babe' Haddon, clearly on a roll, scored a confirmed victory over a Fw.190, with two other German fighters declared as 'damaged'. The only dark cloud that day was the disappearance of Henry 'Desmond' Amor.

On 16 December, the Typhoons of 609 were back on operations, although Jean de Selys' first flight of the day was cut short by dreadful weather. However, he took off again at 2pm with Turek for a 'scramble' that turned into a patrol. Nearing fuel exhaustion, the two pilots spotted two enemy aircraft: Focke-Wulf 190s. Each selected their prey, and the two Typhoons closed in at lightning speed on their respective targets. Jean fired first from 1,300 feet away, scoring clear hits on the Luftwaffe fighter. He did not give up the chase and unleashed another burst as he closed to 650 feet. Luck favoured the German, however, who managed to vanish into the clouds, trailing a puff of black smoke. Jean was on the verge of claiming his first victory but had to settle for an 'enemy aircraft damaged'. Turek fared better, shooting down his 190, which hit the sea, bounced, and crashed on a beach north of Boulogne.

Jean de Selys found more fortune on 22 December during a solo night operation. After taking off at 9:35pm, he attacked and immobilised a high-speed train south of Roeselare. His plane was targeted by intense Flak fire during his two runs, but fortunately, the gunners struggled to gauge his altitude and he escaped unscathed, adding another locomotive (Cat B) to 609's tally. Upon returning, de Selys cheekily reported that the curfew was poorly observed during his attack; many windows were opened, and rooms lit up in response to the commotion his night-time raid had caused. This must have heartened his fellow citizens witnessing the German disarray.

In a twist of fate, Squadron Leader 'Bee' Beamont received a letter of congratulation from Air Marshal Leigh-Mallory for the squadron's feats over the past few weeks. Receiving such a letter would have seemed wildly optimistic just a month previously, but the numbers spoke for themselves: in December, 609 destroyed eighteen locomotives (Cat B), one tug (Cat III), numerous rolling stock, achieved four confirmed aerial victories (Focke-Wulf 190s), three probable victories (190s), and damaged four enemy aircraft (three 190s and one Junker 88). For 1942, this was a remarkable and unexpected tally and closed a year that had been fraught with prolonged doubts about the squadron and its new aircraft. To say that all pilots of 609 Squadron were eagerly awaiting 1943 would be an understatement.

Chapter 12

Befehlshaber der Sipo-SD, 453 Avenue Louise, Brussels, Belgium

(1940–1943)

'Sir, I have the honour to request permission to carry out a Rhubarb operation over Brussels at the next opportunity as the operation will have a private character rather than a military one.'

This draft letter, addressed to his superiors, is the only trace Jean de Selys Longchamps left in his personal documents regarding the project that had been stirring within him for some months. There is little doubt that the prolonged period of near inactivity forced by the Typhoon's laborious operational start kindled significant frustration in him. His arrival at 609, so full of promise, had turned out to be a long series of disappointments. Indeed, barely two months after his arrival, the squadron had been put on a four-month long,

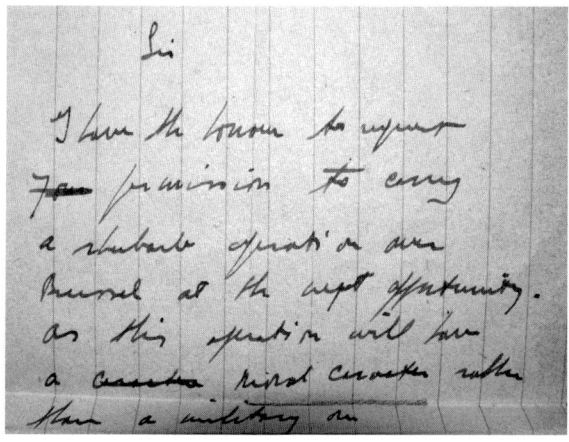

Jean pasted the draft of his request for authorisation to carry out his 'Special Rhubarb' on Brussels into his logbook. Thus, he kept a record of his vain attempts to obtain authorisation from his superiors.

interminable rest 'in the middle of nowhere' (Digby). The subsequent conversion to the Typhoon had proved disappointing, even exasperating, as the aircraft fell short of all hopes placed in it, even displaying some very worrying structural weaknesses. In fact, the aircraft had proved to be a genuine nightmare machine. Operational flights were therefore delayed, and, when they finally began, 609 went through a long period of trial and error to determine what types of operations the Typhoon was genuinely suited for.

For pilots dreaming of engaging the enemy, the situation was despairing, and even the most optimistic had to muster all their patience to maintain some semblance of morale. Fortunately, thanks to 'Bee' Beamont's vision, the Typhoon seemed to have finally found its operational role, and the operations carried out in the very last weeks of 1942 had been very promising.

The previous year had left very little room for Flight Lieutenant de Selys Longchamps to influence a conflict that he had observed too often in a quasi-spectator position. It is therefore not surprising that Jean embarked on a quest for a project that could finally give concrete meaning to his commitment. He knew that we only have one, short, life, so we might as well make sure it is not insignificant. It is likely that his project began to take shape during a period of leave in London. Whenever he had the opportunity, Baron Jean de Selys enjoyed reconnecting with the small piece of Belgium that had formed in the heart of the English capital. He had befriended the Belgian ambassador, Baron Émile de Cartier de Marchienne. The latter, born in Brussels in 1871 (thus 72 years old in 1943), appreciated the 'young' de Selys, and a room at the embassy even seemed to be reserved for him whenever he was in London. Like all other Belgians, Jean was relentless in trying to obtain news from home. Whether through embassy staff, members of the Belgian government, or in more informal circles, one truth became clear to all: the situation in occupied Belgium was increasingly worrying.

To better understand how the situation had deteriorated since the German invasion, it is necessary to look back in time and examine how Nazi Germany decided to administer the country. Following the surrender on 28 May 1940, Hitler ordered that a military administration (*Militärverwaltung*) be established to govern the country.[1] He appointed Baron Alexander von Falkenhausen, from an old Prussian noble family, who boasted a long experience abroad, as the military governor of Belgium and the two attached French departments (Nord and Pas-de-Calais). At 62, von Falkenhausen assumed command, with authority over two general-staffs: one managing purely military issues and another in charge of public life and the daily administration of the country. Heading this second staff was another key figure of the Occupation, von Falkenhausen's true right handman, Eggert Reeder. Aged 46 when he arrived in Brussels, Reeder was a trained lawyer who had quickly climbed the ranks within the German state apparatus and had already presided over some significant regional councils in

Alexander von Falkenhausen, who for four years was responsible, as military governor, for maintaining 'public order' in Belgium.

Germany. Under von Falkenhausen, Reeder took on economic and political affairs as well as liaising with the Belgian administration.

The establishment of a military administration was uncommon in occupied territories where a civil administration (*Zivilverwaltung*) led by a civil governor (called *Reichprotector* in Czechoslovakia, *Generalgouverneur* in Poland, or *Reichskommissar* in the Netherlands and Norway) was usually preferred. The decision to opt for a *Militärverwaltung* in France and Belgium resulted from intense lobbying by Generalfeldmarschall Walther von Brauchitsch (commander-in-chief of the Heer, the German land forces) to Hitler to avoid the incessant tensions he observed in Poland between the Wehrmacht and the SS. The latter quickly began committing mass crimes and did not hesitate to multiply conflicts of authority with Heer officers.

Eggert Reeder, von Falkenhausen's right-hand man. Although hierarchically subordinate to the latter, Reeder played an essential role in the administration and intensified repression over the course of the Occupation.

Von Brauchitsch was right to fear the unbearable sense of omnipotence oozing from the SS ranks. Reichsführer-SS Heinrich Himmler was power-hungry, and since September 1939, had managed to consolidate all police forces under his authority within the *Reichssicherheitshauptamt* (RSHA), a veritable Ministry of Police dominated by National Socialist political ideology. The RSHA merged Nazi Party organs like the SD (*Sicherheitsdienst*) with state services of the Sipo (*Sicherheitspolizei*), such as the Gestapo (*Geheime Staatspolizei*) and Kripo (criminal police). However, the RSHA was a somewhat heterogeneous amalgamation where the hardliners of the party, the SD members, were not particularly thrilled about the integration of the Sipo into their ranks. To manage such a diverse structure required a strong hand, and the fearsome SS-Obergruppenführer Reinhard Heydrich, with his knife-like, long thin face, was promoted to lead this relentless repression machine that would sow terror in all occupied territories.

Even though the military did everything to keep the RSHA at bay from the territories it administered, Heydrich's men remained on the lookout for opportunities to infiltrate the system and expand their power. Thus, as early as July 1940, SS-Sturmbannführer Kriminaldirektor Franz Straub, a former sculptor, arrived in Brussels with twenty agents from the Sipo-SD acting under the authority of the Düsseldorf office. By the end of July, a more ambitious structure was already being established and a representative of

The imposing building at 453 Avenue Louise, as it appeared at the time.

the chief of police was officially appointed for France and Belgium by the name of SS-Brigadeführer Max Thomas, who was based in Paris.

On 27 July, Heydrich himself visited von Falkenhausen and Reeder in Brussels and informed them he had been tasked with organising police activities in Belgium and northern France. He took advantage of his presence in Brussels to inaugurate the building at 453 Avenue Louise, which had been chosen as the central headquarters of the Sipo-SD. While no one had formally invited Heydrich's henchmen, they had indeed begun to extend their web, albeit cleverly, without making too much noise, aware they were flirting with numerous red lines that should not be crossed. For now, at least.

A sign of the RSHA's relative discretion in Belgium was that Reeder's reports to Berlin only mentioned the Sipo-SD for the first time in January 1941. Nevertheless, the new tenants of 453 Avenue Louise did not remain inactive and quickly established a network of regional offices (*Aussenstellen*) in Liège, Ghent, Charleroi, Antwerp, and Lille. Smaller structures (Kommandos) would later be created in Leuven, Dinant, Hasselt, and Arlon. The implacable meshing of the territory had now begun. In the shadows, the Sipo-SD began its investigations and compiled lists of suspects to prepare for 'the future'.

Three SS officers would successively lead the Sipo-SD in Belgium. The first, SS-Sturmbannführer Karl Hasselbacher, made only a brief appearance, as he died in a car accident on 13 September 1940 while returning from a meeting in Paris. In early October, he was replaced by SS-Sturmbannführer Karl Constantin Canaris, the nephew of the chief of the Abwehr (German intelligence), Wilhelm Canaris. A doctor of law and a historian, before the war he worked for the state police in Cologne and Koblenz. But Canaris, who was deemed too docile by Berlin and too compliant with the military administration, was replaced in November 1941 by a far tougher officer, SS-Sturmbannführer Ernst Ehlers. Originally a doctor, Ehlers was 32 when he was promoted to Brussels. Previously, he had been part of the staff of the infamously notorious Einsatzgruppe B (mobile extermination unit), operating in Belarus. Ehlers did not kill with his own hands but organised the killings masterfully. Indeed, it is estimated that between June and October 1941, Einsatzgruppe B eliminated over 37,000 Russians, mostly Jews. The profile of the SS majors successively leading the Brussels office of the Sipo-SD is very telling of the gradual hardening of methods used in occupied Belgium.

Well before Ehlers' arrival on 4 February 1941, the Sipo-SD had received authorisation to conduct arrests, searches, and seizures themselves. Although, in theory, the military command held all policing powers in occupied territory, reality proved far more nuanced, and the Sipo-SD continually gained autonomy. It took control over the concentration camp established in the Breendonk fort, about 12 miles from Antwerp, and the military administration struggled to enforce the rules initially set forth. Indeed, it was von Falkenhausen who established the camp on 29 August 1940 (he would later call it a 'shameful stain' after the war), imposing a strict regulation: only Jews could be interned, their detention should not exceed a fixed time (one month, except with special permission), and the treatment of prisoners had to be 'hard but fair'. Brutality and abuse were prohibited, with violence only permitted in case of resistance from detainees. Needless to say, these 'rules' shattered as the SS took over the place.

One of the first to enforce iron discipline was none other than SS-Untersturmführer Arthur Prauss, who assisted SS-Sturmbannführer Philipp Schmitt in leading the

In this photograph taken at the liberation, a guardhouse still stands in front of the entrance at 453. Marked with the sinister SS symbol, it immediately indicated to those arriving the identity of the masters reigning over the dreadful building.

camp, bringing to Breendonk the terrifying methods he had zealously applied at the Sachsenhausen concentration camp in Germany. Until June 1941, abuses remained exceptional, but would become commonplace thereafter. Berlin continually demanded more severity in the treatment of detainees, and Breendonk's executioners were only too willing to comply. A total of 3,800 Belgians and foreigners would pass through

Breendonk during the Occupation. Of these, 300 died without care, most under torture, and 400 others were executed there.

By June 1941, the role of the Sipo-SD gradually became clearer: it had become the executive arm of the *Militärverwaltung* in political and security matters, its main missions being to neutralise German émigrés and conduct general police duties concerning foreigners.

But the Germans' initial illusions about the Belgians had soon vanished by the summer of 1941, as the population was certainly not as docile as had been expected – hostility grew with food scarcity – and Belgium was soon considered enemy territory. This, of course, benefited the Sipo-SD, which had been waiting for just such an opportunity to significantly expand its influence. Now, the minions of 453 Avenue Louise started monitoring all administrative mechanisms and all political, cultural, philosophical, and religious organisations. Heydrich's strategy of patience paid off, as one by one he removed all obstacles put in place by von Falkenhausen and Reeder, without them being able to do anything about it. This forced evolution of the Sipo-SD's role did nothing to resolve the deep antagonism between the military and the SS, with the latter considering the *Militärverwaltung* 'aristocrats' who were far too lenient towards the Belgians. In turn, the military saw the RSHA representatives as upstarts who had become dangerously powerful.

As the Sipo-SD extended its grip, quarrels with military intelligence and police forces multiplied. Whether it was the Abwehr (espionage and counterespionage) or the GFP (secret military police), opportunities to step on each other's toes abounded. Only with the *Feldgendarmerie* (military police) were relations relatively calm, with the Sipo-SD finding in them resources (a significant force of 1,700 men) that would prove very useful for large-scale operations on the ground, such as roundups.

On 12 July 1941, the Germans' analysis was confirmed: the Belgians were increasingly openly hostile, and sabotage of electricity cabins at Rotheux-Rimière (province of Liège) marked the beginning of a resistance that was no longer content with distributing clandestine pamphlets. Eight people were sentenced to death in retaliation. The infernal machinery was set in motion. Sabotage, arson, the placing of explosives, cable destruction, all acts of resistance multiplied. In response, the Sipo-SD arrested 306 people in September 1941, 538 in October, and 272 in November. The always measured von Falkenhausen had warned the population on 21 August that 'In case of an attack resulting in the death of a German soldier, five hostages will be shot.'

By mid-1941, the Belgian population was clearly divided into three distinct groups: active resistance members, active collaborationists, and the vast majority (estimated today at about 85%) who struggled daily just to survive. When the RSHA pushed again for a harsher stance in Belgium, von Falkenhausen and Reeder countered by

Befehlshaber der Sipo-SD, 453 Avenue Louise, Brussels, Belgium

In this photograph taken inside the Gestapo headquarters after liberation, Resistance member François Dorsaghers (member of the Belgian National Movement, MNB) is seen inspecting a club used to 'interrogate' prisoners.

Photographs taken by Canadian liberation forces showing the cells in the basement of 453 Avenue Louise, where the feared members of the Sipo-SD held their prisoners.

highlighting that '90% of the Belgian population disapproves of the attacks'. Their increasing frequency, however, made their position more and more untenable. 'Enhanced interrogation' (*Verschärfte Vernehmung*) was introduced within the year, allowing the Sipo-SD's men to use baton blows, cigarette burns, and forced baths to loosen the tongues of those arrested. By the end of October 1941, German authorities announced that all political detainees were now considered hostages.

In a clear sign that each territory now required much more attention, the Sipo-SD offices in Brussels and Paris developed independently from December and interacted directly with Berlin headquarters. SS-Brigadeführer Max Thomas, who had overseen both entities, was transferred to Ukraine to command Einsatzgruppe C.

The day after Christmas 1941, the first five Brussels hostages were shot following new attacks. The escalation became irreversible and continued into 1942. On 8 January, a German soldier was killed on Bosquet Street in Saint-Gilles (Brussels), and another was wounded on a tram: twenty 'terrorists' were executed by the occupiers. The attacks were mainly the work of communist militants, who were perfectly organised for clandestine struggle, daring to attack everywhere and anytime. Their motto was 'One Boche each'.

The Sipo-SD was now faced with the thorny problem encountered by all occupying forces: how to defeat nearly invisible and unpredictable internal adversaries? The strategies to try to annihilate this 'terrorist' threat were as old as time: recruit informants and encourage denouncers and so the Germans quickly enlisted V-Mann (*Vertrauensmann*) or V-Leute (*Vertrauensleute*) to infiltrate resistance networks and gather information. The quality of these informants was often quite poor, but there were, unfortunately, exceptions. Prosper Dezitter ('The man with the cut finger') and his partner Flore Giralt caused havoc within the Resistance ranks, managing to dismantle numerous networks, escape routes, and Allied aviator reception centres. Their gang of collaborators was found guilty of at least 700 arrests.

Émile Van Thielen, aka Max Günther, was another example. He took on the responsibilities of Haupt-V-Mann particularly effectively and stood out, among other things, during Operation Sonnewenden (solstice) in June 1941, leading to the arrest of 300 individuals. He was also regularly seen at the Breendonk camp, actively participating in torture sessions.

To combat rampant denunciation, some Belgians set up networks to intercept letters addressed to German authorities. The 'Service D', created as early as July 1940 in Liège by Joseph Joset, specialised in pilfering letters of denunciation thanks to Post Office agents, warning threatened individuals, and identifying denouncers. It is estimated that the 'Service D' intercepted over 14,000 letters during the Occupation.

The beginning of 1942 was also marked by the Wannsee Conference held on 20 January in a villa southwest of Berlin.[2] Chaired by Reinhard Heydrich (assisted by Adolf Eichmann), the conference gathered fifteen senior officials of the Third Reich, all specialists in the 'Jewish question', and lasted less than two hours. It was a meeting of psychopaths. As a true manager of the Final Solution, Heydrich outlined his plan for the industrial liquidation of Europe's Jews using 'cost-effective' methods. Historians consider this conference a decisive step in the implementation of the Nazi regime's genocidal policy and its staggering machinery of death. The esteemed German historian Peter Longerich summarised it as follows: 'The Wannsee Conference protocol is now viewed as the very symbol of the cold, calculated, and bureaucratic organization of the genocide of the Jews in Europe.'

During the conference, Heydrich detailed, country by country, the 11 million people targeted by the Final Solution to the Jewish question in Europe. It is believed that some numbers were significantly inflated (such as those for France), but the figures for Belgium were an exception. The total of 43,000 individuals reported by the Sipo-SD of Brussels was even corrected (and increased) by the very zealous Ernst Ehlers, who sent an amended report, his *Sonderbericht* 'Judaism in Belgium', to his superiors in Berlin ten days after the Wannsee Conference. The documents submitted by Ehlers were drafted by his deputy, SS-Sturmbannführer Alfred Thomas, who now demands our attention as one of the key figures at the Brussels headquarters. As head of the SD, he played an essential role in the deportation of Jews from Belgium, and, as unlikely as it may seem, his fate would intersect with that of Jean de Selys, and their 'encounter' would be fatal.

SS-Sturmbannführer Alfred Hugo Otto Thomas[3] was a zealous officer with a macabre demeanour that exuded Nazism. Born on 8 October 1905, in Bielefeld, before arriving in Brussels in August 1940, he had been part of the Sipo in Stettin (now Szczecin, located in Polish territory, merely 8.7 miles from the current German border), where he had held the title of SS-Sturmbannführer, Inspector of the Sipo and the SD in Stettin. He had a doctorate, earning him the title Doktor Thomas and despite his move to Belgium, his wife and two children remained in Stettin.

In Brussels, Alfred Thomas would play an essential role in identifying and locating Jews in Belgium. Early in the Occupation, it is important to remember that no national

A very rare portrait of SS-Sturmbannführer Alfred Thomas, who can be considered the highly effective and zealous number two of the Sipo-SD in Brussels. He was killed by shells fired by Jean de Selys.

civil registry of the population existed, except for the foreigners' police register, which would prove fatal for many Jewish immigrants. The files of Jewish citizens in Belgium were scattered across all the municipalities where they resided. An insidious paragraph in an ordinance dated 28 October 1940, would, however, open the door to a beginning of a 'solution' for the occupier, specifying that the Jewish registry was accessible to anyone upon request. Anti-Jewish leagues did not hesitate to begin publishing long columns of names and addresses in their vile newspapers.

As an astute observer, Alfred Thomas quickly identified the opportunity for the Sipo-SD to industrialise these sleazy investigative methods. In March 1941, he set up the Antwerp lawyer René Lambrichts and a few elements of his anti-Jewish league on the ground floor of 52 Philippe de Champagne Street[4] – a confiscated 'Jewish enemy' property – in Brussels to create what would later be termed the 'office for research on Jewish questions'. On the first floor, the central office of the *Volksverwering/Défense du peuple* league also moved in. Thomas dreamt of a General Commissariat for Jewish Affairs similar to the one in France and lobbied for Lambrichts to lead it. The commissariat imagined by the SD chief was, however, vetoed by military authorities, but the Propaganda Abteilung let the anti-Jewish leagues seize the concept to create buzz around their fantasised future role. During the transition between Constantin Canaris' departure and Ernst Ehlers' arrival at the head of the 453 Avenue Louise teams in November 1941, Alfred Thomas ensured the continuity of anti-Jewish action. He clearly established himself as the second-in-command in the hierarchy of the Brussels Dienststelle. With the support of SS-Obersturmführer Kurt Asche, the Belgian branch's *Judenreferent*, he had control over all Jewish affairs.

Thomas launched multiple initiatives, and on 25 November 1941, an ordinance announcing the creation of the Association of Jews in Belgium (AJB) was issued based on a project he had presented. By then, seven extremely restrictive and overtly discriminatory anti-Jewish ordinances had already been published in Belgium. Under the reassuring control of the Ministry of the Interior and Public Health, the AJB was, in fact, a dreadfully pernicious Trojan horse that all Jews in Belgium were forced to join and, with supreme cynicism, to contribute to financially. It was a diabolical machine for registration, especially as it became the only Jewish association authorised by the occupier in spring 1942. Completely subservient to the occupying forces, the AJB played a central role in organising the deportation of Jews from Belgium.

Parallel to these disgraceful stratagems concealed under a legal veneer, the monsters at 453 Avenue Louise were also eager to maximize the efficiency of their relentless hunt for Jews and other 'terrorists', incorporating Belgian collaborators who stopped at nothing to please the occupier. Emiel Francken, an Antwerp active anti-Semite before the war, eagerly joined the Sipo-SD's *Judenabteilung*. Alongside him, other Jew hunters also served as translators and interpreters during interrogations.

By the end of 1941, the infernal machine devised by the Sipo-SD was almost ready to accelerate, and now awaited the roadmap that Heydrich and Eichmann were busy finalising in their offices at 101 Wilhelmstrasse in Berlin for the Wannsee Conference.

On 28 May 1942, wearing the yellow star became mandatory in Belgium for Jews over 7 years old when appearing in public. On 11 June, Alfred Thomas was represented in Berlin by Kurt Asche at a meeting where Eichmann communicated to the heads of Jewish affairs from various countries the modus operandi for launching train convoys that would take the 'evacuees' – as the Nazis called them in their euphemism-rich language – to camps where they would be exterminated.

As the Germans left nothing to chance, Alfred Thomas participated in a meeting on 13 July with all organisations involved in deportation to discuss the distribution of future loot.[5] A whole sordid process was established, from sealing seized buildings, retrieving their keys, looting their contents, to finally reassigning them to new 'owners' once emptied. The military authorities insisted that seized furniture be evaluated by a neutral expert, but Thomas opposed this. Everything then accelerated. The transit camp located in the Dossin Barracks in Mechelen opened on 28 July, and the very first convoy to Auschwitz departed on 4 August. On board were 1,005 individuals: 545 men, 408 women, 28 boys, and 24 girls. Only seven of them would return alive in 1945.

Under the authority of SS-Sturmbannführer Alfred Thomas, no fewer than nineteen convoys linked Mechelen to the gates of hell of the Auschwitz extermination camp between August 1942 and January 1943. The numbers are damning: 18,182 people were thus 'evacuated'. Only 367 survived (barely 2%).[6]

Unfortunately, the Germans did not have a monopoly on ignominy, and in these times of unbearable darkness, some still found ways to push the limits of the unbearable further, with Icek Glogowski being a grim example. Also known as 'big Jacques', he was a Belgian Jew of Polish origin living in Uccle, on Vanderkindere Street, and worked as a night porter in the red-light district near the North Station. His wife and three children (aged 9, 7, and 5) were arrested on 3 September and were part of convoy number 12 that left Mechelen on 10 October 1942. Having lost all his family, no one knows what drove Glogowski to start collaborating with the occupier. Was it to save his own skin, to inflict on others the same fate as his family, to negotiate the return of his loved ones? Whatever the truth may be, 'big Jacques' would become one of the Sipo-SD's most feared and effective hunters.

What did the Belgian circles in London, frequented by Jean de Selys Longchamps, understand about what was happening in Belgium at the end of 1942? The magnitude of the nightmare the Nazis were setting up with their convoys to Auschwitz could not be imagined, as it pushed the boundaries of horror well beyond what is conceivable. Yet the dark veil now covering all of Belgium, oppressing all its citizens, could not be ignored by anyone. Many Belgians truly thought in June 1940 that the war was effectively over and that it was now a matter of adapting to life under German occupation. Over time, however, it became clear that the Germans increasingly regarded the Belgians as enemies. Evidently, an explosive cocktail mixing good things – the Wehrmacht's first setbacks on the Eastern Front, the growing influence of Radio London – and less good ones – forced labour, the yellow star, food restrictions, and shortages of almost everything – galvanized resistance movements that increasingly, and aggressively, targeted the occupying forces. And the latter did not hold back: roundups, summary arrests, torture, hostage-taking, deportations, execution squads, all became very visible and very oppressive.

The descent into hell seemed to never end: in just one month, from 12 December 1942 to 13 January 1943, sixty-eight Belgians were executed by firing squad as a form of retaliation. For Jean de Selys, it was clear something had to be done to strike the

Graffiti left by passing prisoners can be seen on the cell walls. Some of these traces, often very moving but sometimes more light-hearted, are still visible today.

enemy at its heart. It had to be a significant symbol, something that would stun the Nazis and boost the morale of the Belgians. For de Selys, this raid was a tribute to his country.

After the war, it was often heard that Jean's raid was motivated by a desire for revenge following his father's arrest by the Germans. There were even claims his father had been tortured and had died as a result. Of course, this is entirely false: Jean de Selys Longchamps' father died peacefully in 1966 and was never bothered by the Sipo-SD. Therefore, Jean de Selys' remarkable raid was a purely patriotic act, not a personal vendetta.

However, Jean may have been inspired by the spectacular feat performed over the Champs-Élysées by a Bristol Beaufighter of 236 Squadron on 12 June 1942. The aircraft, manned by two Englishmen (pilot Ken Gatward and navigator Gilbert Fern), had indeed dropped two French flags over the City of Light: one near the Arc

Jean de Selys in the company of de Ryckman de Betz (standing) and Wouters (seated). It may have been in this office that Jean first shared his raid project.

de Triomphe and another on the Ministry of the Navy at Place de la Concorde. The original idea was to try to throw a flag over the military parade that was organised daily by the Nazis on the Champs-Élysées, but there seems to have been a misunderstanding about the timing, and the Beaufighter flew over the avenue when the troops were not there. It was a pity because the snub would have been perfect. Jean was convinced by this project because the RAF had approved the raid on Paris. It is worth noting that although it was the French of the FAFL who came up with the idea, their staff did not authorise it. This type of operation, therefore, was not carried out on an unfeasible whim. Through conversations with Belgians in London, it appears that the headquarters of the German police, commonly (and incorrectly) referred to as the 'Gestapo', the true arm of Nazi terror, where Belgians are tortured daily, was located in a building

Promotional drawing representing the project of the Belvédère residence, which would become the dreaded headquarters of the Sipo-SD on the prestigious Avenue Louise.

The building housing the Sipo-SD headquarters at 453 Avenue Louise, seen from Avenue Émile De Mot.

Jean knew very well having visited a friend there several times before the war. It was, of course, the building at 453 Avenue Louise.

The Belvédère residence, as it is known, was originally a modernist style apartment building designed in 1936–1937 by Belgian architect Stanislas Jasinski. Deliberately provocative, the architect wanted to elicit 'for or against' reactions, especially through advertisements published in the press. The building is ideally located and offers a magnificent view of the gardens of the Abbey of La Cambre. Yet what distinguishes the building is undoubtedly its size, being twelve stories high, which was uncommon at the time and unique on Avenue Louise. The building was therefore easy to spot from the sky. Moreover, the Brussels-born de Selys knew the building was located in the extension of Avenue Émile De Mot, which would greatly facilitate his approach and create an ideal firing line. Jean was now convinced that it was the perfect target for an air raid, especially at the controls of a Typhoon, which had proven its ease at low altitude and could unleash 640 20mm shells per minute. During the few seconds he would have the building in his sights, he could hope to place between 100 and 200 shells into the target.

Once the objective had been identified, Jean relentlessly sought approval for his raid project from his superiors, with the draft request for authorisation at the beginning of the chapter attesting to this. Yet weeks passed without any response. Frank Ziegler, 609's intelligence officer, even intervened with 11 Group's staff to unblock the situation, but was met with embarrassed silence vaguely tinted with disapproval.

However, the staff's inertia did not seem to worry de Selys, who openly continued preparing his raid, as evidenced by the squadron's Operations Record. For instance, on 1 January 1943, it reads:

> F/Lt de Selys Longchamps is all set for a special 'Greetings' Rhubarb to Brussels. Aim: to drop Belgian and British flags, a lot of miniature flags, leaflets with '1918' on them, shoot up the Gestapo building, raise Belgian morale. At the last minute he is not allowed to go, and the first day of 1943 sees all aircraft grounded on account of the weather.

A second, similar, entry is visible on 12 January: 'F/Lt de Selys is again all set for his special "Rhubarb" and is again disappointed when the Whirlwinds report unfavourable weather on the other side.' In both cases, it was more the whims of dreadful winter weather that thwarted the Belgian's plans, rather than the absence of formal authorisation, which he ultimately seemed to disregard. Some have said that it was the Belgian authorities in London who rejected the project, but nothing can confirm this for certain. In his memoirs, Raymond 'Cheval' Lallemant indicates that Jean's initial idea was for a raid involving four Typhoons. In an interview conducted for the documentary *Jours de Guerre* broadcasted on Belgian television in November 1992, he even asserted that the initial idea was to repaint the roundels of the four Typhoons with Belgian colours for the occasion. Perhaps de Selys convinced himself that the lack of authorisation was related to the engagement of four aircraft and that the staff would be more lenient if he operated solo? It is not really clear, and one may question the reliability of Cheval's recollections on this matter. Lallemant also claims in his memoirs that 350 Squadron had heard of the project and demanded the right, as a 100% Belgian squadron, to carry out the operation. Again, this remains hard to believe, and the reality is certainly more prosaic: Jean de Selys Longchamps was determined to carry out his raid, no matter the cost. Perhaps he had adopted that lovely expression: 'better to ask for forgiveness than permission.'

Chapter 13

Don't Stop Me Now

(20 January 1943)

An unpublished document helps us to understand Jean de Selys' activities during the days leading up to his raid on the Sipo-SD HQ: the personal diary of Flight Sergeant Robert 'Bob' Walling.[1] Part of 609's 'senior' ground staff, Walling assisted Jean in his role as leader of B Flight and reported that on Friday, 1 January 1943, de Selys had one idea in mind: 'to fly over Brussels at low altitude to drop the British and the Belgian flag.' In his diary, Walling describes an astonishing contraption they had come up with to enable this to happen, whereby the flags were attached to a mini parachute (a flare chute, identical to those used for distress rockets) to facilitate their release in the aircraft's wake. Everything seemed ready, but as we have seen in the ORB entry cited at the end of the previous chapter, the operation was canceled at the last minute. Walling specifies that the 'raid' proposed by de Selys was extensively discussed at the group level but was deemed too dangerous for the pilot. Bob Walling notes that following this setback, an angry Jean de Selys went on leave for a few days, and Walling feared that the pilot's wrath would be fuelled further upon learning that his aircraft had been sent to Henlow for modifications. And, indeed, this was what happened when Jean returned to the snow-covered Manston base on Wednesday, 6 January. However, the Belgian's irritation subsided when he learned his Typhoon was at Henlow, as he 'knew someone there' and was confident he could retrieve the aircraft without delay. This seemed to be true, as by Friday, 8 January, he took off three times in the Typhoon registered PR-M. On Saturday, 9 January, Jean returned from patrol with a mysteriously low oil pressure in his engine, and Flight Sergeant Walling seemed confident that the Napier engine manufacturer's representative attached to 609 would quickly identify the bug.

On Tuesday, 12 January, poor weather conditions once again thwarted Jean's aspirations to conduct his raid on Brussels. Nonetheless, he improvised a short 15-minute flight, laconically titled 'air test' in his logbook, during which he attempted to drop his flags over 609's dispersal area. The trial was hardly conclusive, as Bob Walling reports: 'Nobody saw the flags take flight, so I think it's a failure.'

Flight Sergeant Robert 'Bob' Walling is seated at the far right of the second row. He provided invaluable assistance to Jean de Selys in preparing his 'Special Rhubarb'.

Jean de Selys added a hit to his record on Sunday, 17 January, claiming a 'Cat B locomotive' during an 'Intruder' operation that took him near Dunkirk, the northwest suburbs of Brussels, and Ghent, where, not far from Deinze, Jean annihilated his target. On his second pass, he saw a large flash, and his aircraft was shaken by a violent explosion. Despite heavy anti-aircraft fire, he emerged from the hornet's nest satisfied with his accurate aim: he had never been sharper.

Another operation sent him once more toward Belgium on Monday, 18 January, but it was a night 'Intruder' operation that could in no way serve as a springboard for his raid on Brussels. Jean took off early in the evening, at 8:27pm, heading for Chièvres (north of Mons). On the way, his aircraft was again targeted by 'friendly fire' from British anti-aircraft guns near Ramsgate, but he escaped unscathed and the rest of the operation was uneventful.

On the evening of Tuesday, 19 January, Jean read the latest report from the Meteorological Office of the Air Ministry, whose forecast was optimistic for the next

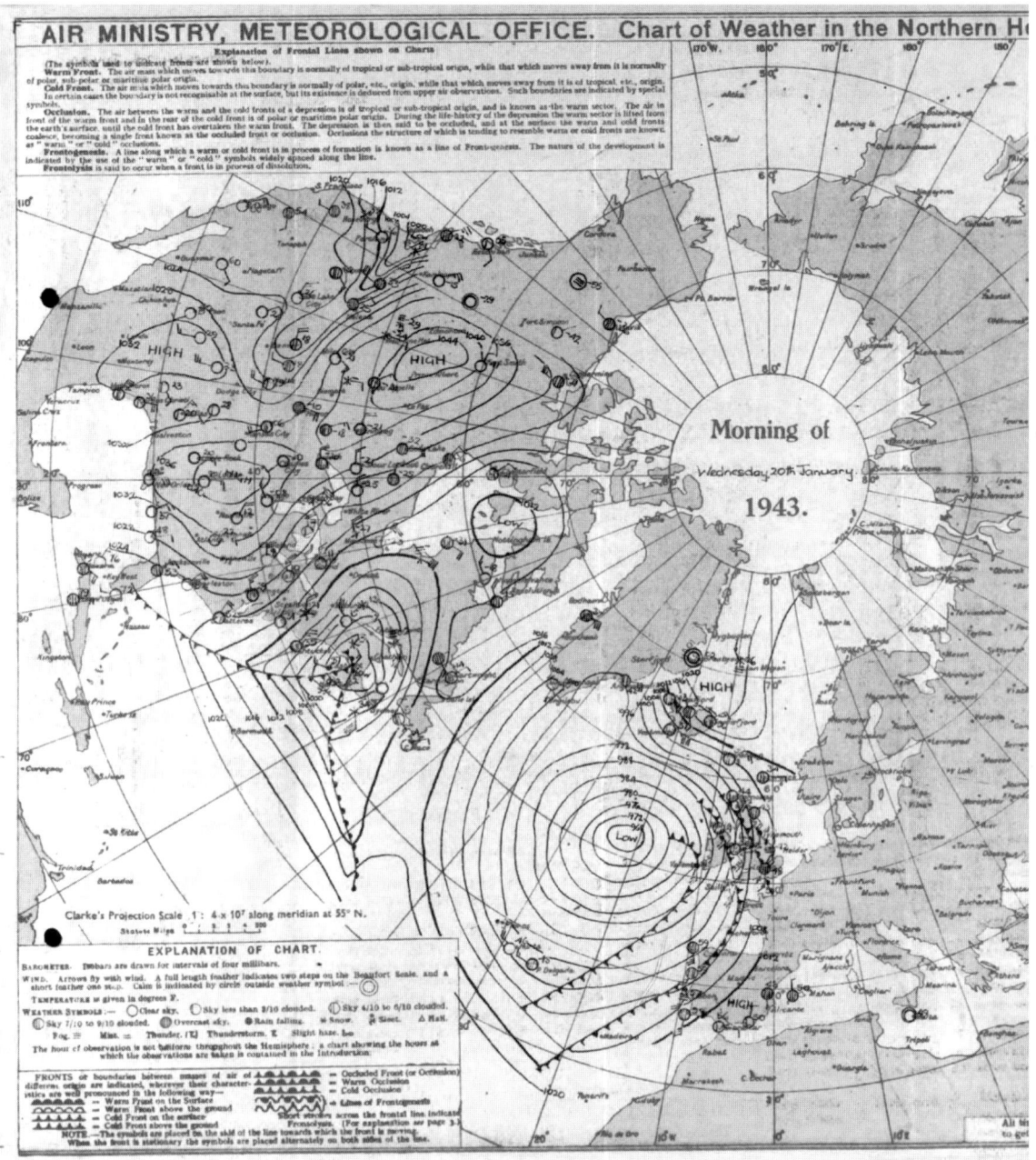

The weather map for 20 January 1943, prepared by the Meteorological Office of the Air Ministry.

day. Could the moment to finally take action have come? Fingers crossed. That night, Jean likely rehearsed once more the route he had envisioned to reach his target without fail. The aerial slalom he was about to perform over Brussels was a first for him, having never flown over the city, his city, at the controls of an aircraft. It was, therefore, essential to rely on visual landmarks he could identify in a split second, which would allow him to navigate his plan without hesitation. He knew time would be of the essence and that there would be no room for improvisation. He probably also glanced at the flags he would carry with him. Would Jean use the makeshift contraption made with a 'flare chute' attached to each flag, or would he ultimately opt to simply throw them through the small side window of his cockpit? No one knew. The only certainty was that he would carry two sizable flags – the British flag and the 'black/yellow/red' of the homeland he so dearly loved – along with a myriad of miniature Belgian flags crafted by young Belgian refugee pupils in England. Little is known about the origin of these children. In 1943, it was estimated that 330 Belgian refugee students were studying in schools on English soil: in Penrith, Braemar, Buxton, and Kingston.[2] The latter was the closest school to Manston, located southwest of London, but nothing confirms its potential role. In fact, how the crafting of these small flags was managed remains a mystery, but one can imagine Jean de Selys' good contacts with the Belgian embassy in London played a part.

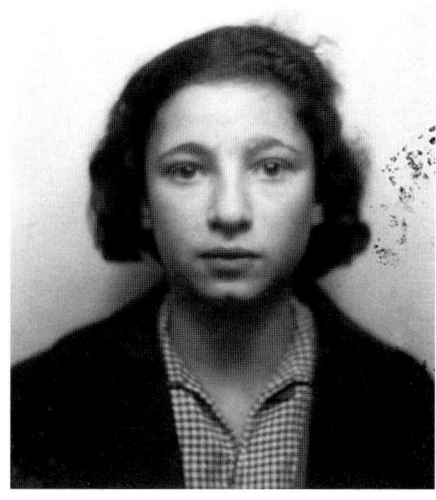

Régine Krochmal was arrested on the night of 19 January 1943 and was imprisoned in the basement of 453 Avenue Louise at the time of Jean's raid.

Did Jean manage to get some sleep on the night of 19 to 20 January? It is doubtful. However, it is certain that the same night was particularly tumultuous and trying for a 22-year-old Brussels woman whom fate would lead to 453 Avenue Louise just a few hours before Jean de Selys would strike the despised building of the Sipo-SD's minions.

This young woman was a nurse called Régine Krochmal.[3] However, because she was Jewish, a sinister ordinance issued by the Nazis forbade her from practising the profession she held so dear. Undeterred, her rebellious nature pushed her to join the ranks of a group of Jewish resistance fighters, the Austrian Liberation Front, to fight against the invaders. Her group's mission was to distribute leaflets and newspapers to reveal Hitler's true intentions to the German troops stationed in Belgium. Régine, born to German-Austrian parents, quickly made her mark in the group. On the night of 19 to 20 January 1943, she was arrested by the Germans following a denunciation while in a Brussels apartment housing the makeshift clandestine printing press where Régine and two accomplices were busy mimeographing their newspaper *Die Wahrheit* (The Truth). When the Germans entered the building, the three comrades hastily hid the mimeograph and printed documents: it was crucial the Nazis did not get hold of them. The two men barely had time to flee across the rooftops before the German policemen forcefully knocked on the door of the apartment, which was fortunately located on the upper floors. Régine, with extraordinary nerve, appeared before them, feigning sleepiness as if pulled from deep slumber. She immediately confessed to the Germans that she was Jewish, delighting the men in the dreaded long leather coats, who believed they had an easy catch. Thrilled to apprehend a Jew who would inflate their grim statistics, 'the life thieves' (as they were nicknamed) conducted a cursory search of the apartment without finding anything and took Régine to the dungeons of 453 Avenue Louise just a few hours before a Typhoon would bring down thunder on the building.

André 'Le Men' Blanco, Jean de Selys' No. 2, who was unaware of Jean's mission when the two Typhoons left Manston for Belgium.

As dawn was about to break on Wednesday, 20 January 1943, it marked one year exactly since the Wannsee Conference, during which Reinhard Heydrich had outlined the diabolical plan conceived by deranged minds to exterminate the Jews. History had now chosen Baron Jean de Selys Longchamps to deliver a spectacular middle finger to the proud Nazis and remind them that their days were also numbered.

In the early morning, as the thick cloak of night covering Manston slowly tore through the Kent sky (the sun rose at 8:56am that day), Jean de Selys headed towards 609's dispersal area. The weather forecast was accurate: it was going to be a good day for flying. There was already a buzz at the dispersal area, as two missions were posted on the operations board. A Flight would conduct the first defensive patrol with Raymond 'Cheval' Lallemant and Peter Raw.[4] To Jean, however, only the second operation scheduled at dawn mattered: an offensive 'Rhubarb' operation for which he would be the leader, and André 'Le Men' Blanco, the No. 2.

Like de Selys, Blanco was from Brussels but had been born in Genoa, Italy, on 5 January 1916. A former member of 3rd Engineer Regiment, he had quickly joined the ranks of the Belgian military aviation, being admitted as a student pilot in March 1938. He bravely participated in the May 1940 campaign as part of 3/2/1Aé Squadron on outdated Fairey-Fox aircraft, and was shot down twice. As a sign of the unequal battles it faced, his squadron was reduced from seventeen to four aircraft in just a few days. Along with other Belgian aviators (including Van Lierde, whom he would meet again at 609), he was then evacuated to France, where he found himself plunged into the infamous chaos now well-known to all Belgian military personnel left to fend for themselves in the days following the surrender on 28 May. Worse still, after

An armourer carrying 20mm shell belts on his back to feed the cannons of a Typhoon. The size of the projectile is impressive.

the French capitulation, Vichy authorities handed Blanco over to the Germans. 'Le Men', as his teammates called him, did not give up and would fight his way to reach England. Escaping from the Germans, he headed to Brussels, then departed a week later with three companions towards southern France, aiming to cross the Spanish border. A French guide led them across but then handed them over to the Spanish police, who quickly turned them over to the French authorities. After three escape attempts, Blanco finally reached Barcelona, where he hid before successfully crossing into Portugal. Arrested again in Portugal, he claimed to be Canadian to avoid expulsion. His ruse worked, and he left Lisbon on 30 May 1941 – a year after the capitulation – aboard the SS *Algerian*, arriving in England on 20 June. Things moved quickly from there and he registered at an RAF recruitment centre on Belgian National Day, a month later, undergoing training at 53 OTU in Kirton in Lindsey, and joining 609 on 13 January 1942.

When he prepared to depart on the operation on the morning of 20 January, André Blanco was unaware that their 'Rhubarb' was actually Jean de Selys' planned raid on Brussels.[5] He had not been informed by his leader, who likely did not want to involve him in an unauthorised operation. Their operation's discussed objectives were fairly standard: hunting for locomotives in the Bruges area. As they finished gathering their flight gear, Jean de Selys and 'Cheval' Lallemant could not help but exchange a knowing glance, aware of what was truly afoot behind what appears to be a routine scene at 609.

It was just past 8am when the pilots headed to their respective aircraft, moving somewhat awkwardly because of the Mae West life jackets they wore over their uniforms and their bulky fur-lined flight boots. A navigation map was tucked in each pilot's boots. On top of their leather flying helmets rested a pair of goggles, while an oxygen mask was attached to the helmet, swinging freely with each step: once the engine started, it must not leave the pilot's face. From afar, the 609 guys might have spotted four Belgian pilots from 350 Squadron, who had spent the night at Manston and were set to take off at 8:25 in their Spitfires towards Hornchurch.

The Typhoon Mk IB, registered DN305 PR-M,[6] awaited Jean de Selys on the edge of the runway, surrounded by two mechanics. Jean circled the aircraft, ever impressed by its massive form. His gaze fell on the formidable cannons that, he hoped, will unleash fury on Brussels that day. As he settled into the cockpit, Jean had to take care not to crush the flags and ensure they would not hinder him, while at the same time remaining easily accessible. Perhaps the faithful Bob Walling had placed them in the cockpit based on Jean's instructions, as it is hard to imagine him transporting all this material from the dispersal area without arousing the curiosity of the other pilots (even Lallemant did not know Jean was carrying flags)[7]. In his cockpit, Jean also carried a small camera to capture his flight over Brussels. Was this confidence or recklessness?

Certainly, it was a sign he felt completely in control and more excited than worried about the raid. A mechanic assisted him in fastening his seat harness and parachute straps. Once securely strapped in, the mechanic connected his flight helmet's headphones to the intercom system. Did Jean have time to feel a slight surge of stress? Probably not, as he quickly secured his mask and connected it to the aircraft's oxygen system, turning the knob to the left to activate it and then checking the flow on the gauge.

It was time to start. A small nod and a thumbs-up to the second mechanic standing by with a fire extinguisher near the engine. The other mechanic closed the cockpit door at the same moment. Everything was set. Contact. The Typhoon used a Coffman starter, activated by the pilot. A starter cartridge was inserted into the cylinder. Two piston injections. The pilot heard a loud noise, a cross between a whistle and a 'bang'. The Napier Sabre engine grumbled, spat, and then roared with a thunderous blast. Flames briefly erupted from the exhaust pipes on either side of the aircraft's nose, followed by thick gray-brown smoke, confirming the engine was alive and eager to unleash its 2,000 horsepower. The mechanic with the fire extinguisher was relieved: everything had gone well this time.

As the engine calmed down, now emitting its characteristic high-pitched growl, a quick check ensured the oxygen was flowing properly. The mechanics positioned themselves at each wingtip, as the Typhoon began to move towards the take off area. Blanco, piloting the Typhoon registered DN300 PR-Z, followed close by. The wind from the engines flattened the grass, as Jean scanned the main indicators on his dashboard and carefully operated all the controls to put his aircraft in optimal take off conditions. Trim, ailerons, rudders, engine mixture, propeller pitch, flap angle, radiator cooling flap, engine RPM kept at the ideal rate… Jean meticulously followed the procedure he had rehearsed countless times. A quick glance at Blanco, now just beside him. It was 8:32am. The sun was almost up, and the morning promised a clear sky, ideal for Baron Jean de Selys Longchamps' task.

Once take off clearance was confirmed by the tower, Jean pushed the throttle all the way, released the brakes, and the aircraft vibrated as the immense engine torque pushed him back into his seat with rapid acceleration. What a thrill! Correcting to keep the aircraft straight as it gains speed, followed by a few more yards of rolling. As the tail lifted and left the ground, the long nose tended to dip, requiring a quick adjustment of the aircraft's attitude. The altimeter span wildly as the plane ascended at a rate of 45 feet per second. Retracting the landing gear, the vibrations continued, conveying an incredible sense of power. This aircraft was a rocket.

Heading straight for Ostend to cover the 60 miles separating Manston from the Belgian coast, Jean was in familiar territory: the English Channel, northern France, and northern Belgium had become the preferred hunting grounds for 609 pilots.

To evade enemy radar, the two Typhoons flew at sea level, an altitude RAF pilots explicitly called 'zero feet'. It was not unusual for the aircraft to leave a wake on the water behind them, created by the high-speed rotation of their propellers, giving the illusion that the two Typhoons had become powerful levitating speedboats. Witnesses report that RAF fighters sometimes returned with damaged propellers after making direct contact with the water from flying so low.

The altitude also led to another hazard: seabirds. Flying over 310mph, a collision with one could cause damage akin to a large piece of shrapnel, or worse, depending on where the aircraft was hit. Fortunately, the Belgian coast appeared on the horizon a few minutes later, laden with many new perils.

Jean de Selys and André Blanco knew where best to penetrate the coast to avoid the formidable hornets' nests of the Flak, the German air defence that vigilantly guarded the occupied territory. Approaching the shore, pilots sometimes made a quick ascent to escape light anti-aircraft guns or even automatic weapon fire, which could be just as deadly, and then immediately repositioned at low altitude towards their target. The radar blip they created vanished as quickly as it appeared on the German operators' screens.

The two Typhoons' hunting zone was reached a few moments later – around 8:45am – and Jean had a stroke of luck as he quickly spotted a target near Ruysseleede (now called Ruiselede), a small municipality in West Flanders, southeast of Bruges. The place was easy to identify as a gigantic radio tower, nearly 980 feet tall, was erected there in the late 1920s for communication with the Belgian Congo. Jean de Selys knew there's no time to waste: his fuel reserve was not unlimited (he took off with just over 500 litres, giving him a range of just over 500 miles), but, more pressing, the number of 20mm shells for his four Hispano Mk II cannons would not magically increase. Each cannon's feed drum only held a reserve of 140 shells, for a total of 560 shells. It was not much. Very little, in fact, for a weapon system capable of firing 600 rounds per minute. Practically, this meant a Typhoon pilot depleted his entire ammunition stock in less than 14 seconds. Precision was, therefore, paramount.

Though tempted to conserve all his fuel and ammunition for the 'Special Rhubarb' on Brussels, the sight of a locomotive stopping for a water refill was too tempting for Jean de Selys. As the two planes approached, their terrifying roar sent the mechanics scurrying away, leaving their machine prey to the Typhoons. As the locomotive widened in his sights, Jean prepared to fire his four cannons by pressing the large button on the top left of his stick. At the right moment, two seconds of pressure were enough to unleash a stream of 20mm shells that effortlessly perforated the boiler, transforming it into a sieve. White steam flared up above the locomotive, as if it had just erupted. Under the watchful eye of his No. 2, there was no doubt this destruction would be confirmed and credited to Jean's tally.

It was now 8:52am, and there was no time left to waste. Jean de Selys informed Blanco they would return separately ('Return independently')[8] and headed directly at 135° to rush at low altitude towards Ghent and then Brussels, where he had a date with destiny.

Probably surprised by his leader's message, André Blanco quickly regrouped and set out in search of his own prey. Near Aalter, he spotted a passenger train on which he simulated an attack. The convoy immediately halted, as passengers panicked and fled the carriages. Then, a freight train arrived on the opposite track and stopped alongside the other locomotive. The two engines were so close together that Blanco could attack them simultaneously. In six passes, the job was done, and two more locomotives were henceforth missing from the inventory of rolling stock the occupiers had seized.

As Blanco completed his pass, Jean's Typhoon had already covered the 43 miles separating him from Brussels. The weather was ideal, and the clouds were low enough to offer refuge in case of trouble. Everything then happened very quickly. He reached the capital via Asse, then flew over Zellik, where he could see the imposing dome of the Palace of Justice, standing 380 feet above Brussels, which was now only 4.3 miles away. It was the first significant visual landmark to guide his navigation.

The path he then took is subject to many debatable theories. Knowing that Jean de Selys had never flown over Brussels, it is very likely he favoured a route following a succession of notorious landmarks, recognisable at first sight from the sky. It is likely that it was towards the concrete colossus that is the Palace of Justice he first headed after briefly flying over the Marolles. From this moment on, he took a few photographs, which, unfortunately, would all turn out to be unusable after development. Next, he headed towards the easily identifiable Royal Palace, then turned right to take Rue de la Loi towards the Cinquantenaire arcades. At this moment, Jean almost flew over his family home at 118 rue de Trèves, and although obviously did not have time to see it, one can imagine his heart tightened for a nanosecond, having not been that close to his loved ones for many months. By now, however, the monumental triumphal arch of the Cinquantenaire, with its quadriga of Brabant at its summit, loomed before him. Raymond Lallemant would later say[9] that Jean confided in him upon his return that he flew so low 'the horses reared as I (he) passed.' With the arch standing only 100 feet tall, one has an idea of how low Jean performed his impressive urban slalom. Louis Robyns de Schneidauer, who was heading towards the Royal Museums of Art and History at the same moment, saw the plane thunder above him.[10] After sweeping over the Cinquantenaire park in an instant, the Typhoon pivoted to the right towards another well-known landmark to Jean: the parade ground facing the barracks district, where he was stationed when he belonged to 1st Guides. In January 1943, the plain was still a vast, easily identifiable open space from the sky. A few seconds later, Jean spotted the Boitsfort racecourse

This photograph, taken from the beginning of Avenue Émile De Mot, shows the unique silhouette of the building, perfectly distinct from other buildings, and presenting a perfect line of fire when Jean discovered it in a low-altitude pass.

in the distance, where he had competed in equestrian events before the war. It was the signal to ascend and head northwest. The attack axis he had identified presented itself as planned when he entered Avenue des Nations (now Avenue Franklin D. Roosevelt). Stunned bystanders struggled to understand what was happening, believing such a plane flying so low, together with that thunderous noise, it must have been in great trouble and was about to crash.

Pulling back the throttles and stabilising his speed at around 125mph (the Typhoon's stall speed was 90mph), he began to climb. The gardens of la Cambre Abbey were now in his sight. After a slight nudge of the rudder to the left, he entered Avenue Émile De Mot without a second thought.

Bingo! Exactly as Jean had imagined: 1,300 feet ahead of him stood the mini skyscraper no one could believe would soon be showered with shells.

It was now 9:05am and although Jean de Selys was unaware of it, the conjunction of two elements would contribute to the success of his daring raid. By the time he

A pre-war photograph from the opposite angle gives an idea of the perspective of Avenue Émile De Mot seen from the Sipo-SD building, where the sentry incredulously saw an aircraft rapidly approaching.

faced 453 Avenue Louise in his Typhoon, it was just past 9am, and the interrogations had not yet begun; the Nazi torturers not beginning their repugnant work until 10am. Prisoners were held in the basement – among them Régine Krochmal, who had arrived a few hours earlier – but most people interrogated by the Sipo-SD's hyenas were transferred daily from Saint-Gilles prison and taken back after interrogations. The building's upper floors were almost exclusively occupied by German personnel or collaborators at the time of de Selys' attack, significantly reducing the probability of collateral damage. Another fortuitous element, however, would maximize the impact of his raid. An important meeting involving several Nazi officers was under way on the building's eighth floor at the same time. There was, therefore, a good concentration of targets with highly harmful potential.

When the German sentry guarding the Sipo-SD building from his sheltered box saw the Typhoon charging down Avenue Émile De Mot, he could not believe his eyes. This astonishing sight soon doubled into a real feel of an impending apocalypse, as the plane opened fire and the sentry distinctly saw four flashes, two on each wing, continuously spitting thunder!

Inside his cockpit, eyes glued to the collimator and the luminous circle that encircled the target like a raptor seizing its prey, Jean indeed began opening fire out of his four cannons. When they activated, they shook the aircraft and even slightly slowed it down due to their significant recoil. Jean exerted slight pressure on the rudder, right then left, to spray the entire width of the building. The attack phase was extremely brief: at 125mph, it would take barely more than 8 seconds to cover the 1,300 feet separating the start of Avenue Émile De Mot from the facade of 453 Avenue Louise. Yet great pilots have a particular talent, having an incredible ability to analyse a situation in milliseconds and react accordingly with composure. In the words of Raymond Lallemant, who expertly described Jean de Selys' strafing:[11]

> You don't see the 'hits' directly, you must wait a bit. Suddenly, Jean realised his shells were hitting the upper floors but not reaching the ground floor or the first floor. He then eased the stick to hit the lower part of the building, and then pulled it back without stopping firing. It was a bit tight. He straightened up, got

A montage made after the war illustrating Jean de Selys Longchamps' raid. Given the limited technical means of the time, the montage is quite realistic, and no doubt many were fooled by what seemed to be a stolen snapshot of the day of the feat.

very close to the building, kept firing. He really grazed the building and when he passed over the roof, he was still firing, the last shots went into the air.

Captain Henri Vanvreckom described the raid from another perspective. At the time, he was employed at the Office of Works for the Demobilised Army (OTAD), whose offices were located on Avenue Émile De Mot. Pierre Stephany reported his testimony:[12]

> He [Vanvreckom] was standing behind a window because that morning German officers had announced they were coming for a visit which he knew would bring nothing good; he heard from his right a world-ending roar and saw the huge silhouette of a plane, its grey colour cutting through the winter sky, and, seeing the leading edge of the wings spit short and regular flames, he understood the pilot was not in distress; he was firing. But the vision only lasted for a flash. The shells, already, finished climbing the facade of the Gestapo building, bursting windows, scattering stone and concrete in all directions.

The apocalyptic noise caused by the Typhoon now flooded the entire Avenue Émile De Mot and undoubtedly drew the occupants of 453 towards the windows to try to understand what was happening outside. Unfortunately for them, they exposed themselves to the terrible 20mm shells, which shattered the windows at a speed of 2,723 feet per second. What made Jean de Selys' feat quite extraordinary, however, was the astonishing precision of his shots: none of his shells hit another facade adjacent

A 20mm shell head that shattered on the facade of 453 Avenue Louise and was given to the de Selys family after the war.

to 453. Did the training at the Central Gunnery School, which he had reluctantly attended last October, bear fruit? If nothing else, it certainly put into perspective the particularly harsh judgment made by his shooting instructor.

An even more astonishing viewpoint, since it came from Hélène Moszkiewiez, who was inside the Sipo-SD offices, describes the chaos that reigned during the attack and the minutes that followed. This testimony is particularly interesting as it comes from a young woman who was part of the Intelligence Service as an undercover agent within the Brussels Sipo-SD headquarters. Thanks to her fluency in German, she was hired as a secretary, and what follows is her account from a letter sent after the war to 'Windmill Charlie' Dumoulin (a Belgian pilot of 609):[13]

> Sitting in my office on the eighth floor (…) where a meeting of bigwigs was currently being held (two soldiers were guarding the door, something which had never happened before), I suddenly heard the muffled sound of a very close airplane engine, intertwined with the sound of a machine gun in action (…) Worried, I went out into the corridor and started heading towards a window overlooking the street – just a few yards away – but from afar, I saw the window obscured by what seemed to be the fuselage of an airplane, and I simultaneously heard the noise of the 'machine gun'. Convinced that it was a full-scale attack by Allied planes, I quickly retreated to my office. The noise stopped as suddenly as it had started. All this took only a few seconds (…) seconds of this kind were etched in memory as if they were hours. After a moment of respite (…) I heard a racket in the corridor. I went out to see what was happening. I was then faced with an incredible scene: a coming and going of soldiers bringing blankets, sheets, and stretchers. The door of Mueller's office was wide open and I got a glimpse of officers lying on the floor, in a pool of blood, a lot of blood.

A final testimony completes the description of the stupor that invaded all floors of 453 Avenue Louise: that of the young Régine Krochmal who was detained in one of the basements at the time of the raid. In the basements, too, the attack did not go unnoticed:[14] '(…) And then, the house was bombed, and all the soldiers came out. I thought to myself, if I go out with them, I'll be shot right away. I stayed in the basement, fortunately.' The attack had a beneficial effect for her: 'They did not have time to torture me', because 'They were shocked enough to have been bombed.' She was transferred to Mechelen the next day without being interrogated and was part of the notorious twentieth convoy to Auschwitz, from which she miraculously escaped. What an astonishing fate!

For now, let us return to the moment when Jean de Selys, throttle forward to release the 2,000 horsepower of his engine, managed to straighten up his Typhoon at the last moment, skimming the top of the twelve-story building now engulfed in dust and smoke. He could hardly avoid letting out a 'phew' of relief, muffled by the oxygen mask clinging to his face. It had been a close call. Very close. But he quickly needed to get back on operation because he was in the heart of enemy territory, over 125 miles from his base, and it would now be more complicated to go unnoticed. As proof of the cool headedness that still inhabited him, it seems that it was while moving away from his target, after making a right turn towards Avenue Louise, that he lowered the left window of his Typhoon to launch his two large flags, the British and the Belgian. Lallemant reported that the flags became caught in the Typhoon's empennage, but eventually detached after Jean shook the aircraft, to finally float in the sky above Brussels.[15] Some claimed that one flag landed near the Royal Palace and the other on a building at the corner of Spa Street and Joseph II Street, where a cousin of the pilot (Baroness de Villegas de Saint-Pierre) resided. After the war, there was also talk of a flag falling on the new junction station, Cardinal Mercier Avenue, but nothing can be said with certainty.

An increasing number of bemused Brussels citizens spotted the mysterious plane as it skimmed the rooftops, no doubt believing it to be the one that had caused the deafening noise that had just shook the city. Léon Nihoul, the famous Brussels pastry chef, was at Cavell Hospital (just over 0.6 miles away) for treatment and heard the explosions' roar. Louis Robyns de Schneidauer, who was on the Cinquantenaire esplanade (1.8 miles from the attack site) when the Typhoon passed overhead, recounted the moments that followed:[16] 'A few seconds later, I heard a monstrous clatter: Jean de Selys was strafing the Gestapo, but at the moment, I thought it was him being caught in German fire.'

Jean now sped away from the capital towards Manston, via Ghent and Ostend. His action was so sudden and lightning-fast that no anti-aircraft battery fired at his Typhoon. Still filled with the incredible images of the low-flying manoeuvre he had just performed over his hometown – he would later tell Lallemant that he was so low he felt 'the tramways were coming towards him'[17]— Jean checked his status. His fuel levels should be fine. As for ammunition, a simple addition of his two firing sequences of the day confirmed what he already knew: he had few shells left. Fortunately, the cloud layer remained conducive to an escape if, by chance, the 'Huns' should engage him. Approaching Ghent, he realised that in the heat of the action, he had forgotten to release the small flags made by the Belgian schoolchildren. Turning back was, of course, impossible, but never mind, the people of Ghent would also receive the patriotic tribute of a pilot determined to boost their morale, so he opened his window again and let the small flags fly over the outskirts of Ghent.

After skimming the modest relief of the Flemish plain, he finally crossed the coast and disappeared into the clouds. There was still no sign of the Luftwaffe; so much the better. Manston was now just 60 short miles away. As he began to spot the English coast, he was intercepted by Raymond Lallemant, whom ground control had sent to check on 'the unidentified aircraft' approaching dangerously the English territory. Jean had not activated his IFF (Identification Friend or Foe) that distinguished 'friendly' from 'enemy' aircraft. Lallemant quickly recognised the silhouette of a lone Typhoon and, as he approached, clearly saw the registration 'PR-M', which he directly attributed to de Selys. The two aircraft now flew side by side, and Lallemant spotted Jean's raised thumb. There was no doubt: he had done it, he had carried out his raid on Brussels. This nice anecdote was reported by Lallemant after the war,[18] but the landing times recorded in the Operations Record Book do not seem to match, and this return flight encounter might well have been invented.

At 9:44am, Jean de Selys Longchamps landed his perfectly intact Typhoon at Manston, which he had left 1 hour and 12 minutes earlier. To the intelligence officer, Frank Ziegler, who came to meet him to collect his flight report, he calmly declared: 'I've done it, Ziegly!'[19] and Ziegler immediately understood that Jean had accomplished the project he had been talking about for weeks. After the liberation of Brussels in 1944, Ziegler would have the chance to meet a lady who was on a tramway at the time of the attack, and who would tell him about the jubilation of the Belgians and the fury of the Germans following Jean's raid. Yet, Jean de Selys' day was far from over, for this Wednesday, 20 January was a date that would enter the legend of 609 Squadron.

Starting at 11:15am, Jean took off again aboard PR-M for a patrol lasting 1 hour and 40 minutes. He spotted the trails left by eight to twelve enemy aircraft at 19,600 feet altitude over the coastal town of Deal, confirming a significantly more intense Luftwaffe activity than usual. Ground control spotted other 'bogeys' at 13,000 feet, even closer to the base. Jean dove in but saw none of them. Unable to continue the chase because he was out of fuel, he had to return to refuel. But it was not the end of surprises, because as he approached Manston, Jean was again engaged by a Spitfire.[20] The Spitfire pilot stopped firing only when Jean lowered his landing gear, instantly realising his mistake: he was not a Focke-Wulf! No doubt the Belgian cursed, wondering when the Typhoon would cease to be targets for other RAF planes?

Back at the base around 1pm, Jean parked his Typhoon and shouted 'Fuel, fuel!' he wanted his plane to be refuelled as quickly as possible so that he could return without wasting a second. However, refuelling was not possible for the moment, and as he climbed out of his plane, he received confirmation that the Luftwaffe was definitely engaged in a large-scale operation. Ziegler assured him that he had not seen so many condensation trails in the sky over Manston since the Battle of Britain. This explains why the Luftwaffe was virtually invisible during Jean's morning raid on Brussels: German squadrons were busy preparing for a raid on London. Indeed, it is estimated that ninety German aircraft were involved in the day's operations.

609 Squadron did not miss the opportunity and multiplied sorties, just like most of Fighter Command squadrons (214 sorties were recorded that day). Jean took off for a third time in a 'scramble' just a few minutes after landing from his midday long patrol. By the evening of 20 January, the squadron's achievements were impressive: the 'White Rose' Squadron had not downed as many aircraft in one day (five) since 8 May 1941! Joe Atkinson even matched Tommy Rigler's record by shooting down three aircraft during the same sortie. The Operations Record Book summarises the day's achievements as follows:[21]

> 1 category B locomotive (F/Lt de Selys), Gestapo HQ attack (Brussels) (F/Lt de Selys), Flags dropped (Brussels and villages) (F/Lt de Selys), 2 category B locomotives (F/Sgt Blanco), 1 Fw.190 destroyed (F/O Lallemant), 3 Me 109 G destroyed (F/O Baldwin), 1 Fw.190 destroyed (F/Lt Atkinson).

With so many reasons to celebrate, it goes without saying that a memorable party was organised at the squadron's 'bistro' (according to Lallemant), the Old Charles in Margate, where eighteen pilots gathered.[22] 'Cheval' Lallemant spoke of it with emotion:[23]

> So, we ended up there in the evening and celebrated. The wonderful thing about those bars was that we met the British people there, we met people who admired us, who found us likeable, and we found them very likeable too, because we must not forget that everyone was at war. There was a cordial understanding and, generally, they already knew the 'score' before we arrived.

The evening was, of course, festive, noisy, and boozy. Jean 'the duck' Creteur insisted on taking down the hunting horns fixed to the oak beam on the ceiling: he wanted to try them all! After countless rounds offered by who knows who, the Old Charles' owner called it a night. But it seems that this now-famous 20 January 1943 was destined to be a special day until the very end. Indeed, once the party ended, the taxi driver who was supposed to take the pilots back to the base was nowhere to be found. His vehicle was, indeed, parked in front of the pub, its engine running, but no one was in the driver's seat. Jean de Selys, accompanied by other pilots, decided not to wait and started driving the driverless taxi. It obviously did not take long for the police to show up in the middle of the night at Doone House (where the pilots were lodged) with a furious taxi driver, and the guilty pilots were taken to the police station. Despite vain attempts, the inspector in charge of the 'dispute' failed to elicit any remorse from the 609 rascals, who spent a few hours behind bars…[24] What a day!

Now that we have followed Jean de Selys through to the end of the night, let us rewind a few hours and find ourselves at the foot of 453 Avenue Louise, just a fraction of a second after the Typhoon made its masterful pull-up above the building and vanished into the Brussels sky.

Countless debris from windows and plaster littered the pavement and the road. The chaos was total. Traffic had stopped, and people were leaving the trams to come and see the damage. From all directions, onlookers were flocking, trying to understand what had just happened. A panicked fear had seized the occupants of the Sipo-SD headquarters, many having hidden like hunted animals, while others had pushed their way into the corridors and rushed downstairs to evade the cataclysm raining down on them. It was a totally unusual sensation for those who usually terrorised innocent victims. Dazed and incredulous, the Germans stared wide-eyed at the damage, with anxiety and simmering anger. Their pride had taken a serious hit.

The people of Brussels, who flocked to the scene, all knew the building had a sinister reputation and was feared by all. At this point in time, most people only had a vague idea about the horrible tortures that took place at 453 Avenue Louise, but no one doubted that it was indeed one of the gates to hell. There was, therefore, a real feeling of triumph and jubilation when it was discovered that the enemy and its most feared armed wing – the Gestapo – had just been spectacularly humiliated.

Despite the cold, people continued to converge on the scene, much to the Germans' displeasure. Enraged, they cursed the mocking onlookers and tried to disperse them, not hesitating to beat those who resisted with rifle butts.[25] Several stubborn individuals were even arrested and locked in the building's basements (a few hours for most, a few days for others). Maxime Carton de Wiart, priest of the La Cambre Abbey (and, in an incredible coincidence, former chaplain of 1st Guides during the First World War), was among them. His crime? He had intervened when the Germans wanted to chastise a group of laughing teenagers. A few days after the raid, witnesses report he still bore the marks of Nazi brutality. Jean-Pierre Hye de Crom, the future right-hand man of the secret agent Pierre Melot, and Henri Van Oost were also among those roughed up by the Germans.[26] After attending a wedding reception, they had detoured along Avenue Louise to admire the damage and were arrested, beaten, and locked up in one of the building's basements. They joined a significant number of other Belgians, kept standing there, packed like sardines against each other, causing some to faint. Noise and commotion were once again to be found there, with whistles resounding in all directions, a mix of shouted orders covering one another. And, on top of all that was the ballet of German ambulances evacuating the wounded to the German military hospital on Avenue de la Couronne, their sirens wailing.

Despite the suffocating tension engulfing the area, the people of Brussels continued to mass and join in what now resembled a pilgrimage. It must be said that the news had spread like wildfire throughout the city, causing considerable excitement. Throughout the day, onlookers who now understood it was better to stay discreet, walked near the place everyone was talking about without stopping. By 4pm, it felt like the whole city had gathered there, so incessant seemed the flow of passersby.

The very next day, the exploits of the English aviator quickly spread across the country (no one knew at this stage that it was a Belgian pilot, but strong suspicions already existed due to the pilot's evidently perfect knowledge of the place and the Belgian flag he had launched, which although very few people had seen, everyone had heard about), and many Belgians felt solidarity with this anonymous hero who had inflicted, in their name, the most stinging humiliation on the proud Nazis.

The collaborationist press obviously gave no echo to the raid, but the underground press and word of mouth did wonders to create what would today be described as a colossal buzz. Herman Bodson, a member of the Resistance, wrote in his memoirs:[27] 'The day of the attack was a day of joy. That week, as the news spread across the country, was a week of joy.'

A report on the population's reactions would later be sent (in May 1943) by the Resistance to the Minister of Defence in London, eloquently narrating the impact on Belgians:[28]

> The population, disconcerted the day before (because it had expected an intervention by the Allied aviation during the Degrelle meeting at the Palais des Sports), fortunately found a glimmer of hope through the daring and very successful blow by a Belgian aviator, it is thought, who, around 9am on 19 January [*sic*], strafed and cannonaded the infamous Gestapo building on Avenue Louise, causing very serious damage: the 2nd and 3rd floors, façade holed, windows broken, interior damage, the 7th and 8th floors frames torn out, windows broken, interior damage, and especially a large number of victims: four dead and 35 wounded. The population was ecstatic when they saw the plane deploy the Belgian flag first and then the English flag. Shouts arose and gestures glorifying the aviators were displayed. At the Gestapo, they did not appear very pleased, as severe orders followed towards the onlookers who went for a walk to the Bois de la Cambre to have the opportunity to pass in front of the building. Germans were seen arresting, hitting, and kicking two young students among others who had laughed out loud while passing in front of the Gestapo. Oh! how grateful we are to this brave aviator

Unpublished photographs of the facade of the Sipo-SD headquarters taken by German correspondent Otto Kropf (no one else would have dared to photograph the building) after the attack. Several things are notable: the impact marks are indeed concentrated on 453, and the depth of some impacts suggests the effect the shots had on the windows; there are impact marks on both the upper and lower floors, confirming that de Selys swept the entire facade; the Germans quickly proceeded with repairs, and many shutters are still lowered where the windows have not yet been replaced: for the Nazis, it was essential that the place quickly regained its 'virginity' to avoid becoming a sanctuary of resistance against the occupier.

who had the audacity to carry out such a feat! It would be desirable for it to be repeated. The Gestapo, indeed, deserves a special punishment.

The minister was so impressed by the account of the attack that he requested a proposal for a commendation, but the commander of the military air force expressed in a handwritten note attached to the letter his fear of nominating Jean de Selys by name and thereby exposing his family, who remained in Belgium, to potential reprisals.[29]

In the days following the raid, the Germans swiftly set about repairing the damage caused by the attack to quickly erase the humiliation they had suffered and to prevent 453 Avenue Louise from becoming a pilgrimage site for the people of Brussels. The Sipo-SD's headquarters were moved to a building a bit further down, at 357 Avenue Louise, whose premises would become just as grimly infamous and dreaded as those at 453 until the liberation. The Germans learned their lesson well: the location of their new headquarters made it very difficult to attack from the air. Additionally, an anti-aircraft battery was installed on the roof of 453, which would continue to be used as an annex for the Nazis' dirty work. Fortunately for Jean, it was a bit too late.

To conclude the story of that epic Wednesday, 20 January 1943, it is necessary to address two topics on which much has been said, starting with several inaccuracies, and sometimes even blatant lies, which contribute to the shrouding of Baron Jean de Selys Longchamps' raid in a veil of dark legend.

The most moving double page of Jean de Selys' logbook, detailing his flights of January 1943 and his audacious first sortie on 20 January 1943.

Let us begin with the number of German victims, as there is no doubt that no Belgian victims were there to mourn. From the day of the attack, the most fanciful figures began to circulate.[30] As Jean Frosty points out, by noon, 'twenty versions were circulating' in Brussels. Caught up in their excitement and eager to see the Nazis pay the heaviest of tolls, every onlooker offered their estimate, and word-of-mouth spread the information at a speed that today's social networks would not deny, but this also tended to distort the figures. Public rumour quickly reported seven deaths and dozens of wounded. In reality, the raid resulted in about a dozen wounded in various states of severity, and five dead.[31] These included SS-Sturmbannführer Alfred Thomas (born in 1905 in Bielefeld), Kriminal Kommissar Werner Vogt (born in 1913 in Vosswalde), *Hilfspolizeibeamte*, interpreter Gustav Peters (born in 1916 in Kiel), *Kriminaloberassistent* Heinrich Beiderwieden (born in 1906 in Schmidthorst), and *Kriminalsekretar* Fritz Knorbin (born in 1900 in Alt Inse). Knorbin, it should be noted, died two days later from his injuries, while all the others died on the day of the raid. All were buried in the Evere cemetery.

Of the five Germans struck down by the Typhoon's shells, the one with the highest rank by far was Alfred Thomas who, as detailed in the previous chapter, played a key role in the deportation of Jews from Belgium. Now that we know the disturbing ease with which the Nazis, including the most murderous among them, managed to escape post-war justice (in a world eager to rebuild, turn the page, and focus on the new communist enemy), it is clear that Jean de Selys, unknowingly, delivered justice by eliminating someone directly involved in the 'evacuation' of 18,182 women, men, and children, of whom only 367 would survive. Without the raid on 20 January, Alfred Thomas might have seen life gently unfold, surrounded by his three children, the youngest of whom was born the day after the raid, on 21 January 1943, in Stettin.[32]

Let us now address the other major controversial topic that has created a halo of dark legend around too many accounts related to the raid: if Jean de Selys' project was not approved by the authorities, it was because a British secret agent was operating under a German uniform within the Sipo-SD headquarters. After being killed during the raid, an astonishing coincidence, the Nazis would have discovered a document in his pockets revealing his double agent status, which would then lead to the dismantling of an entire Belgian resistance network. This plot seems straight out of the pen of a spy novel author, but not everyone is Ian Fleming. The latter would have likely hesitated to have his spy make such a blunder, leaving a sensitive document in a pocket goes against the most basic security rules a covert agent must follow and smacks of dangerous amateurism. So, it is frankly very hard to believe.

Rumours are persistent, however, and it is often impossible to squash them. A more general study on how rumours spread highlights an essential element that allows them to multiply like metastases in narratives. After all, 'There is no smoke without fire'. The mechanism allowing them to bounce back is thus unbeatable: 'I know it is not very credible, but still, if people are talking about it, there must be something true about it.' And off it goes again. Hitler managed to escape. Man never walked on the moon. Elvis Presley did not die in 1977. The American secret services destroyed the Twin Towers, etc., etc.

Let us not give up and try to defuse the rumour mongering with three concrete facts. Firstly, the very careless spy is often presented as a certain 'Colonel Mueller (Müller).'[33] We can smile at the anecdotal fact that this surname was given to one of Tintin's most cunning adversaries (in *The Black Island*, published in 1937 and colourised in… 1943), but it must be acknowledged that no German officer or otherwise named Mueller/Müller is listed among the dead identified by the German military administration following the raid. Better still, there was no 'colonel' (SS-Standartenführer) or even 'lieutenant colonel' (SS-Obersturmbannführer) within the Sipo-SD in Brussels, as the person heading the Brussels site was SS-Sturmbannführer (Major) Ernst Ehlers.

Secondly, Hélène Moszkiewiez, previously mentioned and who was infiltrated at the 453 site on the day of the raid, provided a very explicit response to suspicions of the presence of a killed infiltrated agent that day:[34] 'Personally, I had never heard of this agent. My colleague, Lieutenant François V., also a secret agent at the Gestapo, never mentioned him.' At no point in her memoirs, while she was at the heart of the Nazi system, does she mention the dismantling of a network following the fortuitous discovery of a list of names.

Thirdly, the most enlightening testimony and the one that definitively invalidates the fantasy of 'the clumsy agent exposed by the document stuffed in his pocket' was provided by Léontine Fierens, whose activity in the Resistance was proven and recognised by the State Security Service.[35] In January 1943, Miss Fierens was close to the Van Schelle network, often explicitly identified as the network that would have been dismantled following Jean de Selys' raid. At the head of this network was Martial Van Schelle. Born in 1899, Van Schelle was a former high-level Belgian athlete (among other achievements, he represented Belgium at the 1936 Olympic Games in bobsleigh) who owned several sports stores in Brussels and a swimming pool cum ice rink on Rue de la Glacière. Léontine Fierens was the manager of the sports store on Rue de Loxum. Her boss and friend, Martial Van Schelle, was heavily involved in escape networks and very active within the 'Manipule' network located in the northern zone of France and along the Belgian border.

In a rare interview published by *La Libre Belgique* in 1983, Léontine Fierens looked back on the dark days of January 1943.[36] She confirmed that Martial Van Schelle was indeed arrested based on denunciation on 15 January 1943 – five days before the raid – and that all arrests within his network took place BEFORE Jean de Selys' attack. She herself was arrested on 15 January and released on 12 February, as the Germans were unable to prove her active role in the Resistance and probably judged her importance to be minor. Martial Van Schelle was not so lucky and was executed without trial on 15 March 1943.

In the same interview, Léontine Fierens also shared valuable information that could explain how the fantasy of the infiltrated agent originated. One of the Germans killed on 20 January 1943, whose name she only remembered phonetically as 'a certain Baderwieder', was a corrupt German who 'helped' Martial Van Schelle, against compensation (parties, perhaps even money), by providing administrative documents (driver's licenses, passports etc.) useful for escape networks. She also noted that Van Schelle's 'gestures' in favour of the occupier were vehemently reproved by those who were unaware of his true motives. Thanks to research in German archives, the 'Baderwieder' remembered phonetically by the Resistance is undoubtedly the *Kriminaloberassistent* Heinrich Beiderwieden, who was mentioned earlier. The supposed infiltrated agent of British Intelligence would thus be nothing more than a corrupt German who took bribes in return for favours to improve his living conditions. It is a long way from James Bond.

The ultimate proof of Beiderwieden's very low influence on the affairs of the Sipo-SD in Brussels and his knowledge of the information circulating there, is that he was unable to warn his 'benefactor' Van Schelle of the imminence of his arrest and the dismantling of his network, which has now been proven to have no connection with Jean Selys Longchamps' raid.

Finally, one can also imagine, and this is a hypothesis many have quickly suggested after the raid, that the Germans themselves concocted this dark tale of an infiltrated agent killed by their own allies and whose death had enabled the dismantling of a resistance network.[37] It is a clever strategy to discredit the raid and an attempt, as best as is possible, to save face.

In any case, since the archives of the Intelligence Service will not be declassified for 100 years, fans of fake news will still be able to deny all evidence until 2043. Let us hope, however, that this book helps to silence most of them!

Chapter 14

'The Special One'

(21 January–15 August 1943)

The day after the raid, Thursday, 21 January 1943, Jean de Selys, having been released on bail by the local police, slipped into the cockpit of his faithful Typhoon, registered PR-M. Flight Officer Peter 'Nanki' Nankivell, who had also been involved in the previous day's incident and was still under police supervision, served as his No. 2.[1] Their patrol flight took off at 8:25am, after what had been a very short night, yet the two pilots were sharp and spotted a swarm of about fifteen Focke-Wulf 190s. 'Nanki' managed to shoot one down, its crash in the English Channel being confirmed by Jean. The pilots reported that the Germans likely mistook their Typhoons for 190s so for once, the mistake had worked in their favour, and the squadron continued its successful streak.

The previous day's exploits earned the squadron a cascade of congratulatory messages,[2] including one from Air Marshal Leigh-Mallory ('My heartiest congratulations on the magnificent show yesterday. Well done. Keep it up.'), followed by one from the commander of 11 Group, Hugh Saunders ('Please congratulate all concerned on their very fine show today'). The British press also began to laud the Typhoon's prowess, finally giving Fighter Command's black sheep its moment of glory. It was now time for the Typhoon to start writing its legend.

However, the gentle euphoria enveloping the 'White Rose' Squadron did not exempt Jean de Selys from his responsibilities. By attacking 453 Avenue Louise, he had knowingly acted without authorisation, even though his raid was applauded by his peers and its impact on the morale of Belgians was beyond imaginable, it remained true that Jean had crossed the line in no small manner.

Given the previous day's frenzy, it is likely there was no opportunity for a discussion with Beamont, but it is certain that the squadron leader of 609 finally found the time to reprimand de Selys. The relationship between the two men was not great, with Jean being a 'protégé' of the previous squadron leader, Paul Richey, certainly playing a part. After all, Jean was the godfather of Richey's daughter, and it was Richey who granted him the reins of B Flight. This situation could be seen as a classic territorial conflict in which a new leader wants to impose his mark and make a clean slate of the past. Thus, the relationship between the two men was not first rate, and Beamont acknowledged in a post-war letter (1992) that he saw de Selys as 'an arrogant aristocrat'.[3] Clearly, Jean's aristocratic origins weighed heavily in his relationship with some Belgian pilots in the squadron, and in the same letter, Beamont refers to an altercation between Remy Van Lierde and Jean de Selys, seemingly rooted in class struggle. Jean de Selys was at the crossroads of many antagonisms: a devout Catholic, a staunch royalist despite criticism of Leopold III, a product of Belgian nobility, well-connected in London's power circles, a former cavalryman in the 'rich kids' club' that was 1st Guides, and a latecomer to aviation. Not to mention the fact he was a Francophone from Brussels. Irritation was at its peak.

This uneasiness goes against the idealised image of a fighter squadron traditionally painted as a band of brothers united by unbreakable bonds of friendship. But was it surprising? Of course not: combat pilots are mostly alpha males, full of confidence and with overflowing egos. It is impossible to risk one's life every day in flying coffins without having a true fighter's mindset.

In his personal notes, Count Ivan du Monceau de Bergendal, who interacted with Jean for a few months at 609, probably sums up Jean's personality traits quite accurately, highlighting what endeared him to some and irritated others: 'Courageous, outgoing and enthusiastic. Difficult to live with. Bad temper: abrasive and sometimes unpleasant. Did excellent work. Hated the vulgarity of many Belgians. Great qualities slightly diminished by character flaws.'[4]

This detour into the tensions undermining the Belgians of 609 is far from anecdotal, as it partly explains why Jean was 'demoted' from flight lieutenant to flying officer in the aftermath of the 20 January raid. This loss of rank has always been interpreted as a punishment for disobedience and thus as a direct consequence of his daring move in Brussels. However, some documents in Jean de Selys' military file indicate that the idea of removing him from his flight commander role had been discussed for a few weeks already. On 24 December 1942, nearly a month before the raid, a memo from Group Captain Charles George Lott (11 Group) requested an evaluation of Jean de Selys.[5] Negative feedback from his instructors following his time at the Central Gunnery School (in October 1942) sparked this request. Lott believed that a pilot who showed little interest in learning and sharing the school's excellent training did not deserve the responsibilities of a flight lieutenant.

On 15 January 1943, Squadron Leader Beamont responded unambiguously to Lott's memo,[6] acknowledging Jean de Selys' 'above-average pilot skills', 'good offensive spirit, showing a constant desire to engage the enemy with successful offensive and defensive actions', but also noting his shortcomings in assuming flight commander responsibilities.

Beamont also mentioned Jean de Selys' 'lack of tact in his relations with other Belgian pilots' and his difficulty maintaining discipline and a good atmosphere in his Flight. Beamont concluded that Jean de Selys showed 'no interest in sharing his experience from the Air Gunnery, nor in other subjects, with his pilots… The only thing that interests him is flying.' A handwritten note in French on the memo indicates that Jean de Selys refused to provide a justification memo, as requested by Beamont. This suggests Jean was aware of the doubts about his capabilities as a flight commander but also refused to plead his case. Perhaps he realised that this role was not suited to him and that his deeply individualistic nature did not align with the job description of a flight commander, considering himself a hunter, not a teacher or mentor.

Five days before the 20 January raid, Jean de Selys Longchamps' fate as a flight lieutenant already seemed sealed, and he was aware of it. His decision to carry out his 'Special Rhubarb' over Brussels showed his determination to fulfil his mission, with no intention of keeping a low profile to maintain his. What a snub towards his superiors!

On 21 January, a final memo[7] from Beamont confirmed he had indeed spoken with Jean de Selys, who had 'agreed to acknowledge his incapacity to command the Flight… but wished to remain attached to the squadron.' Beamont, being fair, admitted that given Jean de Selys' 'exceptional pilot qualities', he wished to keep him in the squadron, hoping his transfer to A Flight would allow 609 to continue benefiting from his great potential.

In a letter dated 25 January,[8] signed by Group Captain Adnans (now replacing Lott), it was confirmed that Jean de Selys was relieved of his flight commander duties but remained with 609. All previously listed arguments were repeated, although the unauthorised raid is never mentioned.

His loss of rank was therefore not related to the unauthorised raid, as has been believed for eighty years. This discovery helps to understand why the British and Belgian authorities would award him the Distinguished Flying Cross (DFC) and the Croix de Guerre shortly after, but more on that later. It is also worth noting that this demotion only affected the British side of Jean's military career: at the time of the raid, he was a captain in the Belgian military air force and retained his rank until the end of his life.

However, it seems plausible that the Brussels feat definitively deepened the relational rift between Beamont and de Selys. The Belgian's indiscipline was an extra straw in his long list of grievances about him. Thus, Jean indeed transitioned to A Flight, under the command of Joe Atkinson, but this only lasted for six short weeks before he was moved to another squadron. The atmosphere at 609 may have become suffocating for de Selys. A clear sign that Jean was only slightly affected by this regrettable episode is that he went on to mark some of his greatest combat achievements between 28 January and 10 March 1943, thus making it a point of honour to leave 609 with his head held high.

On Friday, 28 January, de Selys participated in a 'Rhubarb' operation alongside Flight Officer Baldwin. The two pilots took off at 8:45am and separated once they reached the Belgian coast, where Jean destroyed a locomotive carrying three trucks near Dixmude. He then targeted a lone locomotive between Ghent and Deinze. Back on the hunt, he spotted another locomotive leading a long convoy of thirty trucks in the suburbs of Ghent. Again, he destroyed the locomotive, and, engaged by six or seven Flak batteries, he made a low altitude pass over one of them, where his shells cut down a German officer observing the scene with his binoculars. Finally, he destroyed a fourth and final train between Hazebrouck and Saint-Omer. Never before had Jean de Selys destroyed four locomotives in a single operation.

That same 28 January saw two Belgian pilots from 350 Squadron follow in Jean de Selys' footsteps and fly over Brussels. They were Flight Lieutenant Plisnier and Pilot Officer Siroux. Piloting their Spitfire Mk VBs, they took off from Hornchurch at 11:05am and flew over the capital around noon. Plisnier photographed the Palace of Justice with his onboard camera and dropped a Belgian flag over the boulevards. After a flight of 1 hour and 50 minutes, the two aircraft landed at Manston where they likely shared their experience with Jean. Back at Hornchurch, André Plisnier wrote in his logbook: 'This is the happiest day of my life, the pedestrians I see seem overjoyed and wave exuberantly.'

Jean went on leave in London from the 3 to 12 February, and although it cannot be stated with certainty, it is plausible that it was during this stay in the capital that the departure from 609 began to take shape. In London, Jean talked with his contacts at the Belgian embassy at 107 Eaton Square, particularly with the military and air attaché, Louis Wouters, whom he had befriended since his arrival in England. Wouters' former deputy, the very effective Léo De Soomer, had resumed an operational role and was now heading No. 3 Squadron, which was about to start its conversion to Typhoons. The opportunity was certainly very tempting for de Selys to open a new chapter in a more serene context than the one that now surrounded him at 609. He likely did not hesitate for long to seize this new opportunity.

Back at Manston, Jean carried out another seventeen flights in February, including one that definitively entered him into the select circle of great Typhoon pilots. On 14 February, four victories were added to 609's tally. Two were credited to 'Cheval' Lallemant, one to the English pilot 'Roy' Payne, and the last to Jean, thus marking his first confirmed victory.

Everything started for de Selys and Payne at 11:45am with an 'Offensive Sweep' towards Calais and then towards Cap Gris-Nez. As they veered south above Calais,

> *Personal. Air Gunnery*
>
> **PERSONAL COMBAT REPORT.**
>
> P/O de Selys (Belgian) 609 Sqdn.—Manston
>
> A. 14.2.43.
> B. 609 (W.R.) Sqdn.
> C. Typhoon 1 b.
> D. 1200 hours.
> E. 1 mile off Calais
>
> F. 10/10 clouds at 1000 feet.
> G. Typhoon Cat.B.
> H. Nil
> J. 1 F.W.190 destroyed
> K. Nil
>
> I was Red one. Took off at 1145 in order to provide fighter protection to some M.T.B. in Mid-Channel. Another section being with M.T.B. and E/A having been reported in the vicinity I decided make a wide sweep coming from the West towards Calais then to come down the French coast to Gris Nez and rejoin the MT.B.s. As we were nearing Calais and turning South we were attacked by 3 F.W.190s flying North, parallel to the French coast. E/A opened fire on me and I warned my No.2 who was in line astern with me at this moment. E/A missed me as well as my No.2 and I turned steeply to the right. I saw E/A No. 3 continuing North, E/A No.2 going inland over Calais and E/A No. 1 completing a wide turn. This gave me the chance to deliver a head on attack, opening fire at 8 or 700 yards I gave a long burst until he caught fire before flashing over me. I turned and saw it well on fire making a gentle diving turn to the right. At about 300 feet from the water it stalled went in a spin and straight into the water about 800 to 1000 yards off Calais.
>
> My aircraft was slightly damaged by the fire of this E/A during the head on attack.

Combat report of 14 February detailing the aerial battle fought by de Selys, where he achieved his first confirmed victory over an Fw.190.

they were attacked by three Fw.190s flying north. The Germans missed their targets, and Jean de Selys informed Payne that he would make a tight turn to chase the 'Huns'. He noticed one enemy plane escaping north, another returning to the continent towards Calais, and the third completing a long turn to rechallenge the Typhoons. Jean decided to focus on him and engaged in a head-to-head duel that both protagonists were determined to win. What followed was more akin to a medieval joust where two knights challenge each other. Jean fired his cannons with barely 650 yards separating the two fighters closing at full speed. The Luftwaffe pilot unleashed the full power of his BMW engine, and Jean had done the same with all the horsepower of his Napier. When the two planes crossed paths, Jean looked up to see the enemy fighter catch fire. He turned to see the 190 plummeting less than 100 yards above the sea, a fraction of a second before it crashed into the Channel a few miles from Calais.[9] The duel was fierce, and Jean's plane bore the scars: his propeller cone and wings were hit by German shells. It had been a narrow escape.

Needless to say, the day ended at Doone House with a kind of party that 609 was known for. Jean had learned his lesson this time, however, and did not attract the local police's ire. Yet his feats did not go unnoticed, and on 23 February 1943, he was mentioned in the Belgian Army's Orders of the Day and awarded the Croix de Guerre 1940 with the following citation:

> Cavalry officer, driven by high patriotism. Joined Great Britain to continue the fight as soon as Belgium was overwhelmed by the invader in May 1940. Returned to France to resume the battle, he managed in December 1940 to rejoin England where he enlisted in the RAF/VR (Belgian Section). Becoming a fighter pilot and entering into operation in September 1941, he damages a Focke-Wulf 190 on 16 December 1942, and shoots down another on 14th February 1943.

Between 1 and 10 March, Jean de Selys carried out his last flights for 609, flying twenty times in ten days, with several of those last flights being particularly noteworthy.

For instance, on 2 March, a 'Rhubarb' operation sent him almost to Brussels, where low visibility on the ground forced him to turn back. However, his keen eye spotted a locomotive near Courtrai and in two passes, the matter was settled, and another locomotive, his ninth, was added to his tally.

On 3 March, he was credited with a probable victory over a Fw.190 during a patrol he conducts with Pilot Officer Leslie. Two days later, on 5 March, the English press mentioned his raid of 20 January. The *Daily Mail* article that recounted his feat was carefully cut out and pasted into his logbook. Jean took the opportunity to write down the death and injury toll resulting from his attack, not without humour: '5 destroyed – 30 damaged.' He later corrected the thirty to thirty-two. Underground newspapers had begun to cover the event, and his contacts in London might have shared with him what was reported by *Bec et Ongles*, *L'insoumis*, or *La Libre Belgique*. These last two

A rare image of one of Jean de Selys' attacks filmed by his gun camera. The locomotive he destroyed on 2 March 1943 can be seen here.

The *Daily Mail* article recounting his solo raid on the Gestapo headquarters, which Jean pasted into his logbook. In the entry corresponding to his 'Special Rhubarb', he humorously noted the 'damages' inflicted on the Sipo-SD personnel, using terminology typically reserved for aerial victories.

titles even pointed out as early as mid-February that the aircraft was piloted by a Belgian aviator.

On 10 March, Jean took off for the last time at the controls of a 609 Typhoon (PR-I). When he had joined the squadron at the end of September 1941, his flight log totalled 181 hours and 30 minutes, but it now showed 684 hours and 30 minutes.

On 12 March, a note from Frank 'Ziegly' Ziegler formalised in 609's Operations Record Book[10] the posting of Jean de Selys to 3 (Fighter) Squadron. Ziegler's word, delivered with the biting laconism that the English handle so well, captured the mood surrounding Jean's transfer: 'His departure is regretted by the English members of the Squadron, if not so much the Belgians.' Clearly, his divisive personality did not win unanimous approval amongst his Belgian 'brothers in arms', and it was certainly time for a change of air.

The emblem of 3 (F) Squadron, the last squadron in which Jean flew.

On Sunday, 14 March, Jean joined the base at Hunsdon (Essex), 22 miles north of London, where he met his new teammates from the No. 3 (F) Squadron. Unlike 609, which started as an auxiliary squadron that revealed its potential throughout the conflict, 3 Squadron was one of the founding units of the Royal Flying Corps in 1912,[11] the year Jean was born. Its emblem featured a basilisk perched on a grey monolith. The basilisk is a legendary creature, part rooster, part serpent, that has the powers of poisoning and petrification. No. 3 Squadron's motto, '*Tertius primus erit*' (the third shall be the first), refers to the fact that the squadron was the very first to be equipped with 'heavier than air' aircraft, while its sister units still operated with airships. The role of 3 Squadron evolved during the First World War from photographic reconnaissance (with the first aerial victory achieved on 5 February 1915 when an Aviatik was shot down with a rifle at 50 feet), bombing, and finally, fighter operations when the squadron received the legendary Sopwith Camel in September 1917. Captain D.J. Bell ended the war with twenty victories, seventeen of which were with 3 Squadron. By the end of the First World War, the squadron claimed fifty-nine victories, and would shine again in May 1940 when its Hurricanes were deployed in France in support of the British Expeditionary Force (BEF). In just twelve days, the squadron achieved sixty-two victories, but lost eighteen aircraft and seven pilots in the process. It was then assigned to defend the naval base of Scapa Flow, the main anchorage port of the Royal Navy, in Scotland, until April 1941. The unit was then redirected to the base of Stapleford Tawney (Essex) where it received Hurricanes equipped with four 20mm cannons, allowing it to carry out 'Rhubarb' operations in northern France and Belgium. The squadron was later assigned to night fighter operations. In February 1943, it began its conversion to Typhoons, and the timing of Jean's arrival was particularly opportune to bolster the squadron with a pilot who had mastered this demanding aircraft to perfection.

However, even for the experienced Jean de Selys, the weeks ahead did not come under the 'business as usual' routine, because the role allotted to 3 Squadron's Typhoons was very different from that of 609. Indeed, their Typhoons would be used in fighter-bomber operations. Between September 1942 and May 1943, five squadrons (chronologically: 181 Squadron, 182 Squadron, 183 Squadron, 3 Squadron and 175 Squadron) were equipped with 'Bombphoons'. Externally, when not carrying bombs, the 'Bombphoons' were identical to traditional Typhoons, with only a streamlined bomb rack under each wing allowing the discerning eye to differentiate them. Other less visible differences existed, however: the brakes were more powerful to adapt to the increased weight of the aircraft in bomber configuration; a shell ejection system had been added so that the shells from fired rounds did not hit the bombs still attached to the plane; and the rear wheel was equipped with reinforced rubber to improve the aircraft's control when fully loaded. Later, armour (4mm steel protection plates covering the side of the aircraft from the firewall to the rear of the cockpit) would also be added, but this modification was not yet present on the Typhoons piloted by de Selys.

Jean would thus have to familiarise himself with the different techniques for dropping the two bombs the aircraft could carry, either two 500-pound or two 250-pound. Carrying two 1,000-pound bombs was also possible but would not be used in operation by Jean.

Initially, the bombing tactic involved dropping bombs at low altitude, but this approach quickly proved dangerous for two reasons: Flak fire and the shrapnel from exploding bombs (either from the aircraft that dropped them or from the one preceding it), even though the detonators could be set in advance to explode only a few seconds after impact. Hence, dive-bombing was mainly preferred by 'Bombphoon' pilots, who began their dive at a 60°/70° angle from an altitude of between 11,800 and 9,800 feet and dropped their bombs around 5,900 to 3,900 feet above the target.

The technique differed when attacking ships, as bombs were dropped in low-level flight at very high speed so that they bounced on the water's surface and hit the ship's hull. Whichever technique was used, these were extraordinarily perilous manoeuvres that would cost many pilots their lives. (It should be noted that all Typhoons produced from 1943 onwards would be equipped to carry bombs.)

Typhoon of 3 (F) Squadron, on which Jean flew four times. The bomb launcher under the closest cannon to the cockpit can be seen.

Upon arriving at the No. 3 (F) Squadron, Jean found a mix of nationalities similar to the one he had become accustomed to at 609. There were, of course, many British, but also representatives from the dominions (Australia, Canada, New Zealand) and even some Americans. However, there was a significant difference regarding the number of Belgians in the squadron: including Jean, there were indeed only two! The other pilot from the flat country was, of course, Léo De Soomer, the squadron leader, already mentioned earlier.

Born on 30 January 1909, Léo De Soomer, was three years older than Jean de Selys and had joined 2nd Aeronautical Regiment in the early 1930s. Promoted to lieutenant in 1932, De Soomer proved to be not only a good pilot but also a hard worker. Qualified as a staff officer, in 1939 he joined the Air Defence Territory (DAT) staff, where he served during the eighteen-day campaign. Captured by the Germans on 28 May, he managed to escape on 29 May and made his way to England via Dunkirk. He soon became the assistant to the air attaché of the Belgian embassy, Lieutenant Colonel Wouters, and thanks to his perfect command of English (he had found refuge in England with his parents during the First World War), he deployed tremendous efficiency and ingenuity to enable twenty-nine Belgian pilots to participate in the Battle of Britain. Thanks to his efforts, no fewer than 100 candidates for pilots, navigators, or gunners began their training in RAF schools by the end of June 1940. Léo De Soomer was also one of the key figures in creating the pilot training school in Odiham, where Jean took his first steps as an aviator. Léo De Soomer's true nature, however, was to be a pilot, and he soon expressed the desire to be freed from a staff role and to fly again in an operational unit. With the experience gained before the war in the Aéronautique Militaire Belge, he became a pilot officer on 3 March 1941, and, after a brief stint in an OTU, was assigned to 32 Squadron, a fighter unit in Wales. There, he ensured the protection of maritime convoys crossing south of Ireland, but the operations were not very thrilling: many alerts, few results. He then joined the base at Manston and then West Malling, where he was involved in the night defence of London. In June 1942, he was transferred to 174 Squadron, where he took command of a flight. He was involved in day and night attacks on ships, airfields, and factories, and on 19 August 1942, he participated in the Dieppe Raid, earning him the Croix de Guerre. A few days later, on 22 August, Léo De Soomer was promoted to squadron leader and took the reins of 3 Squadron, succeeding Squadron Leader A.E. Berry, who had been killed in action.

The squadron leader of 3 (F) Squadron was an old acquaintance of Jean: Leo De Soomer.

De Soomer had known Jean since his arrival in London in December 1940 and had been a privileged witness to his journey in the RAF. He knew who he was dealing with and was familiar with his qualities and flaws. Undoubtedly, the arrival of a seasoned pilot who had managed to tame the Typhoon was a significant benefit for a squadron leader whose unit had just begun to discover this intimidating new aircraft.

Clearly, the Jean of March 1943 had little in common with the Jean of late September 1941. The latter tiptoed his way into 609, intimidated by the prospect of joining a squadron envied by the entire Royal Air Force and composed of seasoned pilots, some of which already had an impressive tally. In comparison, Jean had still looked like a fledgling apprentice in search of confidence and experience. Yet when Jean joined Léo De Soomer, he arrived with a whole new status. On 20 January, he had pulled off a spectacular feat the entire RAF talked about. His record boasted one Focke-Wulf 190 shot down and two others probable. He had nine locomotives on his list of achievements and was the very first to have successfully bailed out from a Typhoon. And, last but not least, he had logged 257 hours and 10 minutes of flight time at the controls of the Hawker beast.

Jean de Selys, nicknamed 'the Baron' by his new teammates, poses in his very elegant and distinctive RAF 1930 'prestige' flying suit.

However, it is worth noting that 3 Squadron had a few other experienced pilots, including Robert 'Bob' Inwood, who was awarded a DFC in December 1942 and had two victories, one probable, and one enemy aircraft damaged.

For Jean, this move was almost a rebirth and provided the opportunity to completely reposition himself within a squadron. It started with a nickname, 'the Baron', that everyone now used to address him with respect. Then, there was the bold choice to wear an immaculate white RAF 1930 'prestige' flying suit, which gave him a very elegant look. Ron Pottinger,[12] one of the young pilots in 3 Squadron who admired him, noted that he often carried a miniature camera in one of the trouser pockets of his white suit. Within the squadron, it was clear that he enjoyed the role of a free electron and more or less did as he pleased. De Soomer indeed gave him a lot of freedom, and his transfer from 609 to 3 Squadron turned out to be nothing like a banishment to a purgatory squadron as some have sometimes been tempted to describe it.

Jean is part of A Flight, which included the 'red', 'yellow' and 'white' sections, and he operated under the command of Flight Lieutenant Ronald 'Ron' Mackichan (born in 1915, 28 years old), sometimes also nicknamed 'Little Mac'. Jean de Selys began work

Relaxing moment for Jean de Selys with pilots from his new squadron.

on 17 March, the day of his first flight under his new colours. March, April, and early May were devoted to training flights, and Jean familiarised himself with 'low-level bombing' and 'dive bombing' techniques.

On 11 May 1943, a grand 'get together' marked by a lavish dinner was organised jointly by 3 Squadron and 85 Squadron. The two squadrons were neighbours at Hunsdon, and Jean's title of 'Baron' and his exploits of 20 January made him a noted guest.[13]

A few days later, on 14 May, the squadron was transferred to West Malling (Kent), an airfield located 46 miles southeast of London and about 40 miles from the coast. The same day also marked the very first operational sortie of 3 Squadron on Typhoons, involving eight aircraft. Jean did not participate in this but, piloting the Typhoon registered as QO-A, he was part of another formation of eight aircraft conducting an offensive operation on 17 May. Before take off, Jean's aircraft was equipped with two 500-pound bombs, one under each wing. The bomb-loading operation was delicate. An actual train of bombs composed of several carts and pulled by a tractor moved from one aircraft to another. The tractor, sometimes driven by a WAAF, arrived from behind the first aircraft to be armed, with the bombs placed on the last cart. A winch was used to lift the projectiles strapped by cables and the bombs were thus slowly raised and positioned in front of the anchoring points. Once the bomb was secured, the projectile's arming cable was attached to the rack so that when the bomb was dropped, the cable would make it fully operational.

His first bombing operation took him to the Coxyde airfield in Belgium, above which he dropped his two bombs. In the formation, Jean chaperoned a young 21-year-old Canadian pilot, Richard 'Ricky' Purdon.

The next day, Tuesday, 18 May, due to the alternation principle recommending that pilots participated in only one operation out of two, Jean was not involved in a raid on the Poix-de-Picardie (Somme) airfield that turned into a fiasco.[14] The bombing of the site was a success, but five out of eight aircraft did not return to base: one being shot down by Flak and four others destroyed by 190s. It was a severe blow to the squadron, which lost one of its most experienced pilots, 'Bob' Inwood, among others. The atmosphere at West Malling was very grim, and all the pilots were overwhelmed by this terrible twist of fate.

To chase away dark thoughts and doubts, they quickly needed to get back to work, but the 'Rhubarb' operation on 24 May was aborted due to bad weather. So, they had to wait until 27 May for another 'Rhubarb', again in the company of young Purdon, whom Jean seems to have become a mentor to, to get back into action and log his first successes for 3 Squadron.

The operation sent him over Belgium (Furnes, Deinze, Roeselare, Ursel), armed with two 250-pound bombs, allowing Jean to add two locomotives, two tugboats, and a truck to his list of hits. The English press echoed the Belgian's victorious sortie, and Jean stated, anonymously of course: 'Near Roeselare, I came upon a group of soldiers who abandoned their truck to hide under the trees. I strafed them with my cannons.' Jean's return to base was grandiose, and Ron Pottinger, a young English pilot who had arrived a few days earlier, described it in his memoirs:[15]

> Bob Cole was just landing in the 'Hurri' when there was a terrific roar, and the Baron literally hurtled down on the dispersal. He pulled up from about fifty feet and did about three vertical rolls until it seemed he must stall. He finished up with enough speed to rudder it into a steep turn and came whistling down at us again. This time, he was still doing vertical rolls when he disappeared into clouds at about three thousand feet. When he reappeared, he had wheels and flaps down and sideslipped it in to land. It was a fine show of flying. When he taxied in the ground crews crowded around him, helping him out, carrying his parachute, he was obviously their hero at that moment.

On 29 May, Jean again flew in a 'Ramrod' bombing operation, carrying two 500-pound bombs that he dropped over the Maupertus airfield near Cherbourg, facing intense Flak fire, but returning unscathed.

Jean poses with pilots of 3 (F) Squadron. Back row, from left: 'Lefty' Whitman and Hutchinson. Middle row: Jean de Selys, 'Blackie' Schwarz, Chas Tidy, Johnny Foster, Jack Collins and his son, Leo De Soomer, and 'Mac' McCook. Front row: Ray Crisford, 'Buck' Feldman, Ron Pottinger, and 'Kibbie' Reid.

On Monday, 31 May 1943, Jean de Selys celebrated his thirty-first birthday, and his greatest gift came in the form of an announcement: he would be awarded the Distinguished Flying Cross (DFC). The accompanying citation read:

> This officer is a pilot of exceptional ability and keenness. He shows a great offensive spirit and is eager to engage and destroy the enemy whenever possible. He has demonstrated his great courage and initiative in numerous attacks on rail transport and the Gestapo headquarters in Brussels. He has also destroyed at least one enemy aircraft and damaged another.

It was well-deserved and officially confirmed, this time very officially, that the attack on the Gestapo headquarters was not the taboo subject condemned vehemently by the British authorities, as some have claimed. For Jean, it was a magnificent reward that further solidified his status as a 'special one' within the No. 3 (F) Squadron. The official medal presentation ceremony would take place a few weeks later, in July.

On 2 June, another pilot, Bob Barckley, was reported missing. Apparently, his aircraft had hit an obstacle while flying at very low altitude, and his Typhoon made a belly-landing south of Dunkirk. No one knew if he had survived this forced landing.

Pilots of 3 (F) Squadron enjoying the sun between two flights. Jean, visibly very relaxed, is second from left.

Another relocation of 3 Squadron was scheduled for 11 June, this time to Manston. The pilots were dismayed: it would be their third airfield in less than three months! Manston's excellent location, a stone's throw from the coast, justified this new deployment. Now, 3 Squadron, with its extensive experience in night flights, would become one of the few Typhoon squadrons involved in 'night intruders' and 'low-level moonlight' bombing operations.

Fortunately, to mitigate the gloom caused by the announcement of the move to Manston, all the squadron's pilots were invited to a massive 'party' organised by Fighter Command at the Grosvenor Hotel on Park Lane in London on 9 June.[16] The purpose of the celebration justified the grand effort: Fighter Command was celebrating the thousandth enemy aircraft shot down, and all its pilots were invited to an event that promised to be spectacular. The RAF's suppliers – Napiers, Rolls-Royce, Hawker, Supermarine, etc. – had transformed into patrons to finance the fiesta.

Once at Manston, Jean multiplied training sessions aimed at practising ship attack techniques. The weather was very poor, and on two occasions, on 15 and 18 June, he had to drop his bombs into the Channel for failing to reach his target. On 18 June, a new pilot who was part of Jean's formation was reported missing - Bob Moore, an Australian - and the Belgian, along with Vic Smith, set out in a 'Air Sea Rescue' patrol. Unfortunately, in vain.

On Sunday, 20 June, Jean undertook his first 'anti-shipping' night operation, carrying two 250-pound bombs. He attacked two German fast boats 1 mile off the coast near Dunkirk. Not seeing the result of his bomb drops, he decided to destroy them with his 20mm cannons. He attacked the boats five times, seriously damaging one, and causing an explosion that sent black smoke rising into the sky. The two boats responded vigorously, and their fire hit the exhausts and engine cover of Jean's Typhoon. The port's Flak batteries also joined in the chase of the Typhoon. Jean's aircraft manoeuvred through a sky dotted with explosions and swept by searchlights. Hell itself. But it took more to stop the Belgian pilot who, unleashed, launched further assaults on the German E-boats, making three more passes over the Kriegsmarine sailors. The first boat was now motionless, and the second, with only one anti-aircraft cannon working, tried to drag itself toward the port. Jean conducted most of his attacks diving from an altitude of 3,280 feet and only pulled up at the water's edge.[17]

His daring attacks were mentioned in a citation in the Belgian army's order of the day on 24 June 1943:

> Courageous and intrepid aviator officer. On 20 January 1943, he carried out a perilous operation by attacking in broad daylight, in Belgian territory occupied by the enemy, the central headquarters of the German state police, causing a surge of enthusiasm and patriotic emotion among our oppressed compatriots.

This citation earned him the award of a Bronze Lion on the ribbon of the 1940 War Cross.

Four more bombing operations were added to Jean de Selys' logbook. The penultimate one was again marked by the disappearance of a wingman. On 27 June, his No. 2, Sergeant Ernest Ticklepenny (20 years old), hit the steel cable of one of the barrage balloons floating above Dover, to which ground control had inadvertently directed them as they returned from an operation over Dieppe. The night was very dark, and the cables were impossible to see.

On the 28th, Jean undertook an anti-shipping operation with Ricky Purdon, the young Canadian who had already been his No. 2 on numerous occasions, but it was a trouble-free flight. The next day, Tuesday, 29 June, Jean went on leave until 7 July, and would only learn upon his return that his young Canadian protégé, with whom he had flown the day before, had died in an operation the very day he went on leave. Purdon was last seen over the port of Dunkirk. His body would only be washed ashore and recovered by the Germans a month later. He was just 21 years old.

When he returned from leave, Jean also discovered a new Belgian pilot who had joined

Ricky Purdon was 21 years old when he disappeared on a mission off the port of Dunkirk. He had flown barely seven combat missions on Typhoons, four as Jean's wingman. Jean was on leave when Purdon took off for the last time on 29 June 1943.

Hugh Saunders, who led 11 Fighter Group, pins the prestigious DFC on Jean's chest.

Now proudly sporting the distinctive purple and white DFC ribbon under his pilot wings, Jean poses in front of a map, pointing to the location where he accomplished the feat that earned him all the honours: Brussels.

London in the rain, 21 July 1943. Another momentous day when Jean de Selys received the War Cross from Prime Minister and Defence Minister Hubert Pierlot.

3 Squadron: Jean de Callataÿ. Older than Jean (born in 1906), de Callataÿ had come from 350 Squadron. The Antwerp native was a veteran of Aéronautique Militaire Belge, who had distinguished himself during the eighteen-day campaign, securing two victories with his Fiat CR.42 biplane from 3rd fighter Squadron ('*Les Cocottes Blanches*', the white storks).

Group photograph of all the staff of 3 (F) Squadron. Jean is seated on the second row (sixth from left). Léo De Soomer is seated in the same row, four places further (arms crossed).

In July, Jean flew ten times in a Typhoon and participated in three operations, taking the opportunity to add three tugboats to his tally. During his last operation of the month, on 24 July, he damaged a locomotive near Torhout and performed a dive-bombing attack on four Focke-Wulf 190s parked at the Coxyde airfield. The result was uncertain.

For Jean, however, the two major moments of the month occur on 20 and 21 July. On Tuesday the 20th, it was at Manston where Jean finally received his DFC. Pilots from 3 Squadron and those from 609 were all assembled, standing to attention, to witness the official ceremony which honoured two pilots: Jean, of course, but also 'Mony' Van Lierde. The Belgians were in the spotlight. The AOC (Air Officer Commanding) of 11 Group, Hugh Saunders, pinned the coveted medal on their proud chests. That evening, the Belgian authorities organised a big party at the Savoy Hotel to celebrate the heroes.

The next day, Belgium's National Day, Jean was accompanied by Léo De Soomer to Wellington Barracks in central London, a stone's throw from Buckingham Palace, where he was decorated with the Croix de Guerre by the Prime Minister and Minister of Defence, Hubert Pierlot.

This improbable sequence in which, in just two days, he was honoured by both his host country and his beloved homeland, must have stirred a storm of emotions in Jean. The seriousness on his face attests to it. All the sacrifices, the long moments of doubt, the endless gloomy tunnels, the moments when the ground fell from under his feet because he was again at a dead end, the persistent fear that poisons everyday life, the vital decisions to be made on the fly at every crossroad of life… French writer Louis Ferdinand Céline beautifully wrote that sometimes 'one no longer has much music within oneself to make life dance'. Fortunately, Jean had never suffered too much from this state; his volcano never extinguished. His life could have been just a collection of shards and missed opportunities. It was not. He harboured no regrets now, for everything he had experienced had allowed him to reveal the man he was today. Although perhaps he had just one regret: what a pity that his family was not present at these celebrations! He, the distracted schoolboy, the turbulent teenager, the indolent young man, was now a war hero awarded some of the most distinguished military decorations. That was quite something, surely? For his happiness to be complete, it would have been necessary to see the proud and tender looks from his parents, of Monique, François, and Edé. That would be for later: one day, for sure, he would tell them, he would show them the photographs, and together they would finally share his joy.

In his memoirs,[18] Count Georges d'Oultremont (a member of the Comète network) recalls a legendary evening organised in honour of Jean's DFC at the home of Countess Anne de Bousies, sister of the late Rodolphe de Grunne. The house, located at 20

Pembroke Square (Kensington), had become a transit place for high society escapees and a refuge between operations. According to Georges d'Oultremont himself, the evening was so extravagant and noisy that a policeman was dispatched by the neighbours to end the night-time disturbance. Once informed of the reason for the celebration by Bertie de Ligne (Prince Albert de Ligne, who would become an RAF pilot), the policeman joined the 'big binge'!

In August, Jean flew seven more times until the day of his fatal accident: on the 2nd, 3rd, 5th, 8th, 12th, and 13th. Only two dates, the 2nd and the 13th, involved operations. The first involved eight aircraft targeting a German destroyer in the port of Dunkirk. Strong winds complicated the bombing, and the projectiles missed the target. The formation, led by De Soomer, was subjected to intense anti-aircraft fire. On 13 August, a 'Rhubarb' operation with Jean de Callataÿ was cut short because the two aircraft had to abort due to a cloud layer too high up.

On Sunday, 15 August 1943, Jean de Selys visited Lady Ruby Carson at her Cleve Court residence, in Acol, near Minster. Lady Carson was the widow of a prominent Irish politician (Sir Edward Henry Carson), and her house, which had regularly hosted Winston Churchill, had become a favoured refuge for pilots of all nationalities stationed at Manston. Jean de Salis (as she wrote in her journal)[19] was always welcome there, and his charming manners were much appreciated. Lady Carson's only son, Edward Ned Carson, a lieutenant in the army, had married Heather Sclater, and the latter now lived with her mother-in-law as Edward was currently deployed in the Middle East. Heather enjoyed Jean's company greatly. On this Sunday, 15 August, after having tea, the two of them decided to go to the cinema.

After the film, Heather, Jean, and another pilot, Pilot Officer Custance, returned together, and Lady Carson invited them all to join her for dinner. Louis Robyns de Schneidauer related in an article the story of the evening, as told by Lady Carson:

> Jean de Selys was so cheerful, so full of life, light-hearted. Having to execute a night hunting flight over Belgium, he took leave of Lady Carson and her daughter-in-law Heather, and turning around at the moment of departure, he shouted cheerfully: 'I'll shoot down a German plane tonight in your honour. In the morning, I'll call you and say: Lady Carson, I've shot down a Hun for you.' And Lady Carson replied, 'Be careful, don't do anything foolish.'

In her personal journal dated 15 August, Lady Carson summarised the evening with these words: 'It was a glorious night.'

Around 10:00pm, Jean took leave of his hosts and headed back to Manston, for he indeed had an operation scheduled for the night with a take off planned at 1:35am.

Chapter 15

Bad Moon Rising

(16 August 1943)

It is easy to understand why pilots have a special relationship with their dispersal: the life of a squadron beats to the rhythm of this place where operations are posted, and pilots constantly cross paths, some still busy preparing their next flight while others are already debriefing the one they have just completed. Every day, the walls of the dispersal echo with the exploits of some and the tragedies of others. It is often here that concern starts to rise when the clock starts ticking and the pilot who went on an operation fails to return, even though his fuel reserves should have been used up a while ago. For those who do not come back, the dispersal is the last place they saw on earth. The significance of such a place should earn it the utmost attention in terms of decoration and comfort. In wartime, however, everything is somewhat makeshift.

At Manston, the dispersal of 3 Squadron was a large wooden building located to the northwest of the base.[1] Its furniture was made up of mismatched chairs, some comfortable, others back-breaking. The heterogeneity of the ensemble suggested a Salvation Army shelter rather than a RAF fighter-bomber unit. A round cast iron stove with a chimney was the only source of heating, and, like in all squadrons, there was, of course, an old portable turntable next to which sat a large tea box filled with 78rpm records, where the tunes of jazzman Bob Crosby dominated. Was this the influence of the two American pilots – Seymour 'Buck' Feldman and George 'Lefty' Whitman – who had joined the squadron? Quite possibly. Given the late hour, when Jean entered the dispersal, he did not see many people around. The place was bathed in dim light, far from the hustle and bustle of the day. But still, there were four flights scheduled for that particular night,[2] four solitary 'Night Rhubarbs', in which each Typhoon would carry two 250-pound bombs. Jean crossed paths with 'Blackie' Schwarz, who would soon take off towards Abbeville and Amiens, leaving Manston at 11:45pm, while Flight Lieutenant Jack Collins, in charge of B Flight, took off at 1am to bomb an airfield near Laon. The last two pilots, both Belgians, Jean de Selys and Jean de Callataÿ, took off at 1:35 and 1:40am, respectively. The man from Antwerp flew towards Hazebrouck, where he would attack a train. Jean de Selys, meanwhile, headed towards Belgium, in the direction of Ghent. When Jean slipped into the cockpit of the Typhoon registered EJ950 QO-X, perhaps his did not recall that he was only performing this 'Night Rhubarb' by chance, as earlier in the day, he had flipped a coin with 'Lefty' Whitman to determine which of them would undertake the operation.[3]

Jean was insatiable when it came to flying. 'Cheval' Lallemant often repeated in his post-war interviews:[4] 'He would climb down from one aircraft to climb into another. He never had enough and, like in the cavalry, he would ride mount after mount.' A coin toss was the reason Jean took 'Lefty's' place and now found himself taxiing towards the grass runway marked by a long line of lit paraffin pots. Jean had guts, knowing better than anyone that the operations assigned to Typhoons were more dangerous than ever: since joining the squadron commanded by Léo De Soomer five months earlier, no less than seventeen pilots from 3 Squadron had died or gone missing. But Jean believed in his lucky star as he prepared to embark on what would be his very last operation. The night was clear, as the full moon pierced the darkness, and all conditions seemed ripe for a successful hunt.

'Lefty' Whitman, the American pilot with whom Jean played heads or tails for the right to lead the 'Rhubarb' mission that would prove fatal to him.

Within minutes, Jean reached his cruising altitude and speed. He crossed the English coast towards Belgium, the Channel stretching ahead, the night seemingly rendering it infinite. The moon sparkled brilliantly, revealing the sea's relief pulsating under the Typhoon's wings, continuously producing long plains and frothy peaks. It

The very last page of Jean de Selys' logbook.

was beautiful. Soon, using the radio became pointless, as its range did not exceed 12 miles, and the pilot found himself on his own.

Since his first night flights at Tern Hill, Jean had always shown great skill in this delicate exercise. It was not for everyone, especially when it came to the formidable and feared Hawker Typhoon. Over the flights, Jean had understood the survival rules of the nocturnal predator: always trust your instruments, think quickly, and, when necessary, react just as fast. The key was to manage to control your emotions and never panic. The challenge was all the less easy to overcome since 'Rhubarbs' were performed at very low altitude.

Over the various operations, a few adjustments had been made to the Typhoon to boost its efficiency in night flying: the illumination of the cockpit instruments had been dimmed to avoid blinding the pilot, and the gunsight had been considerably modified for more effective night aiming. Tracer bullets were, of course, forbidden to avoid becoming easy prey for anti-aircraft fire and searchlights. The latter were also dreaded as much as the Flak cannons: finding yourself caught in the beams of the searchlights that converged on your aircraft in packs was never a promising situation. The pilot was quickly blinded and knew his seconds were numbered if he could not quickly escape the luminous trap that made him highly vulnerable. If he performed abrupt evasive manoeuvres, which was often inevitable, his artificial horizon and gyro were disoriented for a few long seconds, making instrument flying impossible. It was not easy to stay in control.

All pilots knew that moonlight was ideal for 'Night Rhubarbs', because roads and railways were very visible, even at an altitude of over 3,200 feet. Better yet, the smoke from a locomotive could be seen from 4 to 5 miles away. A feast for the hunter. Jean looked forward to it. But the enemies knew this, too, and their vigilance was at its maximum during the nights when the moonlight spread over the territories they defended, casting a whiteness akin to that of the cold wax of a candle. Since the beginning of the war, everyone was on high alert on the evenings where the moon became a source of terrors from the sky.

Once the target was spotted, it was far from a walk in the park, as the night continued to bring its share of difficulties. When the pilot fired his cannons, the flashes accompanying the departure of the shells impacted his vision and caused temporary blackouts. The flash of light accompanying the explosion of bombs caused the same kind of effects on vision, especially if the timing of the detonation was very short. In these moments of agony for the pilot's pupils, the Flak could unveil its truly lethal prowess.

Jean reached the Belgian coast, but what happened next is unknown since de Selys was flying solo, and radio contact with him was only reestablished when he asked for permission to land at Manston.

The total duration of his operation recorded in the Operations Record Book of No. 3 Squadron – he took off at 1:35am and returns at 3:05am, making his flight 1 hour and 30 minutes – indicates that he had completed a full mission and did not return prematurely. The other three pilots in operations that night flew 55 minutes (de Callataÿ), 1 hour and 10 minutes (Schwarz), and 1 hour and 30 minutes (Collins): Jean de Selys' flight was therefore within a standard time range for a 'Rhubarb' over Belgium and northern France.

Therefore, one can deduce that he carried out his operation successfully without anyone knowing the exact outcome: did his hunt prove to be fruitless? Did he have the opportunity to drop his bombs on a target? Did he use his cannons? It is a mystery. He got rid of his bombs, that is for sure, as no pilot was allowed to land 'armed' for obvious safety reasons.

When he contacted the control tower to ask for permission to land, no mention was made of any particular problem, and he did not issue any 'mayday' nor any request for priority or emergency landing. This seems to indicate he did not notice any specific problem with his aircraft that could endanger his landing. Perhaps his Typhoon was damaged by enemy anti-aircraft fire, and he did not realise the extent of the damage? Did he minimise it? Possibly, but unlikely: Jean de Selys was an accomplished Typhoon pilot, and any anomaly in his aircraft's behaviour would have caught his attention.

The wreckage of the Typhoon EJ950 QO-X in which Jean de Selys lost his life.

All these elements are confirmed by the investigation report established by the British commission under No.W.1619, which detailed the accident as follows:[5]

> This officer had taken off from Manston aerodrome at 1:35am, on 16 August 1943, to carry out a patrol operation over Belgium. As soon as he completed this combat operation, he returned to his base. At 3:02am, he requested radio permission to land, which was granted by the Airfield Control at 3:04am; immediately followed by the pilot's acknowledgment. The weather was clear and there was a full moon at that time, with a light southwest wind. The pilot was very experienced in landing both day and night on Typhoon aircraft and generally made a long gradual approach before landing. His aircraft was seen by ground witnesses at a height of about 1,000 to 1,500 feet. Their attention was drawn by the engine noise, which seemed to indicate that he was diving at quite a rapid speed. A noise was then heard, assumed to be a slight explosion, as a certain part of the fuselage detached from the aircraft. The aircraft immediately went into a spin until it crashed on the runway where it immediately caught fire. The pilot was killed instantly.

Medical Officer MacKechnie, a Scottish doctor serving at Manston since August 1942, could do nothing to save Jean.

The 'certain part of the fuselage' that detached from the aircraft, mentioned in the report, was, of course, the tail of the Typhoon, as confirmed by Sergeant R.W. Cole of 3 Squadron:[6] 'The tail fell in a field behind him.' The inquiry commission's report was diligently requested from the British authorities by a member of Colonel Wouters' staff, who had explicitly required a 'more comprehensive report than those he usually received', which was clear evidence of his deep attachment to Jean de Selys. While the description of the accident is quite precise, the report is very reticent when it comes to determining the causes. The fact that the Typhoon's tail suddenly detached from the rest of the aircraft moments after Jean lowered his landing gear (just before the crash, the aircraft was seen in final approach at an altitude of 1,000 to 1,300 feet: at this precise moment, the landing gear was obviously already extended) supports a quite credible hypothesis. The deployment of the wheels indeed causes the aircraft a significant deceleration, accompanied by a serious jolt, and the conjunction of these two factors considerably strained the aircraft's rivets, especially those of the empennage. Was the tail of EJ950 hit by German anti-aircraft fire? Or did the tired tail rivets simply give way?

This hypothesis is even more credible as it hits a real Achilles' heel of the Hawker Typhoon.[7] As previously seen, among the many ailments suffered by the 'Tiffy', a

On this heavily damaged Typhoon, a few of the alloy plates (fish plates) encircling the tail to reinforce it and prevent detachment can be seen on the white band at the rear of the aircraft.

nasty tendency for the tail to detach from the rest of the aircraft was at the origin of fatal accidents observed as early as July and August 1942. To gauge the problem's magnitude, it should be noted that out of the first 142 Typhoons put into service, only seven were not victims of engine or structural problems. That the aircraft had a rough start has been repeated over and over. Many more incidents would have to be recorded before the issue was finally addressed at the end of 1942, and solutions to the problem of 'tail failures' were sought. Nowadays, entire fleets of the same aircraft are grounded for many months when they encounter issues far less serious than those of the Typhoon and are only allowed to fly again once a validated and revalidated solution has been found. War, of course, imposes a completely different agenda and does not allow entire squadrons to be immobilised before finding a solution. You just have to deal with the situation.

In practice, after some fumbling and a series of modifications, 'MoD. No. TYPHOON/286' was introduced, and a retrofit pack was provided to all units equipped with Typhoons starting in early 1943. This allowed them to reinforce the rear monocoque of the aircraft by fitting twenty alloy reinforcing plates (known as 'fish plates' – Hawker called them 'external butt straps') at the precise spot where the empennage could be dismantled to facilitate the aircraft's transport. The idea was very basic and involved encircling the rear of the fuselage with riveted plates that formed a kind of ring. The interior was also reinforced at several points. This makeshift fix was more of a stopgap than a real solution, and accidents would continue to occur, although less frequently, but this time the breaking point of the fuselage simply shifted on the aircraft's cell.

A proper solution was found from mid to late 1943 (MoD. No. TYPHOON/353), when significant adjustments were made to the aircraft's weight distribution and the elevator's mass balance weight was modified. These changes significantly decreased the resonances on the aircraft, but unfortunately, this long-awaited 'update' was generalised only a few months after the death of Jean de Selys Longchamps.

Jean de Selys' aircraft, the Typhoon EJ950 QO-X, had been built by Hawker at the Langley factory (Parlaunt Park), located west of London, and was part of a batch of 400 aircraft delivered between February and July 1943.[8] The aircraft was therefore quite new and indeed only appears in the ORB of 3 Squadron for the first time on 22 June in the hands of Flight Sergeant M.C. Cook who participated in a 'Fighter Sweep'. From its first combat flight until the day of the fatal crash, the EJ950 was involved in a total of fourteen war operations and three 'scrambles'. Before Jean de Selys first flew the aircraft on 16 August, it had been piloted by nine different pilots. Flight Sergeant Crisford piloted it most often (four times), destroying a lock on the Ypres canal on 11 July while at its controls. On 24 July, the aircraft's tally was enriched by Flight

A Typhoon from 609 Squadron in a poor state, metaphorically summarising the very chaotic operational life of the Typhoon (50% of the total aircraft produced were lost, and two-thirds of these losses were not due to German fighters or anti-aircraft fire).

Officer Foster, who destroyed four barges and damaged a locomotive with the help of his No. 2. Squadron Leader Léo De Soomer also carried out a bombing operation on Coxyde with EJ950 on 30 July. No damage suffered by this aircraft, even minor, is reported in the pages of the ORB.[9] Jean de Selys, therefore, took off on 16 August at the controls of an almost new Typhoon which displayed a relatively low number of hours of flight in war operations and which had never been damaged. This is all reassuring – the EJ950 was not at the end of its operational life – but unfortunately does not erase the Typhoon's intrinsic defects, and one can therefore propose that his landing accident was most likely due to an unfortunate combination of factors: impacts from anti-aircraft fire on the empennage exacerbating the structural weakness of an aircraft that would, moreover, end the war with a rather damning record.

From 1 November 1941 to 8 May 1945, 1,613 Typhoons were lost by the Royal Air Force; more than 50% of the total aircraft produced. The first and last loss bitterly summarise the life of the aircraft and its many vices: in 1941, the aircraft crashed following the pilot's asphyxiation caused by carbon monoxide that invaded the cockpit, while in 1945, it was yet another engine failure that brought down the aircraft. Only sixty-one Typhoons were shot down in aerial combat. While Flak was the aircraft's number one enemy (394 losses), other losses were mainly due to technical and structural problems. Between twenty-four and twenty-eight aircraft were thus

Ron Pottinger (24 years old) was one of Jean de Selys' fervent admirers. He left some beautiful passages about him in his notebooks.

lost due to the aircraft's structural weaknesses and its elusive empennage, causing the death of twenty-four pilots.

It is a strange paradox: the Hawker Typhoon, the aircraft on which Jean de Selys Longchamps would accomplish his most famous exploits, demonstrate extraordinary audacity, and show his exceptional piloting skills, was also the aircraft that would kill him. After engaging in swirling dogfights with Messerschmitt 109s and Focke-Wulf 190s, braving the furious fire of anti-aircraft batteries, attacking locomotives and tugs at treetop level, escaping friendly fire from British anti-aircraft guns and other RAF aircraft, embarking on an unprecedented slalom over the streets of Brussels, it was his own aircraft, perhaps damaged by Flak, that would ultimately be his undoing.

The Operations Record Book of 3 Squadron reports the accident with much emotion in its entry for 16 August:[10]

> The night finished in tragedy as F/O de Selys DFC crashed near the dispersal hut and burst into flames. The squadron suffered one of its greatest losses in losing F/O de Selys who was undoubtedly one of the finest and most highly skilled pilots of his day. He had an outstanding personality, great charm, and by his initiative and great daring set an example to others that was of incalculable value to the squadron. His death was deeply mourned by every member of the squadron as a personal loss.

The young Ron Pottinger, 24 years old, who had joined 3 Squadron at the end of May and had watched Jean with much admiration, noted in his personal diary:[11] 'Sorry to see him go, he was easily the best pilot on the squadron.' Ron would be designated to carry Jean's coffin on the day of his funeral. The news of the tragic accident spread very quickly. Lady Carson, who had hosted Jean the previous evening, received the information shortly after breakfast, after Pilot Officer Custance informed her of Jean's death over the telephone. In her diary, Lady Carson mourned 'such a charming person' and wondered in her journal about the appropriateness of hosting these young pilots when such tragic events could happen.

Later that day, a telegram informed the Belgian embassy of Jean's tragic demise. His funeral was organised three days later, on Thursday, 19 August. Jean had apparently expressed the wish to be buried in the cemetery of Minster-in-Thanet, located a stone's throw from the Manston aerodrome and Lady Carson's house.

The religious service was held in the small chapel at the Manston base. Jean's coffin was covered with both an English and a Belgian flag, while two large wreaths were placed on it, as well as the aviator's officer cap. All pilots of No. 3 (F) Squadron were present, as well as numerous representatives from the RAF, the military aviation,

The religious service held in the small chapel of the Manston base.

The funeral procession walks from the Manston base chapel, where a mass has just been celebrated, to Minster cemetery. The priest and the squadron padre lead the way, followed by Jean's coffin carried by his pilot comrades from 3 (F) Squadron.

The arrival of Jean de Selys' body at its final resting place, carried by his comrades (Pottinger is first on the left, Reid on the right). On the far left is Colonel Wouters. Léo De Soomer follows just behind the coffin.

the Belgian government, and the embassy from London. A few relatives were also present, including Charley de Hepcée who had married Jean's cousin, Micheline de Selys (Charley de Hepcée was a resistance hero who would be shot by the Germans in France in June 1944). After the very moving ceremony was over, as evidenced by the sombre faces of the attendants, Jean's coffin was carried to its final resting place by eight pilots from his squadron, including Pottinger, Reid, and Wingate.

In his memoirs, Ron Pottinger reports that the coffin was extremely heavy, suspecting it was because it was lined with lead in anticipation of his repatriation to Belgium once the conflict had ended,[12] which ultimately never happened. The procession walked to the nearby cemetery, led by the priest who had conducted the service and the squadron's padre. The eight bearers were flanked on their left and right by the other pilots of 3 Squadron, and the slow funeral procession was followed by those attending the ceremony. Along the route, rows of soldiers stood at attention. After the procession's arrival at the cemetery, General Delvoie, the same man who had helped Jean reach Gibraltar for the second time in November 1940, delivered a eulogy that accurately and precisely described his personality and journey.

> Gentlemen, on behalf of the Belgian government and the Minister of National Defence, I come to pay a final tribute to Captain Aviator Baron Jean Michel Paul Marie Ghislain de SELYS-LONGCHAMPS, D.F.C. A cavalry officer serving in 1st Guides cavalry regiment, he distinguished himself in peacetime with his drive and initiative, during cavalry corps manoeuvres as well as in equestrian events, where he was often among the most brilliant competitors. He followed his regiment during the Belgian campaign until the dark moments of defeat when, listening only to the voice of his conscience clearly dictating his duty, he escaped through Dunkirk to place himself under the orders of the Belgian command in France. A few days later, the fight ceased on French territory, but de SELYS LONGCHAMPS understood that the war was not over. He unhesitatingly refused the order given to him to surrender to the enemy since it was still possible for him to fight. Probably, the honour traditions of his regiment were present in his memory: driven by sincere patriotism, he continued the fight and, disregarding the thought of dangers he would face, requested his transfer to the Military Aeronautics.
>
> In January 1941, he joined the Royal Air Force, and a few months later, he was in operation as a fighter pilot. Very quickly, he earned the esteem of his leaders and comrades. On 16 December 1942, he damaged an enemy aircraft, and the following 14 February, he shot down another. de SELYS-LONGCHAMPS became the hero of a series of striking actions, which, unfortunately, can only be

General Delvoie delivered the eulogy before the burial. His text was very inspired and accurately recounted Jean's life and exploits.

recounted later, but which are evidenced by magnificent citations. Last 31 May, His Majesty King George VI awarded him the Distinguished Flying Cross, thus paying tribute to his great courage and audacity. On 16 August, returning from a night operation over the continent, his aircraft crashed to the ground as he prepared to land on the aerodrome from which he had taken off, full of enthusiasm, a few hours earlier.

My thoughts go to the family he leaves in Belgium, and to those of his relatives who are in England, to whom I ask to accept here the sincerest condolences of the Belgian government and the Minister of National Defence. My dear de SELYS-LONGCHAMPS, you have given us an example of courage and patriotism that no one will forget. I say goodbye and thank you.

Eleven British soldiers rendered the final honours to the Belgian pilot.

The attendees then took turns to pay their last respects to the pilot. According to Ron Pottinger,[13] Léo De Soomer seemed the most affected. The sound of trumpets tore through the atmosphere to spread a respectful last burst of military melody. Eleven soldiers then fired their guns towards the sky, where Jean de Selys had lived so many adventures and thrills during the 891 days separating his very first flight from his last. All this had passed so quickly. Too quickly. His grave was located at the end of an alley, with a hedge on the right when facing it. On the left, there was no grave yet. A white wooden cross was placed there, reading: 'CAPTAIN BARON DE SELYS LONGCHAMPS DFC, R.A.F. (VR), BELGIUM, 16.8.43', above a small circle representing a Belgian flag. Two weeks later, the body of an 18-year-old woman, Joan McDonald, a member of the WAAF who had died on 1 September 1943, was buried to his left. She was the only woman among the eighty-five military personnel buried in Minster (seventy-one were soldiers from the First World War, fourteen from the Second). A permanent cross would be placed well after the war at location 3002A, this time in English: 'FLIGHT LIEUTENANT BARON J.M.P.M.G. DE SELYS LONGCHAMPS DFC, PILOT, ROYAL AIR FORCE, 16TH AUGUST 1943, AGE 31'. Jean had thus regained the rank of flight lieutenant that he had lost when he left 609. Above the cross is the official Eagle of the Royal Air Force and its motto,

The first wooden cross standing on Jean de Selys' grave.

The permanent gravestone was put in place well after the war. His rank of flight lieutenant, removed in January 1943, was now listed.

'*Per ardua ad astra*' (Through adversity to the stars), which summarises with great intensity the life trajectory of Baron Jean de Selys Longchamps.

On 27 August, Hubert Pierlot informed all concerned authorities that he had decided to cite to the order of the day of the army Captain Aviator J.M.P.M.G. de Selys Longchamps DFC for the following reasons:

> Fighter pilot driven by remarkable courage and determination. Showed extreme tenacity during a recent night combat against armed boats by returning eight times to the attack despite intense enemy fire and searchlights. Killed on return from an operation, during the night of 15 to 16 August 1943.

The citation was drafted by Flight Lieutenant Léon Terlinden, submitted to the Minister of Defence on 17 August, and published on 9 September 1943.

The news of Jean's death only arrived in Belgium at the very beginning of September. On 2 September, a telegram requested the Red Cross contact Jean's uncle, Edgard de Selys Longchamps, residing at the Château d'Halloy-Ciney, to ask him to inform Jean's parents of his demise. Edgard de Selys was probably identified in his capacity

'Buck' Feldman poses next to the grave of his fallen comrade. Feldman was very attached to Jean, whom he knew at 3 (F) Squadron. He shot down more than ten V-1 flying bombs. Just after the war, 'Buck' joined the Israeli Air Force to fight and achieve a victory flying a Spitfire.

as a Red Cross delegate in Ciney. Following this painful announcement, a mass was celebrated at 11am on Wednesday, 29 September 1943, in the Saint-Joseph Church, located at Square Frère-Orban in Brussels.

In an article published after the war,[14] Louis Robyns de Schneidauer related that a requiem mass might have been celebrated in the crypt of Westminster Abbey. A Belgian delegation, including Minister Gutt and Baron de Cartier, Belgium's ambassador to London, would have attended.

Finally, it seems that a radio message was broadcast on BBC radio in September 1943, probably as part of the programme 'The Belgians Speak to You from London'. The text, found in family archives, was undoubtedly spoken by an aviator since the message is titled 'A Belgian Aviator Speaks to You…' and gives a brief account of Jean's life. The text is signed 'T' and could indicate it was also written by Léon Terlinden. An excerpt confirms it was, indeed, written by someone who clearly understood Jean's personality: 'Jean de Selys brought to his aviator profession the most striking qualities of the cavalry spirit: thoughtful courage, initiative, and intrepidity. He was a superb fighter, characterised by his individualist temperament.' It is difficult to summarise the personality of Baron Jean de Selys Longchamps with so few words as accurately as this.

In closing, it is worth noting that Jean's comrades-in-arms continued to visit him at the Minster cemetery, including the American pilot Seymour 'Buck' Feldman, who was also part of 3 Squadron and was very attached to Jean. 'Buck' also corresponded for a long time with Jean's sister, Monique.

Chapter 16

The Remains of the Day

(From 1946 to Today)

The memory left by Baron Jean de Selys Longchamps would fortunately not fade over time, and his legacy would be honoured in various ways between 1946 and today.

As we have seen earlier, during his lifetime, Jean received the following distinctions for his actions and bravery:

War Cross 1940 with palm (23 February 1942)
Distinguished Flying Cross (DFC) (31 May 1943)
Bronze Lion on the War Cross 1940 (12 June 1943)

Posthumously, other distinctions were also awarded to him:

An additional palm on the War Cross (9 September 1943)
Knight of the Order of Leopold with palm (16 February 1946)
An additional palm on the War Cross (16 February 1946)
1940–1945 Commemorative Medal with two crossed swords (2 May 1946)
1940–1945 Volunteer Medal (18 March 1947)

On Monday, 20 January 1947, exactly four years after his raid on the Sipo-SD headquarters, a grand ceremony was organised in front of 453 Avenue Louise, where a bronze commemorative plaque was affixed to the right of the building's entrance door, bearing the inscription:

IN BROAD DAYLIGHT ON JANUARY 20, 1943 THIS BUILDING, A GESTAPO DEN DURING THE 1940–1945 WAR, WAS STRUCK BY THE AVENGING FIRE FROM THE GUNS OF THE AIRPLANE OF CAPTAIN BARON JEAN-MICHEL DE SELYS LONGCHAMPS, FROM THE 1ST REGIMENT OF GUIDES FLYING OFFICER OF THE R.A.F.

Overall view of the impressive ceremony held on 20 January 1947, for the inauguration of the commemorative plaque placed at the entrance of the former Sipo-SD headquarters.

The RAF wings were placed above the text, and those of the Royal Aero Club of Belgium, which initiated the celebration, just below. The building was beautifully decorated in British and Belgian colours. Several detachments of the Belgian Air Force, created a few months earlier in October 1946, were present in full dress.

The array of dignitaries was impressive. Among others present were the British Ambassador Sir Knatchbull Hugessen, the Mayor of Brussels Van de Meulebroeck, and, among a strong contingent of officers, Colonel Leboutte, the Chief of Staff of the Air Force. Resistance associations and former deportees were also present in force with their banners.

The de Selys family was seated in the front row, including his parents, Raymond and Émilie, his sister Monique, his brother François with his wife Pauline, accompanied by their eldest son Michel.

The de Selys family attended the ceremony. The emotion was palpable. From left to right: François (Jean's brother), Monique (sister), Émilie (mother), Pauline (François' wife), Michel (eldest son of Pauline and François), and Raymond (father).

Detail of the commemorative plaque made by the Compagnie des Bronzes de Bruxelles.

At 11am, the 40-minute ceremony began with the music of the Guides greeting Lieutenant Colonel de Fraiteur, Minister of National Defence and representative of the government, accompanied by his Chief of Staff, Colonel Léo De Soomer, Jean's former squadron leader at No. 3 (F) Squadron.

As the plaque was unveiled, a moving rendition of '*La Brabançonne*' was played, while in the sky, a plane flew over the site. Speeches followed, punctuated by the music of the Guides performing a piece from Beethoven's 5th Symphony, whose first four bars were forever associated with the glimmers of hope for victory spread over the airwaves throughout the conflict. The strong words of the Mayor of Brussels were noteworthy: 'In every war, there are a few audacious examples that History remembers. The feat we are celebrating here is one of those, as it bears an exceptional character in its boldness.'

After all the speeches, Jean's father, Baron Raymond de Selys Longchamps, took the floor to thank the authorities for the tribute paid to his son. In the afternoon, at 2:30pm, a commemorative session intended for schools in the Brussels area and delegations from provincial institutions took place in the vast covered playground of the Éperons d'Or communal school. Over 1,000 schoolboys and girls attended and listened to two talks led by Lieutenant Colonel Aviator Michel Donnet and Captain Aviator Gustave Rens. Both emotionally recounted the story of Jean de Selys and his daring raid. At the end of the event, all the schoolchildren marched in procession to Avenue Louise to lay several wreaths of flowers, accompanied by the music of the Belgian Air Force.

Finally, another commemorative session took place in the late afternoon in the grand hall of the Palais des Académies, located east of the Palais Square.

A few weeks later, on 3 March 1947, Jean's father received a letter from the secretary of King Leopold III, signed by Jacques Pirenne. It read as follows:

> (…) the feat he accomplished, by bombing the Gestapo offices in Brussels, which was the symbol of the oppression our country lived under at that time, was an encouragement, an example, and a beacon of hope for the entire nation. Your son, after this magnificent exploit, continued to give his all in service to the country for which he gloriously sacrificed his life. The King asks me to tell you that he will keep his memory among those of the brightest officers and the greatest citizens who saved the country during the war.

The letter also referred to a letter Jean's father had sent to the King, on his behalf as well as that of Belgian aviators, in which he protested against the removal of the royal monogram from the aviation troops' uniform. The King let him know that 'he was pleased to see that the distinguished group of officers and aviators had retained their loyalty to him.'

The next tribute was more unexpected and took the form of a four-page comic strip published in the weekly *Spirou* magazine on 10 December 1953. Jean also received the honour of an episode of the iconic comic series '*Les belles histoires de l'Oncle Paul*', which thrilled many young readers of that era.

Five years later, in 1958, the coat of arms of the de Selys Longchamps family was adorned with the symbol of the RAF: a golden eagle topped with the British royal crown. By royal letters patent granted in Brussels on 10 March 1958, Baron Raymond de Selys obtained the title of Count as well as a series of modifications to the coat of arms. Jean's aviator exploits thus found a well-chosen place in the family heraldry.

Jean was honoured in a collection of six chromos published by the Liebig brand, dedicated to 'Glories of Belgian Military Aviation' (alongside Jean Olieslagers, Willy Coppens, Jean Offenberg, Michel Donnet, and Léon Divoy and Remy Van Lierde).

In this photograph taken on 20 January 2023, from the balcony of the third floor of 453 Avenue Louise, exactly eighty years after Jean de Selys' raid, a golden dot signals the monument dedicated to the pilot and inaugurated in 1993. His bust has eyes fixed on the horizon, looking at the very spot where the Typhoon PR-M burst one January morning in 1943 to make history.

In the early sixties, Jean had the privilege of appearing in a mini collection of six illustrations issued by the food brand Liebig and dedicated to the 'Glories of Belgian Military Aviation'. Featured alongside him were legendary pilots such as Jean Olieslagers, Willy Coppens, Jean Offenberg, Michel Donnet, Léon Divoy, and finally Remy Van Lierde.

In 1972, the wonderful 'Nos Gloires' collection, published in six volumes by Artis Historia, included an illustration depicting the 20 January 1943 attack, among the 240 collectible illustrations.

On 19 June 1985, the city of Brussels officially named the crossroads formed by Avenue Louise, Avenue Émile De Mot, Rue de l'Aurore, and Rue Paul Lauters as the 'carrefour de Selys Longchamps'.

Mention must also be given to the remarkable series of broadcasts produced by the public Belgian Television channel RTBF for the fiftieth anniversary of the Second World War, *Jours de Guerre*. Hosted by Jean-Jacques Jespers, this monthly TV programme recounted the 2,194 days of the war and aired for over five years (from 1989 to 1995). In 1992, a 20-minute episode dedicated to Jean de Selys was broadcast on 24 November. The narrative, enriched by numerous testimonies, was punctuated by impressive reenactment scenes of the Gestapo headquarters' activities and its attack.

In the early 1990s, a new monument project was proposed in front of the building at 453 Avenue Louise, initiated by the Union of Resistance Fighters. The original plan was to erect a 16-foot-high pylon topped with a Typhoon model identical to the one flown by Jean. However, the project was rejected for being aesthetically displeasing and, more importantly, dangerous in strong winds. It was then replaced by a stone stele project with a gilded bronze statue representing Jean de Selys' face wearing his flight helmet, to be placed on the green facing the building. Fundraising began and the monument was inaugurated on Thursday, 29 April 1993, forty years after the raid. The ceremony was attended by a host of civilian and military personalities, veteran associations, an air force detachment, and, of course, the de Selys family. The bust, sculpted by Paul Boedts in his Watermael-Boitsfort workshop, was unveiled. The de Selys family descendants had called upon one of the last people to have known Jean in real life, Madame Paul de Hemptinne (his first cousin), to ensure the resemblance to its original model and thus validate Boedts' work.

It is worth noting that a scaled-down copy of this sculpture is preserved in the Cinquantenaire Aviation Museum, which also houses in its collection an RAF uniform jacket that belonged to Jean de Selys.

Another tribute was paid when he was chosen as the patron for the wing award ceremony of eight student pilots from the 96B class. The ceremony took place on 17 December 1998, in the presence of General-Aviator Guido Vanhecke, who worked tirelessly to honour the memory of Belgian pilots and is responsible for erecting the moving monument dedicated to Belgian pilots who died in the line of duty, situated in the Cinquantenaire park. Inaugurated in 2000, the sculpture, designed by Claude Rahir (1937–2007), lists Jean's name among the 225 other Belgian aviators who served bravely in the RAF between 1940 and 1945. Today, over 900 names are inscribed on this touching memorial, remembering pilots who have fallen since that time. An annual 'Remembrance Day' ceremony is held every 15 October, the day the independent air force was created in 1946.

In 2009, Dupuis Publishing released a comic book by Schwartz and Yann, depicting an adventure of Spirou and Fantasio in the Brussels of 1942: '*Le Groom vert-de-gris*'.

Jean de Selys' raid plays a key role in the story's resolution, and its integration into the narrative, albeit fantastical, is clever and humorous.

With direct witnesses gradually passing, it was not until 2013 that we witnessed a significant event celebrating Jean de Selys' memory anew. A ceremony organised by the Belgian association Wings of Memory and its dynamic president, Chris Van Heghe, took place at the Thanet cemetery, where Jean had been resting for seventy years. The Wings of Memory team did an excellent job, and the ceremony held on

Preparatory sketch by sculptor Paul Boedts. The golden bronze head created by foundryman Dirk De Groeve of Hansbeke was placed on a blue stone stela representing Jean de Selys, his eyes turned skyward, in the middle of the de Selys Longchamps crossroads, in front of 453 Avenue Louise, and in line with Avenue Émile De Mot. The monument was inaugurated on the fiftieth anniversary of the raid in 1993.

The tribute paid at the Minster cemetery in August 2013 by General aviator Van Caelenberge. Behind him are some members of the de Selys family: Sybille (François' daughter), Ariel (Edé's son), and Mary (Monique's daughter).

Friday, 16 August 2013, gathered military delegations from Belgium (under the direction of General Van Caelenberge) and Britain, as well as associations representing the squadrons Jean served in (609 Squadron and 3 Squadron). The de Selys family was again represented, and Ariel de Selys, son of Edé (Jean's younger brother), delivered a moving speech. The skies of Kent echoed with a loud tribute from Jean's 'descendants' as a Eurofighter Typhoon from 3 Squadron and two Belgian F-16s performed a flypast over the cemetery. Last but not least, a former member of 3 Squadron, a contemporary of Jean's, attended the ceremony: Flight Lieutenant Robert Barckley, who was 93 years old. He briefly knew Jean since he was listed 'Missing in Action' on 2 June 1943, just weeks after Jean's arrival. After a forced landing on French soil, Barckley had managed to return to England through an

Flight Lieutenant Robert Barckley, 93 years old, former member of 3 (F) Squadron who briefly met Jean before being reported 'Missing in Action' in early June 1943.

The tribute of the 'heirs' with a fly over of two Belgian F-16s over the Minster cemetery.

escape network after an epic journey and reached Manston on 25 August 1943, nine days after Jean's crash, to continue fighting in a Typhoon. His memories of Jean were very touching: 'He was a very pleasant person and an extraordinary pilot, the kind of person you don't want to lose.'[1]

Another indirect tribute was paid to him in comic form by Christophe Gibelin, who in 2015 and 2016 published a double album inspired by Jean de Selys' raid: 'Typhoon' (Paquet editions). The artwork is remarkable, but the story, by the author's own admission, is 'largely fictionalised.' Christophe Gibelin very respectfully names his hero Jean de Selys.

More recently (2021), Jean de Selys' 20 January 1943, raid was included in *100 Dates in the History of Belgium* in the eponymous book by Hervé Gérard.

Jean's epic life continues to inspire comic book authors, as he is once again honoured in Volume 3 of the series *Le Petit Théâtre des Opérations* (2022), where Jean's life is humorously (but quite accurately, it must be noted) recounted by the talented duo Julien Hervieux and Monsieur Le Chien.

In 2023, on the eightieth anniversary of the raid on Brussels and the death of Jean de Selys, a moving ceremony was held on 16 August in the Thanet cemetery where Jean rests. Brilliantly organised by a group of dedicated locals who are faithful guardians of memory (John Quittenden, Jonathan Cole, Bernard Perkins, Leanne McCarthy, Annette Hearn-Gibson and Derek Crow-Brown) and the Royal British Legion Minster and Monkton, the event was marked by the presence of an impressive delegation from the de Selys family who wanted to mark the occasion. 609 Squadron Association was worthily represented as well as No. 3 (F) Squadron Association.

A very moving ceremony was organised at the Thanet cemetery on 16 August 2023, on the eightieth anniversary of Jean de Selys' death.

Heather Carson shared a poignant testimony about the last moments spent with Jean de Selys just hours before he tragically disappeared.

During the ceremony, a Belgian F-16 from the Kleine Brogel base (349 Squadron) paid tribute to the glorious elder by tearing through the magnificent blue sky of Minster. There were many speeches, but one in particular stood out. Indeed, the ceremony truly soared when a 96-year-old lady took to the floor to share the poignant memory she had kept of Jean de Selys Longchamps. Her delicate words fluttered through the cemetery's pathways with the subtle grace of a butterfly carried by a gentle breeze. This lady, extraordinarily alert despite her old age, was Heather Carson, with whom Jean had spent his last carefree hours on 15 August 1943. Heather was one of the last people still alive to have met him. Perhaps even the very last. The words and adjectives she summoned to evoke him confirmed that beyond his ardour and courage, Jean de Selys Longchamps was an extraordinary inspirer of enthusiasm, who managed to give life so much more than was expected of him.

Another exceptional event also took place at the 'Jean Offenberg' base in Florennes, (Belgium) in the week of 16 October 2023. For several days, a delegation of three Eurofighter Typhoons from the No. 3 (F) Squadron of Coningsby participated in a squadron exchange with 1st Squadron ('Stingers', equipped with F-16s) to pay tribute to their former lost pilot. On 18 October, the base, expertly led by Colonel Cédric Kamensky, organised a 'Spotters Day', allowing the many present fans to admire a stunning formation composed of a Spitfire (piloted by the passionate Brice Ohayon), an F-16, and an EF Typhoon, which paid an unprecedented and vibrant flying tribute to Jean de Selys.

The remarkable formation of three aircraft paying a vibrant tribute to Jean de Selys over the Florennes airbase (October 2023).

To conclude, one cannot be comprehensive without mentioning the fate of one of the key protagonists of this story: the building at 453 Avenue Louise, which was the headquarters of the Sipo-SD agents. Once the war ended, the building regained its real estate potential and became one of the capital's most sought-after locations, a stone's throw from the La Cambre Abbey. The spacious apartments (2,150 square feet each) occupy each an entire floor. Fully renovated, they are very bright and are leased for just under 3,000 euros per month (January 2023). The building is far from being classified as a place of memory. This is obviously debatable, especially since the building's basements, which served as a prison during the war, house moving testimonies left on their walls by the unfortunate folk who were detained there by their Nazi tormentors.

The rediscovery of these inscriptions and sketches, echoing the despair and last wishes of the prisoners, goes to the credit of two gentlemen. In 1995, as part of his documentary film 'À mon père résistant', historian and filmmaker André Dartevelle had the opportunity to visit four basements (out of twenty) at 347 Avenue Louise (where the Sipo-SD had moved after Jean de Selys' raid). The walls revealed numerous inscriptions etched into the lime. Unfortunately, he was not authorised to document those at 453. In 2009, Daniel Weyssow, the ever-active and determined project manager at the Auschwitz Foundation in Brussels, brought the issue to the attention of Monuments and Sites. The problem he faced, however, was how to inventory the graffiti in the basements when the owners refused access. In October 2011, a seminar organised by the Auschwitz Foundation brought together a panel of people concerned by the issue (historians, survivors, political figures, journalists, and even a 453 landlord). A few days earlier, thanks to the intervention of the TV channel RTBF, another owner at 453 granted access to his basement, and numerous inscriptions were discovered thus proving the existence of graffiti in the basements of 453. However, this discovery did not mobilise all the owners of 453, and only three of them would break their silence.

In 2013, Julie de Groote, a Brussels Parliament member, revived the case and addressed the Minister-President of the Brussels-Capital Region, Rudi Vervoort, who declared that no measure would be excluded to protect the sites. In January 2014, RTBF produced a new report on the subject. Interviews were recorded in the basements of 453, whose owners/tenants had become more cooperative. The day after the broadcast, a proposal to classify the basements was submitted to the parliament by Rudi Vervoort. In January 2016, the Brussels government approved the definitive classification order of the basements of the two buildings that housed the Sipo-SD headquarters at 357 and 453 Avenue Louise. The opinion issued by the Royal Commission for Monuments and Sites stated that these basements 'have a unique memorial value that exceeds mere heritage interest.' Thus, it took twenty years of effort to finally begin removing these places from the sad status of 'non-places of memory' into which a disheartening passivity had cast them.

Chapter 17

The Incredibles

(1939–1948)

As I delved into the epic saga of Jean de Selys Longchamps, spending countless hours digging through family archives and engaging in fascinating conversations with his nieces and nephews, it became glaringly clear that his biography could never be considered complete without acknowledging the incredible bravery and extraordinary sense of duty displayed by his sister and two brothers during, and sometimes after, the Second World War. It is apparent that the four siblings shared the same shimmering genes that have distinguished the de Selys family for generations. The inadvertent shadow cast by Jean's feats could easily obscure the achievements of this formidable sibling quartet, but to overlook their contributions would have been an unforgivable mistake. Thus, let me briefly recount the roles they played, often at great personal sacrifice and sometimes at the risk of their lives, to aid their beloved homeland.

Like the three musketeers, Raymond and Émilie de Selys Longchamps' children were actually four, as we've seen at the beginning of this book, so let us start with the eldest, Monique.

Monique

Monique's engagement in action was the longest of all the siblings, spanning from 1940 to 1948. Her service to her country was not in the khaki or aviator blue uniforms, however, rather, Monique's uniform often consisted of a white work apron, matching the colour of her cap, and a red cross armband bearing the number 4802 on her left arm. Indeed, it was through her service with the Belgian Red Cross that Monique would make her mark.

In the interwar period, the Red Cross managed to establish itself as a national-scale organisation in Belgium, significantly expanding its membership from barely 3,000 in 1922 to 105,000 in 1938. Towards the end of the decade, the Belgian Red Cross embarked on an intensive female personnel recruitment programme. To this end, a committee for female mobilisation, exclusively composed of women – a very innovative move for the time – was created in 1938. Facing the looming threat of an increasingly belligerent Germany, its goal was to organise female mobilisation in case of conflict. Queen Elisabeth of Belgium, the honorary president of the Red Cross since 1910, supported this significant initiative with this appeal in 1939: 'I'm certain that Belgian women will understand the necessity of cooperating with the Red Cross' Female Auxiliary Service and that they will respond in large numbers to its call.'

Her past as a nurse made Queen Elisabeth particularly legitimate to actively participate in the mobilisation of women: during the First World War, she had donned the nurse's uniform to provide care to the wounded at the military hospital 'L'ambulance de l'Océan' in De Panne, earning the nickname 'Queen-Nurse' and an indelible aura. Undoubtedly, the Queen's call resonated in a family as deeply royalist as the de Selys Longchamps, further encouraging Monique in her commitment.

Anticipating that an imminent conflict would inevitably lead to the mobilisation of a large part of the medical staff, the Red Cross embarked on training ambulance drivers among other roles. Training was provided at the Red Cross health centre in Brussels and was complemented by a three-month internship in a hospital. Monique underwent this training and completed her internship at the Brussels military hospital from 18 December 1939 to 18 March 1940. Her performance there was highly praised,

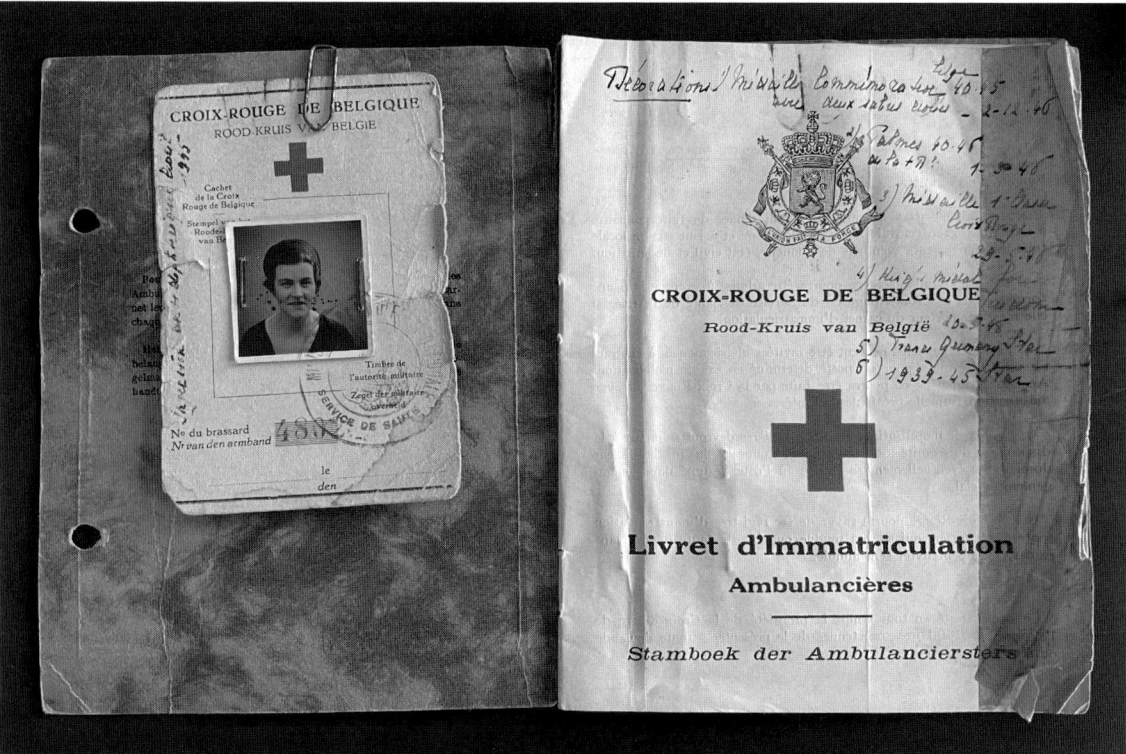

The registration booklet and Belgian Red Cross card of Monique de Selys.

as noted in her registration booklet: 'Very dedicated and hardworking, showed a lot of initiative, competence, and discretion both in wards and the operating room.' Another doctor noted she had 'exceptional qualities for fulfilling the role of a nurse.' No doubt, Monique de Selys had found her calling at the age of 34. The outbreak of the war would prove her commitment even more concretely as she joined the teams of the military hospital that had moved to Berck-Plage, where the Belgian army was evacuating wounded soldiers from 18 May. There, amidst a hellish concentration of soldiers severely affected by the battles, she devotedly cared for the wounded until the end of June 1940, when she received her demobilisation orders on the 25th. But for Monique de Selys, the war was far from over. Standing tall at 5 feet 6 inches, she had no intention of being intimidated by the occupier and was determined to use her recognised qualities – intrepidity, courage, pugnacity, and a big heart – for those in dire need. The Red Cross soon assigned her to a new service where her multiple talents would excel: the sanitary train service. More accurately, this was about the service of a single hospital train that made numerous trips to Germany to periodically repatriate prisoners of war who had been released for health reasons.

In early 1941, third-class carriages were transformed into sanitary wagons in the central workshop in Mechelen. These wagons were part of convoys which, for example, could consist of seven sleeping cars for the sick and wounded, one sleeping car for staff, one kitchen wagon, one dining wagon, one pharmacy-laundry wagon, one office wagon, and one reserve wagon. The number of sleeping cars could vary based on needs.

The Belgian crew accompanying each train typically included five nurses, six ambulance drivers, two doctors, one pharmacist, two secretaries, four cooks, a mission leader, and a chief guard. Sometimes, a Red Cross chaplain would join them. Additionally, two Germans accompanied them: a doctor from the DRK (German Red Cross) and a sergeant from the Wehrmacht. Queen Elisabeth would sometimes lend her support to the crew before departure and sign the top of the first page of the train's journey log.

As one might guess, the logistics surrounding these convoys were complex, and Miss Rondeau, secretary for the general management of the Red Cross, efficiently orchestrated the multiple

Monique de Selys posing in her nurse's uniform. The qualities everyone recognised in her – fearlessness, courage, combativeness, and a big heart – are evident in her gentle yet determined gaze.

parameters (equipment, personnel, itinerary, and administrative formalities) that allowed the sanitary trains to perform their missions effectively. The German authorities selected the prisoners to be repatriated and set the departure dates for the convoys. The local Red Cross committees in Brussels and Antwerp were the only ones involved in receiving the prisoners.

Between 9 August 1941 and 27 June 1944, no less than twenty-three Sanitary Trains (ST) were deployed to bring back 8,415 prisoners of war. Ordinary trains repatriated an additional 2,671 prisoners, whose health was less concerning, during the same period. Finally, 276 other prisoners were repatriated by two German sanitary trains in August 1944. Thus, approximately 11,362 prisoners of war unfit for camp life returned to Belgium by train before the end of the Occupation.

The exact number of sanitary train convoys Monique participated in is not precisely known. Her registration booklet mentions a few (ST No. 5, 8, 9, 18, and 23), but the exhaustiveness of these notes is questionable, as Monique appears in a photograph of the crew from ST No. 10, which is not listed in her booklet.

The crew accompanying the Sanitary Train (ST) No. 10. Monique is recognisable in the foreground, in profile. The Red Cross chaplain, Henri Van Oostayen, a true resistance hero, is the second from the left in the front row.

This photograph of ST No. 10 is particularly interesting because it features a highly inspiring figure that Monique de Selys encountered during these gruelling journeys: the Red Cross chaplain Henri Van Oostayen. This Jesuit father, a former missionary in India, was a true hero who was part of the Comète network. He risked his life hiding Jewish children in Brussels and was eventually arrested by the German police on 25 July 1944. Interrogated and tortured by his captors, he was deported to Bergen-Belsen, where he died on 19 April 1945, just days before the camp's liberation. It is unknown if the chaplain confided in Monique about his underground activities, but this reminds us that opportunities to interact with active members of the Resistance were plentiful, which could lend credence to family accounts suggesting Monique occasionally hid weapons destined for the Resistance under her nurse's cape.

While unproven, everything about Monique's character seems to indicate that this was entirely plausible. It is also symptomatic to note that relations between the occupiers and the Red Cross deteriorated over the course of the Occupation, with the Germans deeming the institution 'too patriotic and too Francophone'. Transporting these sick and wounded was no easy task, requiring resilience to endure the considerable fatigue it caused. Stress was also a constant companion, as the convoy members' greatest fear was finding themselves in a German area targeted by Allied bombings. According to her superiors, Monique managed extremely well and displayed 'unshakeable good humour' in all situations.

Once Belgium had been liberated, the role of the sanitary trains did not diminish but became even more crucial. After aiding in evacuating military and civilian victims of the Battle of the Bulge, the sanitary trains increased their trips to Germany to repatriate survivors of concentration camps as well as wounded Allied soldiers being transported to England. Monique de Selys devoted herself tirelessly, participating in an impressive number of sanitary convoys from the end of the war to 1948. She made twenty-nine trips on behalf of the British Army of the Rhine, twenty-three to Switzerland, five to the Czech Republic (to repatriate elderly people and Czech children exiled to England), and a few more to Denmark and France. Nothing seemed to stop her. Nothing? Well, love did: in 1949, she married Squadron Leader Patrick Smith DSO, a former liaison officer of the SAS brigade with the Belgian parachute regiment. The list of decorations awarded for her extraordinary commitment eloquently includes the Commemorative Medal of the War 1940–1945 with two crossed swords, King George's Medal for Service in the Cause of Freedom, The France-Germany Star, The 1939–1945 Star, First Class Medal of the Belgian Red Cross, and the 1940–1945 Palms of the Belgian Red Cross.

In 1949, Monique married Squadron Leader Patrick Smith DSO, former liaison officer of the SAS brigade with the Belgian paratrooper regiment.

François

François de Selys Longchamps was 29 years old when he was mobilised in 1939.[1] Married to Pauline Cornet de Ways Ruart since 1937, his first child (Michel, 'Mickey', the eldest of five) was born in 1938. François followed family tradition by voluntarily enlisting in 1st Guides Regiment for three years in 1932. He participates in all

The three brothers (François, Edé, and Jean) with their grandmother in Haren, September 1931.

call-ups while pursuing a brilliant career at the Ministry of Foreign Affairs and International Trade. When he received his mobilisation order on 1 September, François was on a mission in Colorado Springs, USA, and only joined his unit on 15 September. Like Jean, his status as a reserve officer in 1st Guides led him to a squadron attached to a first reserve infantry division: the Cyclist Squadron of 7th Infantry Division (7 ID). He was appointed lieutenant on 26 March 1940, as the German threat looms larger, and commanded the second platoon.

François de Selys joined the prestigious 1st Guides Regiment in 1932.

On 10 May 1940, François' unit, stationed at Glons, was alerted in the middle of the night, around 1:15am. The soldiers of 7 ID moved shortly after, some stationed near the exit of the Tongres-Visé tunnel. From there, they watched in awe as gliders dropped German paratroopers who quickly seized the nearby, supposedly impregnable, fort of Ében-Émael. What a shock! And that was not all: more German paratroopers were dropped near the bridges of Vroenhoven, Veldwezelt, and Kanne. The infantry troops of 7 ID found themselves in the midst of turmoil and were thrust into war around 4:30am. The entire division was battered and never recovered: on the first day alone, 7 ID simply disintegrated.

Orders and counter-orders abounded throughout the day, and 7 ID's cyclist platoons, including François', retreated after briefly considering attacking the paratroopers who had landed near Ében-Émael. For 7 ID, the eighteen-day campaign effectively lasted a single day.

The following weeks were exceedingly chaotic. No. 7 ID retreated to the vicinity of Heysel in Brussels, and by 14 May, as 7 ID's various components regrouped in the assembly area, it became clear that only 3,500 men remained of the 16,679 who were present on the morning of 10 May. The unit was then directed to Poperinge before being evacuated to Brittany for reorganisation and rearming. Upon arrival in the Malestroit area in Morbihan on 27 May, 7 ID faced more challenges when the next day, the news of the Belgian capitulation was received. The Belgian government in exile in France decided that Belgian units not in the Flanders army zone on 28 May were not bound by the capitulation. Under the command of the Minister of National Defence, General Denis, it was planned for them to continue fighting alongside the Allies. Despite being in tatters, 7 ID paradoxically became the only major unit of the

The wedding of François de Selys and Pauline Cornet de Ways Ruart.

Belgian army still available. The cyclist squadron, having suffered relatively few losses, was stationed in the Breton village of Pleucadeuc, 5 miles south of Malestroit.

At this point, fate mischievously smiled down on the de Selys brothers. On 4 June, about 400 Belgian soldiers who had made it to England at the end of the campaign were transported to the port of Brest by the *Batavia II*. This was the same boat Jean de Selys had used to reach Brest that day: unknowingly, the two brothers were now in the same region. Better yet, most soldiers who disembarked from the *Batavia II* arrived in Malestroit on 6 June. Among them, at least two (Lieutenant Terlinden and Second Lieutenant Vanderstraeten) were even assigned to the cyclist squadron alongside François. The two brothers were so close to being reunited.

All efforts to make 7 ID operational for deployment alongside the French army were in vain, and the swift progression of German troops forced France to capitulate on 17 June.

To avoid capture by the advancing Wehrmacht, 7 ID kept retreating until it finally settled in an unoccupied part of the zone. By the end of June, the cyclist squadron of 7 ID had established a cantonment in Le Houga, east of Mont-de-Marsan and north of Pau. This is where François had the road accident that plunged him into a coma for sixteen days, as previously mentioned. The accident allowed the two brothers and their father to briefly reunite for the very last time. Once recovered, François returned to Belgium, released from his military obligations, likely towards the end of August 1940.

François de Selys, his wife Pauline, and their son lived in the family Château de Ruart, near Glabay, where their family soon expanded with the arrival of Sybille in August 1941 and Anne in October 1942. Yet, appearances were deceiving: François was not one to be content with the role of a family man, passively witnessing his country's occupation by the Nazis. In May 1943, he actively joined the Resistance, becoming a liaison officer for Zone IV in the Secret Army. Little is known about his activities except for two events that presumably represented the kind of role he willingly played in the shadows.

On 19 August 1943, three days after his brother Jean's death, two agents were parachuted above the castle, and François provided all the necessary assistance for them to continue their mission. At the end of January 1944, an American bomber crashed near Glabay, and three crew members were briefly hidden in the château before being exfiltrated. François buried their parachutes, and his wife Pauline escorted one of the Americans to a meeting point in Uccle (Brussels), where the other two Americans were brought by other Resistance members.

Pauline Cornet de Ways Ruart, François' wife, showed great courage during the Occupation.

Unfortunately, they were betrayed, and the Resistance members were arrested by the Germans with the two Americans they were escorting. By a stroke of luck, Pauline and the American she was escorting managed to avoid the trap.

With the situation worsening and fearing for his family's safety due to his clandestine activities, François decided to leave for London to continue the fight. He departed Belgium on 4 April 1944, travelled to Paris, Lyon, and Toulouse, crossed the Pyrenees to reach Barcelona, and finally arrived in Gibraltar on 8 May, almost four years after Jean's arrival on the rock. He landed in England on 21 May 1944.

Quickly approaching the military authorities, he provided a detailed report on the state of the Secret Army in Belgium to the SOE, who were keen to learn more just days before the launch of Operation Overlord on 6 June 1944. He was then recruited for a mission during which he was to be parachuted back into Belgium at the end of August.

The operation, named 'Reynaldo', with François' code name 'Gabrielle', was meticulously planned according to the standards of perilous missions in enemy territory.[2] Note that only 284 Belgians were sent by London on missions to occupied Belgium.[3] The operation's objective was to deliver London's latest directives to Major Bastin (commander of Zone V) and then assist in creating a region under the Secret Army's control for future mass weapon drops under special order No. 18. François was given a fake identity card issued in Liège under the name François Michel Marie Lahaye. He carried 4,000 Belgian francs on his person, plus 46,000 Belgian francs and 20,000 French francs in his toiletry kit for emergency funds. He also had access to a mission fund of $100,000 for the secret troops.

The reception committee, led by Count d'Aspremont Linden, greeted him upon landing with the password 'Dyle' in response to 'Arlon'. It was planned that the resistance networks involved received confirmation of his drop through a message broadcast on Radio Belgium at 7:15pm on the first, third, and fifth days after his departure from England.

François met Major Bastin on 1 September at the Château de Fisenne, owned by Count Philippe de Cherizey. He quickly learned that due to the rapid and massive retreat of German forces, creating controlled zones in the Ardennes was now impossible, making his mission null and void. Undeterred, François decided to report back to 'Osric', the code name for the head of the Secret Army, to explore if other zones could be suitable for creating controlled areas for drops. After a long bike journey, François finally met 'Osric' at La Rosières to hear the confirmation he dreaded: the Allies' advance made order No. 18 inapplicable. A SHAEF telegram confirmed no more weapon drops would be conducted in Belgium. François had to accept that he had been parachuted in ten days too late and, in his mission report, he regretted that 'everywhere, the lack of arms and ammunition prevented the troops from giving their full measure.'

François de Selys ended the war in a newly formed armoured car regiment, which he joined on 13 February 1945. He remained active until the end of the conflict on 8 May 1945. The Ministry of Foreign Affairs and International Trade had vainly attempted to reintegrate him in December 1944, but evidently, François could not envisage ending the war in any way other than in uniform.

He was awarded multiple decorations, notably the Member of the British Empire (MBE) for his 'great courage and determination', standing proudly alongside, among others, the 1940 War Croix de Guerre and the Knight of the Order of Leopold.

Edmond

Edmond, known as Edé, followed in his brothers' footsteps, performing his military service in 1st Guides. Appointed as a reserve sub-lieutenant in March 1939, he was mobilised on 16 August 1939, aged 26.[4] Unlike François and Jean, he was not detached to a divisional cyclist squadron and instead joined 1st Guides as a platoon leader of 4/II (4th Motorcyclist Squadron of 2nd group) under Captain Prince Amaury de Mérode.

Edmond was the only one of the three brothers to experience combat at the heart of a motorised cavalry regiment. As previously mentioned, 1st Guides began to be motorised as early as 1936, and its theoretical order of battle at the dawn of conflict included 230 motorcycles, 274 sidecars, 16 Ford Marmon-Herrington armoured artillery tractors, 4 T13 self-propelled guns, and 7 T15 light tanks.

When the Germans launched their assault on 10 May, 1st Guides left their encampments in the Borsu and Maffe region (west of Durbuy) to head for Halen, about 12.5 miles west of Hasselt. Edmond's squadron occupied the southern edge of Halen and the bridge over the Gette at Zelk. On the afternoon of 13 May, the positions of 1st Guides and 2nd Cyclist were attacked by German tanks, but they offered fierce resistance, and the front remained intact.

As the German offensive forced Belgian positions to continually retreat, the Guides moved towards Kampenhout and then headed north, to the edge of the Dutch border. Reconnaissance missions were conducted into Dutch territory near Zwijndrecht. On 23 May, 1st Guides, along with 3rd Cyclist, once again stood out, thwarting the enemy's attempt to cross the canal at Terneuzen and Sluiskil. The Wehrmacht's push failed completely, causing heavy losses. Unfortunately, this would be the last brilliant action of the Guides, as the shadow of 28 May already loomed ahead.

Edmond and his squadron were in Dudzele (4.5 miles north of Bruges) when they learned of King Leopold III's declaration. The instructions he received from his

The 1st Guides in manoeuvres before the war. The motorisation of the unit is evident, and the regiment no longer has anything of a cavalry unit.

superiors were brief: 'Stay with your men, keep them orderly and grouped.' Among the soldiers under Edé's command was Jean Terlinden, to whom he confided, 'This is not over!' His statement turned out to be eerily prescient, as the two men would fight together again during the country's liberation at the end of 1944.

But in these dark days at the end of May 1940, the prospect of liberation barely crossed the minds of even the most optimistic men. From 1 June, the Germans gathered their prisoners in columns, under the watch of a motorcycle platoon, and led them to Berchem, where all vehicles and cannons were placed in an open-air depot. The men then crossed Antwerp on foot and were briefly locked up in the Brasschaat camp. They were subsequently transported by train from Sint-Mariaburg station to their prisoner-of-war camps in Germany. The officers, meanwhile, were imprisoned in Oflags (*Offizierslager*).

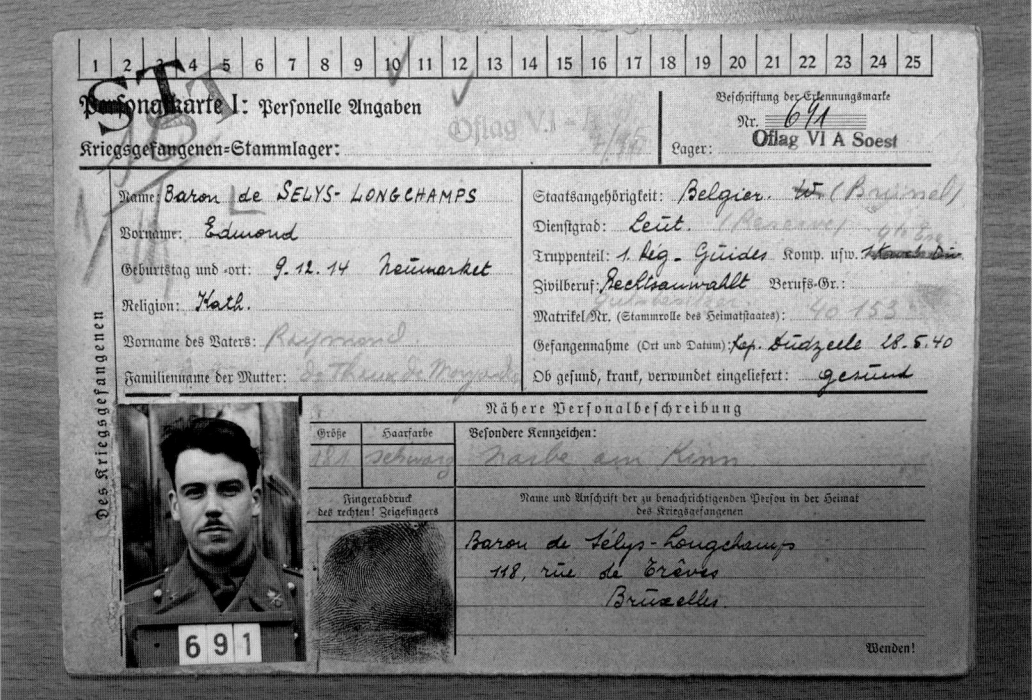

Identification card of prisoner '691' issued by Oflag VI-A in Soest.

During his captivity, Edé would stay in five different Oflags. The first he was directed to was Oflag VI-A in Soest, east of Dortmund. This Oflag had been set up in a former infantry barracks converted into a prison, and 2,000 Belgians were imprisoned there. Edé stayed there for about two months before being moved to Oflag III-B in Tibor (now Cibórz), near the Polish border, where 2,500 Belgian officers, both from Brussels and Wallonia, were held. This Oflag was located in a forest, near a lake, and the winter was particularly harsh for the prisoners, whose barracks were unheated. In early March 1941, Edé was transferred to Oflag II-A in Prenzlau, located just over 55 miles north of Berlin. In this camp, also housed in a former barracks, the Belgian officers replaced Polish officers. Edmond de Selys only stayed there for five months before being moved again, this time to Oflag VIII-C, which he reached in early August 1941. This Oflag was in Juliusburg, now the Polish city known as Dobroszyce, in Silesia. Edé had never been in a camp so far from Belgium and was now over 600 miles from Brussels.

The distance from his loved ones, however, did not quell the escape attempts that had been stirring in him since the beginning of his captivity, especially since Dutch officers had already managed to fool the guards of this Oflag. Edé's first escape attempt was thwarted in December when he tried to blend in with a group of Flemish non-commissioned officers being repatriated to Belgium. Perhaps he had been a tad too optimistic.

In the family album, some souvenir photographs of life in the Oflags.

His second escape attempt also took place in Oflag VIII-C in August 1942 and was much more elaborate. With the help of two other officers, de Vogel from 2nd Lancers and Weimvikisch from 1st Lancers, Edé began digging a hole in a small chapel built against the barbed wire fences enclosing the camp. The presence of this chapel might seem odd, but it was because the Oflag was partly set up in a former orphanage for girls, the Amalienstift, a charitable institution created by Princess Amelia, sister of Emperor Wilhelm II.

Once they had dug through the wall, the Belgians began cutting the barbed wire and clearing a path at the base of the wooden palisade surrounding the camp. The operation was long and carried out in several stages with the cooperation of other officers who kept watch and, if necessary, distracted the soldiers guarding them. But all these efforts were in vain: just as he took his first steps outside the camp, Edé was spotted by a sentry, and all his hopes of escape evaporated. But he did not give up.

Edmond de Selys was moved again at the end of August 1942 to his fifth Oflag, X-D, located in Fischbeck, 9 miles southwest of Hamburg. The Germans had decided

3. All information regarding Louis Wouters' military career is from his personal military file (matricule 16268) held at the Royal Museum of the Army and Military History (Brussels).
4. Brown, Alan, *Flying for Freedom: The Allied Air Forces 1939–1945*, The History Press, 2011; Donnet, Mike, *Les aviateurs belges dans la Royal Air Force*, op. cit., pp. 35–36.
5. The diary of a French pilot provides an interesting portrait of the life of trainee pilots at Odiham: Chéron, Philippe, *Bonsoir Nadette: journal d'un pilote, Marc Hauchemaille, de la France Libre, 1940–1942*, Éditions Petit à Petit, 2004, pp. 11–17.

Chapter 8
1. Taylor, Jim and John, 'A link to victory', Vintage Wings of Canada, https://www.vintagewings.ca/stories/a-link-to-victory.

Chapter 9
1. de la Poype, Roland, *L'épopée du Normandie-Niemen*, Perrin, 2007, pp. 68–73 (this book provides a good idea of the life of trainees at Tern Hill).
2. Taken from the full transcript of Raymond Lallemant's interview for the TV documentary *Jours de Guerre* kept at the General Archives of the Kingdom 2 (Brussels) M236.
3. Brooks, Robin, *Thames Valley Airfields in the Second World War*, Countryside Books, 2000.
4. Houart, Victor, *Les carnets d'Offenberg*, Pensée Moderne, 1956.

Chapter 10
1. For essential information about 609 Squadron, see: Ziegler, Frank H., *The Story of 609 Squadron: Under the White Rose*, Crécy Books, 1971. It greatly contributed to this biography.
2. Among the important works to understand the life of the Belgians in the 609 Squadron, see: Lallemant, Raymond, *Rendez-vous avec la chance*, Robert Laffont, 1962; Demoulin, Charles, *Mes oiseaux de feux*, Éditions Julliard, 1984; Celis, Peter and De Decker, Cynrik, *Mony Van Lierde: van volksjongen to volksheld*, Uitgeerij Flying Pencil, 2007.
3. Taken from the full transcript of Raymond Lallemant's interview for the TV documentary *Jours de Guerre*, op. cit.
4. Roumieux, Koen, 'Les pilotes belges du 609 (WR) Squadron de la Royal Air Force pendant la secondes guerre mondiale', *VTB Magazine*, number 4/21, pp. 27–28.
5. Ziegler, Frank H., *The Story of 609 Squadron: Under the White Rose*, op. cit., pp. 211–212.
6. The mascot of the 609 Squadron even has its own biography: Waite, Brian, Squadron Leader RAF, *William de Goat*, Athena Press, 2008.
7. O'Malley, Dave, 'Of goats and men', Vintage Wings of Canada, https://www.vintagewings.ca/stories/of-goats-and-men.
8. Goya, Michel, 'Les as, qu'ont-ils de plus?' (Dossier on aviation aces in *Guerres et Histoire*, number 46), 2018, pp. 34–35.
9. Olmsted, Merle C., *The 357th Over Europe: the 357th Fighter Group in World War II*, Phalanx Publishing, 1994.
10. http://www.conscript-heroes.com/Art07-Alex-Nitelet-960.html.
11. Cited by Jean de Selys in a letter to Sam Heapy (14 April 1942).

Chapter 11
1. The Hawker Typhoon is a privileged aircraft as it has Chris Thomas as its highly talented biographer. Chris has authored several reference books on the subject: Thomas, Chris and Shores, Christopher, *The Typhoon & Tempest Story*, Arms and Armour Press, 1988; Thomas, Chris, *Hawker Typhoon 1940 to Spring 1943*, Wingleader, 2022. Also: Townshend Bickers, Richard, *Hawker Typhoon: The Combat History*, Airlife, 1999; Buttler, Tony, *Hawker Typhoon*, Key Books, 2021.
2. Richey, Paul and Franks, Norman, *Fighter Pilot Summer*, Grub Street, 1993.

to gather all Belgian officers from Oflags VII-B, VIII-C, and IX-A/Z there. Now, officers were imprisoned in only two camps: II-A in Prenzlau for active officers and X-D in Fischbeck for reserve officers. One hundred Belgian soldiers were also incarcerated in Fischbeck to serve as attendants to the officers. Escaping remained a persistent obsession, and Edé was even punished in early April 1943 when he was caught stealing an identity card and a pass in a guardhouse at the camp's entrance. Sentenced to ten days in solitary confinement, Edé was weighed down by the forced inactivity and by the disheartening behaviour of men, whether high-ranking officers or even chaplains, willing to quarrel over scraps of food. Plunged into boredom, human nature revealed its most mediocre facets.

In the Oflag, a parcel system set up by the Red Cross allowed prisoners to send clothes back to Belgium once a month for repairs and then get them back. They quickly found a way to hide messages in these parcels to communicate with their loved ones. Most of the time, this was done under the watchful yet indulgent eyes of the Germans, who were either not fooled or turned a blind eye in exchange for a few cigarettes. Edé paid close attention to the logistics surrounding the sending of parcels and soon saw a new opportunity for escape.

The parcels were indeed loaded by Belgian soldiers into a covered truck and unloaded by other Belgian soldiers at the nearby station, where they were transferred to a train bound for Belgium. The truck was, of course, driven by a German, and sentries were everywhere, but Edé believed in his luck and took action on 13 September 1943. Dressed in a pair of British battle-dress trousers and a shirt, he stealthily slipped into the truck and hid under the parcels with the help of the soldiers in charge of loading. At the station, another accomplice signalled the right moment for him to leave the truck without attracting the sentries' attention and sneak into one of the train's wagons preparing to depart for Belgium, still hidden amidst a pile of parcels. It was bold, but it worked! The train was a real slowpoke, progressing very slowly for four days that seemed endless to Edé. He was hungry – a soldier at the station had given him some chocolate and six apples – but he kept faith as he watched Belgium draw closer: Osnabrück, Münster, Krefeld… And then, finally, a 'Visé' sign confirmed he had indeed arrived in Belgium! At night, taking advantage of a slowdown, he jumped off the train near Paifve, close to Glons. He then began searching for someone willing to help. He was turned away at the first house he approached ('Leave, or I'll release the dogs!'), but received a much warmer welcome at a farm a little further on. The next day, he reached Baron de Rosen's castle in Bilzen, where acquaintances enthusiastically welcomed the emaciated but still spirited escaped prisoner. There, he contacted his brother François, who sent him fake papers in the name of Albert Carlier to move around more easily. Then, Edé headed back to Brussels where he daringly visited his parents at 118 rue de Trèves, accompanied by François. The two brothers made a surprise visit to their mother, who had learned of Jean's death a few days earlier, and was worried about Edé's fate, imagining him in great danger under the Allied bombings targeting Hamburg. 'But no, Edé is doing very well', François told her upon arrival, 'I just met him, in fact, here he is…': Edé then appeared before an incredulous but overjoyed mother, blessed to see both her sons reunited. If only Jean could have been there too…

Edmond then hid for several weeks at the Château de Ruart, where François lived. His brother provided him with new fake documents (Belgian and French) and money so he could reach England with the help of the highly efficient Comète escape network. On 10 November 1943, less than two months after his return to Belgium, Edmond's long journey to London began. He took the train, via Tournai, to Blandain near the French border. Crossing fields for more discretion, he entered France and reached Lille, from where he travelled to Paris by train. He stayed for two days with Countess de Brie in the sixteenth district. Then, from Austerlitz station, he departed for Bayonne. Edé was incredibly lucky, escaping all document checks. It was almost miraculous.

Upon arriving in Bayonne, following instructions, Edé went to a small restaurant near the station (the Restaurant d'Agneau) where he asked the only waiter present if he was 'Arthur', before telling him in return that he was 'Ambroise.' The contact was established. He spent a night upstairs, and the next afternoon, another Frenchman came to take him outside the city. In an orchard out of sight, he met two Frenchmen aged 35–40 and two Basque guides in their twenties. Crossing the Pyrenees into Spain took no less than eighteen hours, mostly by night. The small group crossed the border on 15 November, passing over a summit at an altitude of 2,600 feet, where several inches of snow covered the ground. A few hundred yards past the border, they reached a small farm near Urdax. One of the guides then demanded the agreed amount for their passage: 5,000 francs. The paths of Edmond de Selys and his two French escape companions diverged, as he aims to head to San Sebastian where the Belgian consul, Mr De San, a friend likely to assist him, resided. But things did not go as planned, and the Guardia Civil arrested Edé and took him to Irun, where he is interrogated. He deliberately remained vague about his nationality, stating, which was true, that he was a Belgian officer but was born in England. His money, between 3,000 and 4,000 francs, was seized, and he was given a receipt for 1,000 francs. The Spanish police, clearly satisfied with the profits of their racketeering, allowed him to move freely to San Sebastian where he made contact with the British, American, and Belgian consulates. He eventually obtained the necessary papers to travel first to Madrid (where he stayed from 2 to 15 December) and then to Lisbon, from where he departed for England, finally arriving on 23 December 1943.

Once in London, Edé stayed with Countess de Bousies, but his only desire was to return to the fight. His dual Belgian-British nationality spared him from the interrogations of the Patriotic School, tasked with vetting new arrivals eager to join the Allied forces in order to weed out potential spies or, more simply, to discard dubious profiles and ambiguous backgrounds. However, Edé did not escape an extensive interview with MI5, where his entire journey since 28 May 1940 was dissected with precision.[5] A copy of his interview report was sent to MI6 on 9 January 1944; tangible proof of Edé's eagerness to serve his country

Edé photographed during his integration into the Belgian forces in England.

again. His military file indeed specified that he joined the Belgian forces in Britain on 24 December 1943, the day after his arrival. He still had to undergo a convalescence period to regain his strength after his long captivity and challenging escape journey, so at the end of January, he took the opportunity to visit the cemetery in Minster-in-Thanet where Jean was buried and to visit the pilots who knew him at Manston, sharing all his emotions in a lengthy letter written to his parents. He then underwent paratrooper commando training, among other things, at the Achnacarry school in Scotland, where Belgian, French, Dutch, Norwegian, and Czech commandos had trained since the beginning of the conflict.

Returning to uniform allowed him to distance himself from the official circles in London he found 'lamentable' and which hardly inspired confidence for the future. Edé was promoted to lieutenant on 26 March 1944. He had completed his training by the end of August 1944 and managed, a few days later, to join a Belgian commando unit parachuted over the Ardennes on 9 September. Edé's participation in this mission was not initially planned, but he quickly managed to unlock all hierarchical barriers to secure his place in the group of about ten men. He was so eager to participate in the liberation of Belgium that nothing seemed able to stop him. Finally, he found what he had been looking for: action. Indeed, just a few days after his arrival on Belgian soil, Edé took part in the fierce battles waged to liberate the east and northeast outskirts of Antwerp.[6] Accompanied by other Belgians who had just arrived from England (Jean de Cartier de Marchienne, nephew of the Belgian ambassador in London, Pierre Carton de Wiart, Édouard and Teddy d'Oultremont), Edé joined the Brumagne squadron commanded by Jean del Marmol and Robert Tumelaire.

The Brumagne squadron was a mobile unit of the AS (Secret Army) composed of nine platoons of about thirty men each. As part of the operations around Antwerp, the squadron was assigned to the Canadian army (Royal Hamilton Light Infantry Battalion). The battles in which Edé participated take place in Wilmarsdonk on 20 and 21 September.[7] The German counterattacks were violent, and Jean de Cartier de Marchienne died in combat on the 21st, while Edé was wounded in the hand. In the final months of the conflict, Edé participated in the rebuilding of the Belgian army, which was expanding with the incorporation of a particularly heterogeneous mix of profiles: soldiers released from prisoner camps, young people eager to participate in the end of the war, and all those, like him, trained in England, some of whom were true veterans who had distinguished themselves on multiple fronts. Rivalries between old and new were inevitable.

Edé concluded the war within an armoured car unit – 1st Armoured Cavalry Regiment, also known as 1st Hussars – joining on 8 March 1945 to participate in the occupation of defeated Germany. He had his hands full with the young Belgian recruits who were sometimes tempted to humiliate German prisoners, which he did not accept. Not forgetting his comrades still in captivity in Fischbeck, Edmond organised a truck convoy to repatriate them. It was also during this period that the ever-royalist Edmond de Selys Longchamps undertook to cross Germany by jeep with two other soldiers to persuade Leopold III, detained in Austria, to return to Belgium and enter Liège at the head of the Belgian troops. To Edé's great dismay, Leopold III did not even deign to receive the Belgian military personnel who came to meet him. Edmond de Selys' spectacular journey earned him the medal of Knight of the Order of Leopold with palm and the War Cross with palms.

In a questionnaire he filled out in 1953, where asked to specify the decorations received, he wrote, 'I did not apply for the Escaped Prisoner's Cross. In my opinion, a distinction was received, but not requested.' This statement succinctly captures all of Edé's character. In fact, the character, values, and ethics of the de Selys Longchamps siblings are magnificently crystallised by these few words.

Acknowledgements

This book owes a great deal to the individuals who opened the family archives related to Jean de Selys Longchamps for me. I am particularly grateful to Mary Cornet d'Elzius (daughter of Monique), Michel de Selys (son of François), and Ariel de Selys (son of Édé). Their continuous support and numerous encouragements were crucial in bringing this biographical project to fruition.

The invaluable contribution of the very dynamic 609 (WR) Squadron Association must also be highlighted. Driven by the very enthusiastic Conrad Roumieux (Vice-President and Belgian Representative), the association gave me access to a wealth of documents and photographs, masterfully curated by Mark Crame. Many thanks also to Jocelyn Leclerq for his valuable insights.

My gratitude also extends to Chris Thomas, the world's *true* expert on the Hawker Typhoon, who answered all my questions with precision and speed.

Charlie De la Royère, head of the documentation and archives centre at the Royal Museum of the Armed Forces (Brussels), deserves a special mention for his warm support and the extraordinary archives he manages with great skill.

The contribution of Daniel Weyssow (Auschwitz Foundation) was also essential, and his remarkable work on the Sipo-SD headquarters in Brussels proved extraordinarily valuable.

During my research, several encounters were decisive in organising my thoughts and guiding me through the maze of archives. I am grateful to Fabrice Maerten, historian at CegeSoma/State Archives and specialist in the history of the Resistance, as well as Marc Brans (Royal Museum of the Armed Forces), Alicia Wampach, and Eva Muys (Algemene Dienst Inlichting en Veiligheid) for their professionalism and availability.

The first version of this book was written in French, and a few people greatly helped me adapt it into English. I am especially thankful to Michel Miller, who invested himself tirelessly (and with talent) in this difficult exercise. To Mark Crame for his expertise on everything concerning 609 Squadron and the RAF. Finally, to John Bates for agreeing to cast a keen eye over the book. I thank them immensely.

Finally, my gratitude goes to Heather Williams (Pen and Sword) for the trust she immediately showed me and the invaluable help she provided in the publication of this English version.

Notes

Chapter 1
1. Coen, Jules, *Michel Edmond de Selys Longchamps*, 1981, pp. 1–5; de Stein d'Altenstein, Isodore (Baron), *Annuaire de la noblesse de Belgique*, 1853, pp. 177–180.
2. Lameere, Auguste, 'Edmond Selys Longchamps et liste de ses publications scientifiques' in *Mémoire de la Société Entomologique de Belgique*, Tome 9, 1902.
3. De Nayer, Christine, *Raphaël de Selys Longchamps: Un photographe amateur au XIXème siècle*, Musée de la photographie de Charleroi, pp. 7–14.

Chapter 2
1. All information regarding Raymond de Selys Longchamps' military career is sourced from his personal military file (matricule 13609) held at the Royal Museum of the Army and Military History (Brussels).
2. Note addressed on 23 April 1919 to the head of the Belgian mission at the British General Headquarters (Raymond de Selys' military file, op. cit.).

Chapter 3
1. Cited by Louis Robyns de Schneidauer in an article published in issue 73 of the *Bulletin de l'Association de la noblesse du Royaume de Belgique*.
2. Most of the information regarding Jean de Selys Longchamps' Belgian military career comes from his personal military file (matricule 38160) held at the Classified Archives of Defence (Quartier Reine Elisabeth, Evere).
3. Warnauts, Jean Claude (co-author), *La cavalerie belge au fil du temps*, Editions du Perron, 2014, pp. 105–118.
4. Most information on the Cyclist Group of the 17th Division comes from the unit's file held at the Classified Archives of Defence (Quartier Reine Elisabeth, Evere).

Chapter 4
1. All information about Henry Van Derton's military career is from his personal military file (matricule 19032) kept at the Royal Museum of the Army and Military History (Brussels).
2. The majority of information regarding the actions of the Cyclist Group of the 17th Division during the eighteen-day campaign comes from the unit's file held at the Classified Archives of Defence (Quartier Reine Elisabeth, Evere) and the excellent site managed by Walter Van Opstal, www.18daagseveldtocht.be.
3. Handwritten report by Jean de Selys Longchamps found in the unit's file kept at the Classified Archives of Defence (Quartier Reine Elisabeth, Evere).
4. Mathot, René, *Hitler en Belgique et en France*, Racine, 2021, pp. 73–74.

Chapter 5
1. Guérisse, Patrick, *Albert Guérisse alias Pat O'Leary*, biographical document, 20 pages, p. 3.
2. VanWelkenhuyzen, Jean, and Dumont, Jacques, *1940 Le grand Exode*, Duculot, 1984, pp. 122–123.

3. VanWelkenhuyzen, Jean, and Dumont, Jacques, *1940 Le grand Exode*, op. cit., p. 123.
4. Article published by *Mémoires de guerre* on 15 February 2021 (www.mémoiresdeguerre.com).
5. The anecdote is recounted by Jean de Selys in the film shot at Manston in 1942, *Between Friends*, and by Raymond Lallemant in the RTBF TV documentary *Jours de Guerre* (1992).
6. Mace, Martin, *The Royal Navy at Dunkirk*, Pen & Sword Books, 2017, p. 218.
7. Data extracted from various sources: Bourey, Maurice, *Dunkerque 350 000 hommes à la mer*, Heimdal, 1991; Exhibition 'Operatie Dynamo in De Panne' (2021); Speech by Professor Luc Devos at the seventy-fifth anniversary of Operation Dynamo (2015); Larson, Erik, *La splendeur et l'infamie*, Le Cherche-midi, 2021.

Chapter 6

1. Weber, Guy, *L'heure du choix*, Editions Louis Musin, 1985, pp. 43–59; Segers, Carlo G., *Donnez-nous un champ de Bataille*, Pierre de Méyère, 1969, p. 29; Presentations held on 3 February 2023 at the study day in military history and public history 'La création des forces belges libres à Tenby en 1940', UCL.
2. Jamart, Jean, and Colonel B.E.M. Hire, *L'armée belge de France en 1940*, self-published, is an essential work to understand this often-overlooked episode and has largely helped document the pages of this chapter.
3. Information confirmed by the military file of Jean de Selys, op. cit.; Warnauts, Jean Claude (co-author), *La cavalerie belge au fil du temps*, op. cit., p. 140.
4. Études Héraultaises, number 56, 2021.
5. Jullian, Marcel, *H.M.S. Fidelity bateau mystère*, Presses de la Cité, 1972, p. 29. This work will serve as a guide to describe all the episodes on board developed in the following pages.
6. Muselier, Renaud, *L'amiral Muselier, le créateur de la Croix de Lorraine*, Perrin, 2000.
7. Guérisse, Patrick, *Albert Guérisse alias Pat O'Leary*, op. cit., pp. 5–12.
8. Van Der Bijl, Nick, *Commandos in Exile: The Story of 10 (Inter-Allied) Commando 1942–1945*, Pen & Sword, 2008.
9. Jamart, Jean, and Colonel B.E.M. Hire, op. cit.: this work once again proved invaluable in understanding the wanderings of the flight school in the turmoil of 1940.
10. Buzin, Jean, 'Du crépuscule de l'aéronautique militaire à l'aube de la force aérienne', *Vieilles Tiges* magazine, 4–2019, pp. 46–48.
11. Weber, Guy, *Evadés de guerre : souvenirs de la seconde guerre mondiale*, Bourdeaux-Capelle, 1997, pp. 62–66.
12. Jaspar, Marcel-Henri, *Souvenirs sans retouche*, Fayard, 1968.
13. All travel dates are based on tickets and other documents (passport, visas, etc.) kept by Jean de Selys in one of his photograph albums (de Selys family collection).
14. Personal journals and memoirs of Louise de Roubaix and Gérard Thys were kindly made available to the author by Stéphane de Potter. These pages are invaluable for capturing the atmosphere within the Belgian refugee community in Pau.
15. D'Udekem d'Accoz, Marie-Pierre, *Pour le Roi et la patrie : la noblesse belge dans la résistance*, Racine, 2002, pp. 298–301.

Chapter 7

1. Excellent works cover this period, such as: Donnet, Mike, *Les aviateurs belges dans la Royal Air Force*, Racine, 2006; Donnet, Mike, *50 ans d'aivation militaire*, self-published, 1997; Rens, Gustave, *Les Belges de la bataille d'Angleterre*, Louis Musin, 1980; Rens, Gustave, *Pas de panache en altitude*, La maison des Ailes, 1963.
2. The instruction given by the Minister of Defence, General Denis, is explicit: 'Formal prohibition to join Great Britain under penalty of being brought before the War Council and being condemned as a deserter.'

3. This sad episode is recounted with much emotion by 'Cheval' Lallemant in his first book: Lallemant, Raymond, *Rendez-vous avec la chance*, op. cit.
4. Shores, Christopher and Williams, Clive, *Aces High: A Tribute to the Most Notable Fighter Pilots of the British and Commonwealth Forces in WW2*, Volume 1, Grub Street, 1994, Chapter five; Thomas, Chris, *Typhoon and Tempest Aces of World War 2*, Osprey Publishing, 1999.
5. https://www.youtube.com/watch?v=5m7zoPYVMUc.
6. Bamford, Joe, Williams, John, and Gallagher, Peter, *A Detailed History of RAF Manston 1941–1945: Invicta – The Undefeated*, Fonthill, 2016.

Chapter 12

1. This important chapter is heavily drawn from the works of three essential authors: Maxime Steinberg, Laurence Schram, and Daniel Weyssow. The essential works are: Steinberg, Maxime, *Dossier Bruxelles Auschwitz*, Belgian Committee of Support for the Civil Party in the SS Officers' Trial, 1980; Steinberg, Maxime, *La persécution des juifs en Belgique (1940–1945)*, Éditions Complexe, 2004; Schram, Laurence, *Dossin, l'antichambre d'Auschwitz*, Racine, 2017; Weyssow, Daniel, *Les caves de la Gestapo: reconnaissance et conservation*, Éditions Kimé, 2013. Daniel Weyssow is also the author of a remarkable series of articles on the subject listed in the bibliography.
2. Longerich, Peter, *La conférence de Wannsee : le chemin vers la solution finale*, Éloïse d'Ormesson, 2019.
3. Elements compiled based on research conducted at the Bundesarchiv (Berlin) – 'NSDAP-Zentralkartei', 'NSDAP-Gaukartei', 'Rasse- und Siedlungshauptamt' (RS), SS-Offizier-Akte (SSO) (2022).
4. Steinberg, Maxime, *La persécution des juifs en Belgique (1940–1945)*, op. cit., p. 119.
5. Schreiber, Marion, *Rebelles silencieux : l'attaque du 20e convoi pour Auschwitz*, Racine en poche, 2006, pp. 72–73.
6. Detailed tables of deportations from Malines are available in this work: Schram, Laurence, *Dossin, l'antichambre d'Auscschwitz*, Racine, 2017, pp. 26–36.

Chapter 13

1. The document 'The diary of Bob Walling July 1941 – September 1943' was provided by Mark Crame, curator of the 609 Squadron Association archives.
2. Conway, Martin, and Gotovitch, José, *Europe in Exile: European Exile Communities in Britain*, Berghahn Books, 2001.
3. The following narrative is based on a long video interview with Régine Krochmal kept by the Auschwitz Foundation (Brussels) (1999 – YA/FA/153).
4. Lallemant, Raymond, *Rendez-vous avec la chance*, op. cit.
5. Video interview with Raymond Lallemant conducted by Bernard Cornet ('Jean de Selys: le chevalier du ciel') as part of a school project (2002).
6. Operations Record Book 609 Squadron (20 January 1943), The National Archives AIR 27/2103/2.
7. Video interview with Raymond Lallemant conducted by Bernard Cornet, op. cit.
8. Lallemant, Raymond, *Rendez-vous avec la chance*, op. cit.
9. Video interview with Raymond Lallemant conducted by Bernard Cornet, op. cit.
10. Robyns de Schneidauer, Louis, article published in issue 73 of the *Bulletin de l'Association de la noblesse du Royaume de Belgique*.
11. Video interview with Raymond Lallemant conducted by Bernard Cornet, op. cit.
12. Stephany, Pierre, *1943: le grand tournant de la guerre et le commencement de la fin*, F. Baurtembourg, 1993, p. 66.
13. Letter dated 4 January 1983, a copy of which is in the production file of the program *Jours de Guerre* that RTBF dedicated to Jean de Selys and broadcast on 24 November 1992.
14. Interview with Régine Krochmal kept by the Auschwitz Foundation (Brussels) (1999 – YA/FA/153).
15. Video interview with Raymond Lallemant conducted by Bernard Cornet, op. cit.

16. Robyns de Schneidauer, Louis, article published in issue 73 of the *Bulletin de l'Association de la noblesse du Royaume de Belgique*.
17. Video interview with Raymond Lallemant conducted by Bernard Cornet, op. cit.
18. Video interview with Raymond Lallemant conducted by Bernard Cornet, op. cit.
19. Ziegler, Frank H., *The Story of 609 Squadron: Under the White Rose*, op. cit., p. 258.
20. Operations Record Book 609 Squadron (20 January 1943), The National Archives' reference AIR 27/2103/1.
21. Operations Record Book 609 Squadron (20 January 1943), op. cit.
22. Operations Record Book 609 Squadron (20 January 1943), op. cit.
23. Video interview with Raymond Lallemant conducted by Bernard Cornet, op. cit.
24. Operations Record Book 609 Squadron (20 January 1943), op. cit.
25. Delandsheere, Paul, and Ooms, Alphonse, *La Belgique sous les nazis*, tome 3, Edition Universelle, pp. 31–32.
26. D'Udekem d'Accoz, Marie-Pierre, *Pour le Roi et la patrie: la noblesse belge dans la résistance*, op. cit., pp. 367–368.
27. Bodson, Herman, *Agent for the Resistance: A Belgian Saboteur in World War 2*, Texas A&M University, 1994.
28. Attachment to the letter from the Minister of Defence addressed to Louis Wouters on 19 May 1943; document kept in Jean de Selys' personal military file, op. cit.
29. Letter from the Minister of Defence addressed to Louis Wouters on 19 May 1943, op. cit.
30. Fosty, Jean, journal *Cité Nouvelle*, 18 January 1947.
31. Death certificates from the Bundesarchiv (Abt. Miltärarchiv) in Berlin.
32. Schreiber, Marion, *Rebelles silencieux: l'attaque du 20e convoi pour Auschwitz*, Racine en poche, 2006.
33. Demoulin, Charles, *Mes oiseaux de feux*, Éditions Julliard, 1984, p. 84.
34. Moszkiewiez, Hélène, *Ma guerre dans la Gestapo: l'incroyable destin d'une femme juive dans les réseaux nazis*, Albin Michel, 1992, p. 204.
35. Interview with Fabrice Maerten (CegeSoma), specialist on the Belgian resistance (23 May 2022).
36. Rosart, Roger, article in *La Libre Belgique*, 5 May 1983.
37. Hypothesis proposed by Gustave Rens in the following work: Crahay, Jean, *20 héros de chez nous 1940–1964*, Editions J.M. Collet, 1983, p. 76.

Chapter 14

1. Operations Record Book 609 Squadron (20 January 1943), op. cit.
2. Documents provided by Mark Crame (609 Squadron Association).
3. Celis, Peter, and De Decker, Cynrik, *Mony Van Lierde: van volksjongen to volksheld*, Uitgeerij Flying Pencil, 2007, p. 65.
4. Copy of a handwritten document provided to the de Selys Longchamps family and kept at the Kleine Brogel Air Base Museum.
5. The original of this letter is in Jean de Selys' military file, op. cit.
6. The original of this letter is in Jean de Selys' military file, op. cit.
7. The original of this letter is in Jean de Selys' military file, op. cit.
8. The original of this letter is in Jean de Selys' military file, op. cit.
9. Personal Combat Report 14 February 1943 (The National Archives) AIR 50/171/20 and Operations Record Book 609 Squadron (14 February 1943), op. cit.
10. Operations Record Book 609 Squadron (12 March 1943), op. cit.
11. Long, Jack T.C., *Three's Company: An Illustrated History of No. 3 (Fighter) Squadron RAF*, Pen & Sword, 2005.
12. Pottinger, Ron, *A Soldier in the Cockpit: From Rifles to Typhoons in WWII*, Stackpole Books, 2005, p. 88.
13. Collins, Michael, *Discovering My Father: The Wartime Experiences of Squadron Leader John Russel DFC & Bar (1913–1944)*, self-published, 2012, pp. 27–28.

14. Operations Record Book 3 Squadron (18 May 1943), The National Archives AIR-27-33-53.
15. Pottinger, Ron, *A Soldier in the Cockpit: From Rifles to Typhoons in WWII*, op. cit., pp. 88–89.
16. Pottinger, Ron, *A Soldier in the Cockpit: From Rifles to Typhoons in WWII*, op. cit., pp. 94–95.
17. Operations Record Book 3 Squadron (20 June 1943), The National Archives AIR-27-33-53.
18. d'Oultremont, Georges, *Souvenirs d'Oultre-bombes: une guerre très personnelle*, self-published, 2020, p. 64.
19. A copy of the pages from Lady Carson's journal relating to Jean de Selys was given to the de Selys family.

Chapter 15
1. Pottinger, Ron, *A Soldier in the Cockpit: From Rifles to Typhoons in WWII*, op. cit., p. 95.
2. Operations Record Book 3 Squadron (16 August 1943), The National Archives AIR-27-33-53.
3. Franks, Norman, *Typhoon Attack: The Legendary British Fighter in Combat in WWII*, Stackpole, 2003, pp. 51–52.
4. Lallemant, Raymond, *Rendez-vous avec la chance*, op. cit., p. 157.
5. The document summarising the investigation report in French is in Jean de Selys' military file (matricule 38160), op. cit.
6. Franks, Norman, *Typhoon Attack: The Legendary British Fighter in Combat in WWII*, op. cit., p. 52.
7. The following summary compiles information from the following reference works: Thomas, Chris, and Shores, Christopher, *The Typhoon & Tempest Story*, Arms and Armour Press, 1988; Thomas, Chris, *Hawker Typhoon 1940 to Spring 1943*, Wingleader, 2022. Also: Townshend Bickers, Richard, *Hawker Typhoon: The Combat History*, Airlife, 1999; Buttler, Tony, *Hawker Typhoon*, Key Books, 2021.
8. Townshend Bickers, Richard, *Hawker Typhoon: The Combat History*, Airlife, 1999, p. 103.
9. Operations Record Book 3 Squadron (June, July, August 1943), The National Archives AIR-27-33-53.
10. Operations Record Book 3 Squadron (16 August 1943), The National Archives AIR-27-33-53.
11. Pottinger, Ron, *A Soldier in the Cockpit: From Rifles to Typhoons in WWII*, op. cit., p. 107.
12. Pottinger, Ron, *A Soldier in the Cockpit: From Rifles to Typhoons in WWII*, op. cit., pp. 107–108.
13. Pottinger, Ron, *A Soldier in the Cockpit: From Rifles to Typhoons in WWII*, op. cit., p. 107.
14. Robyns de Schneidauer, Louis, article published in *Le Soir* on 12 December 1952.

Chapter 16
1. Interview conducted by the regional BBC channel (Southeast) on 16 August 2013.

Chapter 17
1. Most of the information about François during this period comes from his military file (matricule 35777) kept at the Classified Archives of Defence (Quartier Reine Elisabeth, Evere).
2. Dossier 'Reynaldo mission', The National Archives, HS/6188.
3. D'Udekem d'Accoz, Marie-Pierre, *Pour le Roi et la patrie: la noblesse belge dans la résistance*, op. cit.
4. Most of the information about Edmond during this period comes from his military file (matricule 40 153) kept in the Classified Archives of Defence (Queen Elisabeth Quarter, Evere). Additionally, there is a very interesting and rich biographical typescript written by his son, Ariel.
5. File obtained from The National Archives (HS9/937/9).
6. D'Udekem d'Accoz, Marie-Pierre, *Pour le Roi et la patrie: la noblesse belge dans la résistance*, op. cit., p. 363.
7. Marquet, Victor, Journal of Belgian History, 'Wilmarsdonk cahiers_marquet_1990_1_part2'.

Selected Bibliography

The Eighteen-Day Campaign and the Following Months (May-August 1940)
Bernard, Henri, *Panorama d'une défaite. Bataille de Belgique-Dunkerque 10 mai - 4 juin 1940*, Duculot, 1984
Bourey, Maurice, *Dunkerque: 350 000 hommes à la mer*, Éditions Heimdal, 1991
Du Ry, Jean-Pierre, *Allons enfants de la Belgique. Les 16–35 ans mai-août 1940*, Éditions Racine, 1995
Jamart, Jean, *L'armée belge de France en 1940*, autoédition, 1994
Leclercq, Alain, Hoeve, Nathan, *Belgique Mai 40. La campagne des 18 jours*, Éditions Pixl, 2014
Leclercq, Alain, *1940. 18 jours de résistance en Belgique*, Éditions Jourdan, 2020
Mace, Martin, *The Royal Navy at Dunkirk*, Pen & Sword Books, 2017
VanWelkenhuyzen, Jean et Dumont, Jacques, *1940 Le grand exode*, Duculot, 1984
Vanwelkenhuyzen, Jean, *1940. Pleins feux sur un désastre*, Éditions Racine, 1996
Weber, Guy, *L'heure du choix ou les séquelles du drame belge de 1940*, Éditions Louis Musin, 1985

Occupation in Belgium, Deportation, The Holocaust 1940–1945
'La vie quotidienne en Belgique', catalogue, Galerie CGER, 1984
De Launay, Jacques, Offergeld, Jacques, *La vie quotidienne des Belges sous l'occupation (1940–1945)*, Paul Legrain, 1982
De Vos, Luc, *La Belgique et la seconde Guerre Mondiale*, Éditions Racine, 2004
Devos, Wannes, Gony, Kevin, *Guerre occupation libération. Belgique 1940–1945*, Éditions Racine, 2019
Gérard, Jo, *La Belgique sous l'occupation 1940–1944*, Les Ateliers d'Art Graphique Meddens, 1974
Guillaume, Lucien, *Les trains sanitaires*, Weyrich, 2010
Kesteloot, Chantal, *Bruxelles sous l'occupation*, Luc Pire, 2009
Moszkiewiez, Hélène, *Ma guerre dans la Gestapo*, Albin Michel, 1999
Nefors, Patrick, *Breendonk 1940–1945*, Éditions Racine, 2005
Shram, Laurence, *Dossin. L'antichambre d'Auschwitz*, Racine, 2017
Shreiber, Marion, *Rebelles silencieux. L'attaque du 20e convoi pour Auschwitz*, Racine en poche, 2000
Sommerhausen, Anne, *Journal d'une femme occupée, Rheto éditions*, 2011
Steinberg, Maxime, *Dossier Bruxelles Auschwitz. La police SS et l'extermination des juifs de Belgique*, Le Comité, 1980
Steinberg, Maxime, *La persécution des juifs en Belgique (1940–1945)*, Éditions Complexe, 2004
Stephany, Pierre, *1940, 365 jours d'histoire de Belgique et d'ailleurs*, F. Bourtembourg, 1990
Stephany, Pierre, 1943, *Le grand tournant de la guerre et le commencement de la fin*, F. Bourtembourg, 1993
Von Falkenhausen, Alexander, *Mémoires d'outre-guerre*, Éditions Jourdan, 2019
Weyssow, Daniel, *Les caves de la Gestapo. Reconnaissance et conservation*, Éditions Kimé, 2013

Belgian Government in France and London, Belgian Refugees in England
Conway, Martin, Gotovitch, José, *Europe in Exile: European Communities in Britain 1940–1945*, Berghan Books, 2001
Crombois, Jean-François, *1940–1945, Quorum-Ceges, 2000*
Denuit, Désiré, *L'été ambigu de 1940*, Louis Musin éditeur, 1978
d'Oultremont, Georges, *Souvenirs d'Oultre-bombes: une guerre très personnelle*, auto-édité, 2020

Dutry-Soinne, Tinou, *Les méconnus de Londres. Journal de guerre d'une belge 1940–1945* (2 tomes), 2006
D'Ydewalle, Pierre, *Mémoires 1912–1940 aux avant-postes*, Éditions Racine, 1994
Grosbois, Thierry, *Pierlot 1930–1950*, Éditions Racine, 2007
Gutt, Camille, *La Belgique au carrefour 1940–1944*, Fayard, 1971
Hermanus, Merry, Paul Hymans, *Carnet d'exode 1940*, Belg-o-Belge, 2022
Jaspar, Marcel-Henri, *Souvenirs sans retouch*, Fayard, 1968

Resistance in Belgium, Escape Networks
Bodson, Herman, *Agent for the Resistance: A Belgian Saboteur in World War 2*, Texas A&M University, 1994
Debruyne, Emmanuel, *La guerre secrète des espions belges 1940–1944*, Éditions Racine, 2008
D'Udekem d'Acoz, Marie-Pierre, *Pour le Roi et la patrie. La noblesse belge dans la résistance*, Éditions Racine, 2002
Le Blanc, Philippe, *Comète. Le réseau derrière la ligne DD*, MeMograMes, 2015
Maerten, Fabrice, *Papy était-il un héros?*, Racine, 2020
Rens, Gustave, Weber, Guy, Deheusch, Willy, *Évasions de guerre*, J.M. Collet, 1995
Stephany, Pierre, 1941, *Les misères et les chagrins de l'année la plus noire*, F. Bourtembourg, 1991
Ugueux, William, *Le passage de l'Iraty*, Armand Henneuse, 1962
Weber, Guy, *Évadés de guerre*, Bourdeaux-Capelle, 1997

Belgian Airmen (Aéronautique Militaire, RAF, Air Force)
Anthoine, Roger, Roba, Jean-Louis, *Les Belges de la R.A.F.*, Éditions J.M. Collet, 1989
Bar, André, Brackx, Daniel, De Decker, Cynrik, Lacoste, Georges, Roba, Jean-Louis, Schelfaut, Jacques, *Ailes brisées de l'aviation belge*, Éditions Flying Pencil, 2010
Celis, Peter, De Decker, Cynrik, *Mony Van Lierde: van volksjongen to volksreed*, Uitgeverij Flying Pencil, 2007
De Decker, Cynrik, Roba, Jean-Louis, *Duel over Belgïe*, Uitgeverij De Krijger, 1996
Demoulin, Charles, *Mes oiseaux de feux*, Julliard, 1982
Donnet, Mike, *Ils en étaient. Les escadrilles belges de la R.A.F.*, Les presses de l'Avenir, 1991
Donnet, Mike, *50 ans d'aviation miltiaire*, 1997
Donnet, Mike, *Les aviateurs belges dans la Royal Air Force*, Éditions Racine, 2006
Gérard, Hervé, *Les as de l'aviation belge*, J.M. Collet, 1994
Houart, Victor, *Les carnets d'offenberg*, Éditions de la pensée Moderne, 1956
Lallemant, Raymond, *Rendez-vous avec la chance*, Éditions J'ai Lu, 1964
Lallemant, Raymond, *Rendez-vous avec le destin*, 2004
Rens, Gustave, *Pas de panache en altitude*, 1963
Rens, Gustave, *Les Belges dans la bataille d'Angleterre*, Louis Musin éditeur, 1980

Royal Air Force (Pilots, Aircraft, etc.)
Bamford, Joe, William, John, Gallagher, Peter, *A Detailed History of RAF Manston 1941–1945*, Foothill Media, 2016
Brown, Alan, *Flying for Freedom: The Allied Air Forces in the RAF 1939–1945*, History Press, 2000
Buttler, Tony, *Hawker Typhoon*, Key Books, 2021
Collins, Michael, *Discovering My Father*, 2012
Collet, Patrick, *Jacques-Henri Schloesing: itinéraire d'un Français libre*, Heimdal, 2014
De la Poype, Roland, *L'épopée du Normandie-Niemen*, Tempus, 2007
Earnshaw, James D., *609 At War*, Vector Fine Art, 2003
Franks, Norman, *Typhoon Attack*, Stackpole Books, 2003
Long, Jack T.C., *Three's Company: An Illustrated History of N°. 3 (Fighter) Squadron RAF*, Pen & Sword, 2005.
Mister Kit, Thomas, Chris, *Hawker Typhoon*, Éditions Atlas, 1980
Pottinger, Ron, *A Soldier in the Cockpit*, Stackpole Books, 2005

Richey, Paul, *Fighter Pilot's Summer*, Grub Street, 1993
Thomas, Chris, Shores, Christopher, *The Typhoon and Tempest Story*, DAG Publications, 1988
Thomas, Chris, *Typhoon and Tempest aces of World War 2*, Osprey publishing, 1999
Thomas, Chris, *Hawker Typhoon 1940 to Spring 1943*, Wingleader, 2022
Thomas, Chris, *Hawker Typhoon Summer 1943 to early 1944*, Wingleader, 2023
Townshend Bickers, Richard, *Hawker Typhoon: The Combat History*, Airlife Publishing, 1999
Waite, Brian, *William de Goat*, Athena Press, 2008
Ziegler, Frank, *The Story of 609 Squadron*, MacDonald, 1971

The Belgian Army, Before and During the Second Word War
Brabant, Willy, *La cavalerie belge au fil des siècles*, Éditions du Perron, 2014
Crahay, général, *20 héros de chez nous 1940–1964*, Éditions J.M. Collet, 1983
Gérard, Jo, Gérard, Hervé, Rens, Gustave, *Se battre pour la Belgique*, Éditions J.M. Collet, 1984
Jullian, Marcel, *H.M.S. Fidelity. Bateau mystère*, Presse de la cité, 1972
Leclercq, Alian, Hoeve, Nathan, *Les Belges en guerre*, Éditions Pixl, 2014
Seger, Carlo G., *Donnez-nous un champ de bataille*, Pierre De Méyère, 1969
Van Der Bijl, Nick, *Commandos in Exile: The Story of 10 (Inter-Allied) Commando 1942–1945*, Pen & Sword, 2008
Van Hammée, Ernest, *La Belgique en guerre et dans la paix*, Weissenbruch, 1953

Index

1st Regiment of Guides 11, 25–9, 30, 33, 84, 101, 149, 187, 196, 205, 238, 244, 247, 263–4, 268–9, 273
1st Squadron (Stingers), 80, 255
3 (F) Squadron, 207, 211–19, 221, 222, 224, 226–7, 229, 230, 232, 235, 237–8, 242–3, 247, 252–3, 255
17 DI Cyclist group, 29, 30, 32–4, 36–7, 39–40
61 OTU, 63, 101–102, 105–106, 114
349 Squadron, 109, 255
350 Squadron, 109, 139, 177, 184, 207, 221
609 (WR) Squadron, 45, 75, 96, 106–30, 132–51, 153, 155, 158–60, 177–8, 182, 184–5, 192, 194–6, 204–207, 209, 211–13, 215, 224, 233, 240, 252–3, 276

Adnans, A.G., 206
Albert 1, King, 3, 16, 19
Alexandre, Robert, 91
Atkinson, Joe, 119, 150, 195, 206
Armor, Henry (Desmond), 158
Asche, Kurt, 171
Auschwitz, 172, 192, 256, 276

Baldwin, J.R., 195, 207
Barckley, Bob, 218, 252
Barnham, Dennis, 119
Bastin, Jules, 45, 48
Beamont, Roland (Bee), 151–3, 155, 158–9, 161, 204, 205–206
Beiderwieden, Heinrich, 201, 203
Belgian Congo, 3, 63–4, 68, 120, 186
Bell, D.J., 211
Berry, A.E., 214
Biggin Hill (RAF Station), 107, 109, 110–13, 116, 118–19, 121, 128, 147–8, 153, 155
Billy de Goat, 113–14, 121, 129
Blairon, Arnold José, 91
Blanco, André (Le Men), 133, 140, 182, 184–7, 195

Bodson, Herman, 197
Boedts, Paul, 250, 251
Breendonk, 164–6, 169
Brest, 54–5, 57, 128, 265–6
Buchin, Maurice, 72

Cajot, Robert, 64, 87
Camm, Sydney, 135
Canaris, Karl Constantin, 164, 171
Cantillo, André, 91
Carton de Wiart, Maxime, 196
Carson, Edward Henry, 225
Carson, Edward Ned, 225
Carson, Ruby, 225, 235
Central Gunnery School (CGS), 154, 192, 205–206
Claesen, Antoon, 91
Cole, Bob, 217, 230
Collins, Jack, 218, 226, 229
Coltishall, 133
Comète (escape network), 224, 261, 273
Cook, M.C., 232
Choron, Maurice, 111
Churchill, Winston, 16, 18, 42, 51, 107, 225
Coppens, Willy, 80, 248, 249
Cornet de Ways Ruart (de Selys), Pauline, 65, 245–6, 263, 265–7
Creteur, Jean, 139, 195
Crisford, Ray, 218, 232
Custance, P/O, 225, 235

Danloy, Georges (George Chesty), 54, 57, 59, 61–2, 68
Dartevelle, André, 256
d'Oultremont, Georges, 224–5
d'Ursel, Jacques, 75, 82
de Bousies, Anne, 79, 224, 274
de Callataÿ, Jean, 221, 225–6, 229
de Cannart d'Hamale, Roger Émile, 72
de Cartier de Marchienne, Émile, 53, 161, 243

de Hepcée, Charley, 238
de Hemptine, Baudoin, 109, 118, 224
de Hemricourt de Grunne, Rodolphe (Dolfo), 79, 80, 96, 109, 224
de Liederkerke, Anne, 68
de Ligne, Bertie, 225
De Panne 43–5, 47–50, 53–4, 74, 88, 95, 117, 258
de Patoul, Guy, 91
de Rancourt de Mimérand, Henry, 75
de Ryckman de Betz, 174
de Selliers de Moranville, Frédéric, 69
de Selys Longchamps, Edgard, 241
de Selys Longchamps, Edmond, 4–6,
de Selys Longchamps, Edmond (Edé), 19, 22–3, 27, 80, 138, 224, 252, 263, 268–75
de Selys Longchamps, François, 3, 14–15, 19, 22–3, 65–6, 146, 224, 245, 246, 252, 263–8, 272–3, 276
de Selys Longchamps, Micheline, 238
de Selys Michel (Mickey), 245, 246
de Selys Longchamps, Monique, 3, 14–15, 19, 22–3, 26–7, 224, 243, 245, 246, 252
de Selys Longchamps, Raphaël, 5–9
de Selys Longchamps, Raymond, 3, 4, 10–12, 15–21, 65, 174, 245, 246, 247, 248, 257–62
de Selys Longchamps, Sybille, 146, 252
de Spirlet, François, 108–109, 112, 119, 123, 125, 140, 142–3, 155
de Theux de Meylandt, Émilie, 3–4, 11, 13–14, 19, 245–6, 257
de Theux de Montjardin, Alain, 68
Decloedt, Jean, 62, 91
Delvoie, Maurice, 69, 238, 239
Denis, Henri 55, 264, 278
De Renzi, Godfrey, 127
De Soomer, Léon (Léo), 74, 207, 213–15, 218, 222–5, 227, 233, 237, 240, 247
Dezitter, Prosper, 169
Dickson, George (Russ/Reg), 126, 132
Dieu, Giovanni, 75, 81–5, 89, 109, 130
Digby (RAF Station), 119, 120–3, 125–32, 148, 154, 160
Divoy, Léon, 248, 249
Donnet, Michel (Mike), 247, 248, 249
Dopéré, Raymaond, 139, 140, 153, 155
Dossin Barracks (Mechelen), 172, 192
du monceau de Bergendal, Ivan (the Duke), 109, 122, 129, 130, 144, 205
Dumoulin, Charles (Windmill Charlie), 192

Dunkirk (and Operation Dynamo), 42–5, 49–54, 57, 108, 238
Duxford (RAF Station), 131–4, 136, 140–8, 153

Ehlers, Ernst, 164, 170, 171, 202
Eichmann, Adolf, 169, 172
Ellis, Francis, 70
Ester, Jean, 91
Evans, George (Moose), 119

Feldman, Seymour (Buck), 218, 226, 242, 243
Fern, Gilbert, 174
Feyten, Édouard, 91
Fierens, Léontine, 202, 203
Flohimont, Louis, 91
Florennes, 255
Foster, Johnny, 218, 233
Francken, Emiel, 171

Galloway, Kenneth, 119
Gascoine, Alvary, 69–70
Garward, Ken, 174
Gibraltar, 57–64, 69, 70, 88, 125, 238, 267
Gilroy, George Kemps (Sheep), 112, 118, 123, 130, 133, 140
Giralt, Flore, 169
Glasgow, 70
Glogowski, Icek (Big Jacques), 172
Goblet, Henri, 91
Goethals, Carlos, 75
Gonay, Henry (Moustique), 75, 83
Greenfield, W, 119
Guérisse, Albert (Pat O'Leary), 45–6, 48, 54, 56–7, 60–3, 68
Gutt, Camille, 65, 87, 100, 120, 140, 243

Haddon, Alan (Babe), 155, 158
Hansez, Louis, 91
Harmel, Léon
Hasselbacher, Karl, 163
Hawker Hurricane, 44, 72, 80, 92–4, 98–9, 100–104, 107, 123, 135–6, 141, 150–1, 153, 211–12
Hawker Typhoon, 122, 126, 132–48, 150–1, 153–6, 158–61, 177–8, 182–9, 191, 193–4, 196, 201, 204, 207–208, 211–13, 215–16, 218–20, 224, 226–33, 235, 249–50, 253
Hawkinge (RAF Station), 118, 148
Heapy, Sam 27, 74, 80, 121, 123, 138
Henlow, 178
Herreman, André, 91

Heston, 101
Heydrich, Reinhard, 162–3, 166-70, 172, 182
HMS *Argus*, 70
HMS *Westward HO*, 48–50
Hornchurch (RAF Station), 184, 207
Hunsdon (RAF Station), 211, 216
Hutchinson, 'Hutch', 218
Hye de Crom, Jean-Pierre, 196

Innes, J.G., 133
Inwood, Robert (Bob), 215, 217

Janssens de Vaerebeke, William, 63
Jasinski, Stanislas, 176
Joset, Joseph, 169

Kamensky, Cédric, 255
Kaspar the cat, 120, 121, 123, 124
Knorbin, Fritz, 201
Krochmal, Régine, 181, 182, 189, 192

Laing, Ken, 119
Lallemant, Raymond (Cheval), 91, 1001, 108, 110, 112, 119, 128, 140, 142–3, 177, 182, 184, 187, 190, 193–5, 207, 227
Lambotte, André, 91, 105
Lambrichts, René, 171
Leboutte, Lucien, 74, 245
Lemaire, André, 91
Leopold III, King, 31, 38–9, 42, 54, 80, 139, 205, 247, 268, 275
Leslie, J., 209
Link Trainer, 89–90, 100, 106
Lott, Charles George, 205
Lunden, René, 132, 138
Lympne (RAF Station), 148

McConnel, Charles (Mac), 126
McCook, 'Mac', 218
MacKechnie, Doctor, 230
Mackichan, Ronald (Ron, Little Mac), 215
Malan, Adolph (Sailor), 154
Malengreau, Roger, 109, 125, 133, 140, 146, 149
Mallory, Leigh, 120, 151, 159, 204
Manston (RAF Station), 52, 112, 130, 148, 155–6, 158, 178, 181–2, 184–5, 193–4, 207, 214, 219, 224–6, 228, 230, 235–7, 253, 274
Marchal, Henri, 85, 91
Margate, 52–3, 195
Melot, Pierrre, 196
Miles Magister (Maggie), 81–6, 91–3, 103, 122

Miles Master, 91–7, 99, 100–101, 105, 155
Milford Haven, 54
Minster-in-Thanet, 225, 235, 237, 240, 243, 252–5, 274
Montgomery, Bernard, 44
Moore, Alfred, 126
Moore, Bob, 219
Moszkiewiez, Hélène, 192, 202
Muller, José, 109
Muselier, Émile, 59–60
MV Northmoor, 57

Nankivell, Peter (Nanki), 204
Nash, Peter, 119, 125
Nitelet, Alex, 109, 123, 125, 141

Odiham (RAF Station), 74–7, 81–2, 85–91, 93, 97, 99, 102, 107, 114, 122, 214
Offenberg, Jean (Le Pyker), 64, 106, 108–12, 118, 120–1, 125–8, 155, 248–9, 255
Oujda, 63–4, 75, 88
Olieslagers, Jean, 248, 249
Ortmans, Christian, 108–109, 112, 117, 119, 123, 126, 140, 142, 150
Ortmans, Victor (Vicky), 109, 112–13, 117–18, 122–3, 129
Osborn, Bruce, 126

Palmer, Allan George (Goldie), 117
Patterson, H, 126
Pau, 65-6, 68, 111
Payne, Roy, 153, 207, 208
Peeters, Louis, 91
Péri, Claude, 58–60, 63
Peters, Gustav, 201
Philippart, Jacques, 72
Pierlot, Hubert, 65, 22, 224, 241
Plisnier, André, 207
Poitiers, 54-5, 88
Pottinger, Ron, 215, 217, 218, 234, 235, 237, 238, 240
Prauss, Arthur, 164
Prévot, Léon, 75, 83, 84, 85
Purdon, Richard (Ricky), 217, 220

Raes, Maurice, 91
Rahir, Claude, 250
Raw, Peter, 143, 182
Reeder, Eggert, 161–4, 166
Reid, 'Kibbie', 218, 237
Renier, Jospeh, 158

Rens, Gustave, 247
Richey, Paul, 137, 140–2, 145, 146, 147, 148, 150, 151, 204
Rigler, Thomas (Tommy), 119, 125–6, 128, 133–4
Robyns de Schneidauer, Louis, 187, 193, 225, 243
Robinson, Michael, 111–12, 141
Roelandt, Robert (Balbo), 126, 133

Saunders, Hugh, 204, 221, 224
Schlossing, Jacques-Henri, 101
Schmitt, Phillip, 164
Schwarz, 'Blackie', 218, 226, 229
Sclater, Heather (Carson), 225, 254, 255
Seghers, Eugène (Strop), 109
Sète, 57, 88
Signeux, Eugène, 95
Siroux, Paul, 207
Smith, 119
Smith, Patrick, 261, 262
Smith, Vic, 219
SS Rhin (HMS *Fidelity*), 58–9
Spaak, Paul-Henri, 65, 100
Spit, 114, 115, 119
Stock, William (Bill), 126
Staub, Franz, 162
Supermarine Spitfire, 44, 62, 91–3, 96, 98, 101–109, 112, 114–17, 121, 126, 130–1, 133–7, 142, 145, 147, 149, 153, 155, 184, 194, 207, 242, 255
Sutton Bridge (RAF Station), 154-5

Tenby, 53–4, 61-2, 71, 88, 149
Terlinden, Léon, 132, 243
Tern Hill (RAF Station), 91, 93–7, 99–101, 123, 228
Thomas, Alfred, 170–2, 201
Thomas, Max, 163, 169
Ticklepenny, Ernest, 220

Tidy, Chas, 218
Tiger Moth, 81
Turek, Tadeusz, 158, 159

Van Arenbergh, Louis, 108–109, 115–16, 119, 122
Van Caelenberge, Gerard, 251
Van Cromphout, Georges, 75
Van Derton, Henry, 33–7, 39–40, 42
Vanhecke, Guido, 250
Van Oostayen, Henri, 260, 261
Van Hoost, Henri, 196
Van Leerberghe, Jean, 91
Van Heghe, Chris, 251
Van Lierde, Willy, 109
Van Lierde, Remy, (Mony), 129, 140, 142, 182, 205, 224, 248, 249
Van Moffaert, Henri, 91
Van Schaik, John, 119, 125
Van Schelle, Martial, 202, 203
Van Strijdonck de Burkel, Victor, 53, 149-50
Van Thielen, Émile (Max Günther), 169
Vanvreckom, Henri, 191
Vogt, Werner, 201
von Falkenhausen, Alexander, 161, 162, 163, 164, 166
von Brauchistch, Walther, 162

Wannsee, 169-70, 172, 182
Walling, Robert (Bob), 178–9, 184
West Malling (RAF Station), 116, 130, 133–4, 214, 216-17
Weyssow, Daniel, 256
Wilmet, Robert, 109, 129, 132, 142, 149
Withman, George, (Lefty), 218, 226, 227
Wingate, H.R. (Dickie), 238
Wouters, Louis, 73, 74, 149, 150, 174, 207, 214, 230, 237

Ziegler, Frank (Ziegly), 117, 145, 177, 194, 211

Dear Reader,

We hope you have enjoyed this book, but why not share your views on social media? You can also follow our pages to see more about our other products: facebook.com/penandswordbooks or follow us on X @penswordbooks

You can also view our products at www.pen-and-sword.co.uk (UK and ROW) or www.penandswordbooks.com (North America).

To keep up to date with our latest releases and online catalogues, please sign up to our newsletter at: www.pen-and-sword.co.uk/newsletter

If you would like a printed catalogue with our latest books, then please email: enquiries@pen-and-sword.co.uk or telephone: 01226 734555 (UK and ROW) or email: uspen-and-sword@casematepublishers.com or telephone: (610) 853-9131 (North America).

We respect your privacy and we will only use personal information to send you information about our products.

Thank you!